MILTON AND THE POST-SECULAR PRESENT

Cultural Memory
in
the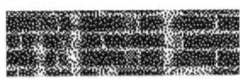
Present

Mieke Bal and Hent de Vries, Editors

MILTON AND THE POST-SECULAR PRESENT

Ethics, Politics, Terrorism

Feisal G. Mohamed

STANFORD UNIVERSITY PRESS
STANFORD, CALIFORNIA

Stanford University Press
Stanford, California

© 2011 by the Board of Trustees of the
Leland Stanford Junior University. All rights reserved

No part of this book may be reproduced or transmitted in any form or by any means, electronic or mechanical, including photocopying and recording, or in any information storage or retrieval system without the prior written permission of Stanford University Press.

Printed in the United States of America
on acid-free, archival-quality paper.

Library of Congress Cataloging-in-Publication Data

Mohamed, Feisal G. (Feisal Gharib), author.
  Milton and the post-secular present : ethics, politics, terrorism / Feisal G. Mohamed.
      pages cm. — (Cultural memory in the present)
  Includes bibliographical references and index.
  ISBN 978-0-8047-7650-9 (cloth : alk. paper) —
  ISBN 978-0-8047-7651-6 (pbk. : alk. paper)
    1. Milton, John, 1608–1674—Criticism and interpretation.
  2. Ethics in literature.   3. Politics in literature.   4. Terrorism in literature.
  5. Religion and politics.   6. Postsecularism.   I. Title.   II. Series: Cultural memory in the present.
  PR3588.M57 2011
  821'.4 —dc22   2011006590

Typeset at Stanford University Press in 11/13.5 Garamond

For my parents

Contents

	Acknowledgments	xi
	A Note on Texts	xiii
	Introduction	1
1	'Not but by the Spirit understood': Milton's Plain Style and Present-Day Messianism	19
2	*Areopagitica* and the Ethics of Reading	43
3	Liberty before and after Liberalism: Milton's Politics and the Post-secular State	66
4	Samson, the Peacemaker: Enlightened Slaughter in *Samson Agonistes*	87
5	Can the Suicide Bomber Speak?	107
	Epilogue	127
	Notes	133
	Index	163

Acknowledgments

This book has grown out of lively conversation with other scholars, many of whom have offered both encouragement and critique (in its own way a valuable form of encouragement). I am especially grateful to those who have commented on earlier drafts of its chapters, both in writing and in conference settings: Phillip Donnelly, Stephen Fallon, Stanley Fish, Eliane Glaser, Kenneth Graham, Marshall Grossman, Christopher Kendrick, John Leonard, Michael Lieb, David Loewenstein, Leah Marcus, Ryan Netzley, Mary Nyquist, Annabel Patterson, Balachandra Rajan†, Bruce Rosenstock, Stella Purce Revard, Carter Revard, John Rumrich, Regina Schwartz, Jeffrey Shoulson, Eric Song, Mihoko Suzuki, Paul Stevens, Gordon Teskey, David Urban, Nicholas von Maltzahn, and Susanne Woods. Deserving special acknowledgment are Peter Herman and Joseph Wittreich, valued friends with a very different take on Milton.

Completion of this project coincided with a move to the University of Illinois, which has proven to be as intellectually lively a campus as one could wish for. My colleagues in early modern studies have been enormously generous (that's you, Curtis Perry) and equally tough (that's you, Carol Neely); I am very fortunate to be a member of this scholarly community. That is also true of my colleagues in the Unit for Criticism and Interpretive Theory, of whom I thank especially Michael Rothberg and Lauren Goodlad. The Illinois Program for Research in the Humanities provided a fellowship at a key moment in this book's composition, which afforded precious release time and valuable conversation with faculty and graduate students from across the humanities; particularly helpful were Dianne Harris and Sarah Projansky.

An earlier version of chapter three appeared as 'Liberty Before and After Liberalism: Milton's Shifting Politics and the Current Crisis in Liberal Theory,' in the special issue, 'Milton in America,' ed. Paul Stevens and Patricia Simmons, *University of Toronto Quarterly* 77 (2008): 940–60. © 2008 University of Toronto Press Incorporated. Reprinted by permission of University of Toronto Press Incorporated (www. utpjournals.com) and the Graduate Centre for the Study of Drama at the University of Toronto. An earlier version of chapter four appeared as 'Confronting Religious Violence: Milton's *Samson Agonistes*,' *PMLA* 120 (2005): 327–40, © 2005 by the Modern Language Association of America. Reprinted by permission of the Modern Language Association. An earlier version of chapter five appeared as 'Reading *Samson* in the New American Century,' *Milton Studies* 46 (2007): 149–64. I thank the publishers of these journals for granting permissions.

I am grateful to the anonymous readers and editorial staff of the Stanford University Press, especially Emily-Jane Cohen, whose interventions have made the book more clear at key points; Sarah Crane Newman and John Feneron shepherded the manuscript into production with care and efficiency.

This space allows me to give thanks for the thankless task of preparing the index, which fell to Erin Chandler, doctoral candidate at the University of Illinois.

My deepest debts are personal and cannot be expressed on an acknowledgments page. As ever, nothing would seem possible or worthwhile without my wife, Sally. I've dedicated this book to my parents: my father, who taught me to value knowledge, and my mother, whose warmth and humor made me a humanist.

A Note on Texts

Unless otherwise indicated, all references to Milton's poetry are to *Paradise Lost*, ed. Barbara K. Lewalski (Oxford, 2007), and *Complete Shorter Poems*, ed. Stella P. Revard (Oxford, 2009). References to Milton's prose are to the *Complete Prose Works*, 8 vols. in 10, ed. Don M. Wolfe et al. (New Haven, 1953–82), and are indicated in parentheses by the abbreviation *YP*.

MILTON AND THE POST-SECULAR PRESENT

Introduction

> Since I became a tramp, I'm a somewhat better man. I couldn't preach to 'em anymore.
> —The Chaplain in Bertolt Brecht's *Mother Courage and Her Children*

Bertolt Brecht perceived clear parallels between the human cost of religion in the seventeenth century and the human cost of radical politics in the twentieth century. In the wake of the Munich agreement that opened Eastern Europe to Nazi expansion, and the growing recognition among communists of the excesses of Stalinist absolutism, Brecht composed the *Life of Galileo,* a play, as he describes it, concerned not with ecclesiastical resistance to scientific inquiry so much as with 'the temporary victory of authority,' and meant to reflect upon 'present-day reactionary authorities of a totally unecclesiastical kind.'[1] If the moment of the play's initial composition suggests a comment upon Nazism especially, its subsequent revisions and performances suggest other reactionary authorities: staged in the wake of the nuclear annihilation of Hiroshima and Nagasaki, the 1945 American version raises questions on the ethical content of scientific discovery; and the 1955 performance in Cologne, Germany—the final one that Brecht oversaw—seemed to speak to the death of Stalin in 1953. In the former context, Brecht toys with including a Hippocratic Oath for the natural sciences, the absence of which has reduced its investigators to 'a race of dwarfs who can be hired for any purpose who will, as on islands, produce whatever their masters demand.'[2] In the latter context, his editors note, '[T]he parallels are too clear: the Catholic Church is the Communist Party, Aristotle is Marxism-Leninism with its incontrovertible scriptures, the late "reactionary" pope is Joseph Stalin, the Inquisition the KGB.'[3] Similar concerns animate *Mother Courage and Her Children*, which was initially intended to raise the memory of the Thirty Years' War as Europe seemed ready to run headlong into conflagration yet again: 'As I wrote,' Brecht later declared, 'I imagined that the playwright's warning voice would be heard from the stages of various great cities. . . . Such productions never materialised. Writers cannot write as rapidly as governments can make war, because writing demands hard thought.'[4]

Brecht's turn to the seventeenth century at the outbreak of the Second World War implies that comprehensive doctrines lend themselves readily to the assertion of oppressive authority, be they religious or secular, be they of the political right or left. But he is equally skeptical of the lack of conviction serving the interests of the bourgeois 'center.' On one hand, the passage spoken by the Chaplain in *Mother Courage* that is the epigraph of this introduction suggests that something of humanity is lost in an absolute fidelity to principle. On the other hand, Brecht claims that the politicians faced by Galileo were refreshingly guided by spiritual and scientific commitments in a way that their bourgeois counterparts are not.[5] Adherence to doctrine can elevate human endeavor beyond mere interest; in the same stroke doctrine denies non-adherents full participation in the society it imagines.

That Brechtian concern is very much at the heart of this book, which explores the turn in current thought to the realm beyond contingent events. Skepticism on its own, the worry seems increasingly to run, can devolve into a nihilist acceptance of the given eschewing strong ethical and political engagement. And despite its critique of axio-teleology, current skepticism can take as axiomatic the ambiguity of phenomena and see its own rationalism and self-conscious discursiveness as the end of a *telos* where grand narratives are meant to be outgrown. In this climate contingency and ambiguity have become the Castor and Pollux of the humanities in whose temple books and articles are blindly offered. Devotion to these twin gods can be as uncritical as any doctrine, and have its own troubling implications.

Perhaps more than any other poet, John Milton makes us keenly aware of the limits of an emphasis on ambiguity, for his writings continually subsume contrary energies to a truth presenting itself phenomenologically through the workings of an enlightened soul. With iconoclastic verve he launches salvoes of believed truth against tyranny in church and state.

As we shall see, Milton makes us equally aware of the limits of a view of human liberty growing out of an adherence to truth, a view that does not fully accept the principle of equality. That shortcoming can be reproduced in the present-day thought that we will explore.

I. *The post-secular defined*

Which life is more human, Brecht leads us to wonder, the tramp's disengagement from the bloodsport of asserting truth, or the preacher's commitment to a cause larger than material life? Negotiations of that question tend in our moment to be gathered under the broad, and slightly nebulous, category of the 'post-secular.' To clarify this term, we might identify three of its tendencies, and point to thinkers significant to this book exemplifying each one: (1) an argument for subjectivity grounded fully in belief, rather than a dialectic of intuition and knowledge (Alain Badiou); (2) a renewed interest in what Immanuel Kant would call a 'theological philosophy' (late Jacques Derrida), which can at times make strong claims for the metaphysics of a particular religious tradition (John Milbank); and (3) an adjustment of liberal views of modern civil society responsive to the growing relevance of religiosity (Jürgen Habermas).

Badiou offers an ontology of truth fully divorced from the constraint of a theological transcendence. 'Mathematics is ontology' in his formulation, because set theory provides a model of infinite multiplicity that does not imply the existence of an external referent, a multiplicity that Badiou attributes to the realm of Being.[6] The point may be clarified by comparison to a more familiar Neoplatonic ontology, where the realm of Idea has less multiplicity than that of matter, narrowing to the One above Being from which all necessarily proceeds and to which all returns. For Badiou, there is no limit to the multiplicity of Being, no constraining One above Being, and nothing requiring Being to be presented to the realm of intelligibility. Being does not, however, stand entirely apart from experience. Presentation occurs in an 'event,' the 'immanent break' in which a truth appears. No existing knowledge can account for the event, making adherence to the truth it offers not a matter of learning but of faith, and not the province of an expert but that of a militant. Because the realm of truths is one of unending multiplicity, no single believing community can claim a monopoly on truth itself, even as it is defined by adherence to a point of truth.

In his arguments against transcendence, he suggests that belief can take on forms beyond those abstract absolutes that have been associated with divinity: one can be faithful to the truth of romantic love, or to Cubism, or to the *Sans culottes* uprising of 1792. Because he is an avowed atheist who places belief at the center of his vision, he represents to my mind the post-secular at its purest, and figures prominently in this book: he provides a glimpse of the possibility of a fully unreligious turn away from a secular view of belief. Charles Taylor avers that secularism is that condition where one recognizes adoption of a belief system as one option among many. Badiou imagines fidelity to truth as effecting a removal from this arena of contending options: '*To the extent that it is the subject of a truth,*' he claims, '*a subject subtracts itself from every community and destroys every individuation.*'[7]

Reason does have a role in Badiou's thought, though that role is not disjoined from truth. Drawing on the recent work of Philip Gorski and Gauri Viswanathan, we might query the valuation of reason that is often taken to be a defining mark of secularism. The rationalistic faith of the early modern period, Gorski observes, was faith nonetheless, but one different in kind to its medieval predecessor, which tended to emphasize institutions and ceremonies as mediating divine mystery.[8] More productive in defining secularism may be the dissociation of belief and imagination: it is when myth serves as epistemic ground that we are in a frame of mind at odds with secularism, though that frame of mind can still give ample space to reason as a hermeneutic tool and can interrogate institutions and ceremonies claiming to embody divine will.[9]

In placing reason within the framework of belief, Badiou is a current thinker with particular relevance to discussion of Milton and to the seventeenth-century idea of *recta ratio*, or 'right reason.' Unlike instrumental reason, *recta ratio* is a mental unfolding of right order. It does not cast rival claims in the scales and decide which carries the greater weight of evidence; it seeks to determine the terms consistent with divinely ordained principles, placing reason in the service of faith. As Milton describes it in *De doctrina Christiana*, the divinely implanted capacity for *recta ratio* 'establishes a dividing line between right and wrong.' Without this guide, '[W]hat was to be called virtue, and what vice, would be guided by mere arbitrary opinion' (*YP* 6: 132). Marking his distance from Taylor's secular age, Milton describes every mind as carrying this divinely granted brand of conscience, so that denial of God's existence is equivalent to insanity (*YP* 6: 130). His rationalism is what Gorski has called the 'religious rationalization' of the early modern period, which rejects a 'magical, ritual, and communal' religiosity in favor of an 'ethical, intellectual, and individual' one. These are not, Gorski observes, 'so much different *levels* of religiosity, one of which is less Christian than the other, as two different *kinds* of religiosity, one of which is less rationalistic than the other.'[10]

As in Badiou's post-secular formulation, Milton's pre-secular reason is the means by which the subject cleaves to the path of truth in the wild wood of competing claims. The reader of Milton will instantly apprehend what Badiou is driving at when he tells us that democracy is necessary to philosophy, which removes the search for truth from princes and priests, but a difficulty after philosophy, which offers a truth that becomes a positive obligation for every fit mind. The younger Sir Henry Vane (1613–62), a contemporary who shares a good many of Milton's opinions, defines freedom as the 'power to will immutably that which is good . . . not only without any resistance or hindrance from within him that wills or does it, but against all the tempting or attempting power of any other person or thing without him.' Badiou analogously claims that 'being free does not pertain to the register of relation (between bodies and languages) but directly to that of incorporation (to a truth).'[11]

Much less strident in its defense of belief, the late Derridean ethics that we shall explore in chapter two argues for a 'messianicity without messianism' or, in another of its phrases, for the adoption of a 'nondogmatic doublet of dogma . . . a thinking that "repeats" the possibility of religion without religion.'[12] In this view the inscrutable Other makes demands of infinite love never fully discharged, calling us to strive for fuller manifestations of justice and democracy, always in the mode of 'to come.' Derrida confesses his proximity to Kant, to Walter Benjamin, and to Emmanuel Lévinas. Like Kant and Lévinas, he avers that we cannot fully know the transcendent Other who makes these constant demands. But unlike Kant he does not adopt an Aristotelian *telos* where imperfect human virtue necessarily implies the existence of perfect virtue in the afterlife, being more interested in the ethical pressure felt by the subject than in metaphysical questions of whence that pressure arises and where it ends. The paradox of 'religion without religion' that he employs is a device suggesting the existence of moral intuitions constantly urging us to make the world fit for messianic arrival. Though Derrida's late affinity for theological language is sometimes deemed a post-secular turn, it is also consistent with his long-standing worrying over the pursuit of the good deferred by the language games he famously describes.

Metaphysics are taken up more fully by John Milbank, who argues for the possibility of infinite truths within an ostensibly Christian account of transcendence. There are, as he describes it, 'infinitely many possible versions of truth. . . . Objects and subjects are, as they are narrated in a story. . . . If subjects and objects only are, through the complex relations of a narrative, then neither objects are privileged, as in premodernity, nor subjects, as in modernity.'[13] If Kant responds to the 'immense depth behind things' by distinguishing 'what is clear from what is hidden,' Milbank would 'trust the depth, and appearance as the gift of depth, and history as the restoration of the loss of this depth in Christ.'[14] His 'Postmodern Critical Augustinianism' adds a theistic strain to post-modern emphasis on contingency and narrativization. Rather than a void beyond the perceptible, we find a benevolent divinity and the possibility of harmonious society, or what Milbank describes as an Augustinian *societas perfecta*.

His 'radical orthodoxy' is 'orthodox' in its reclamation of actual divine presence in the universe, as opposed to the liberal theology that it accuses of giving over God's transcendence, and in its rejection of Protestant historical teleology in favor of the pure contingency of the given.[15] It is 'radical' in the sense that it conceives of this return to orthodoxy as a critique, indeed as the strongest possible critique, of the nihilist materialism that the secular tradition breeds. 'The secular natural law model,' Milbank argues, 'establishes "autonomy" with the fiction that fundamental social arrangements can be deduced simply from the formal requirements of reason. (These deductions then, of course, unconsciously reproduce bourgeois property laws and understandings of the individual.)'[16] This is equivalent to the public space of violence that Augustine finds in Rome, against which the Church offers a 'new social order based on love and forgiveness.' Only through the example of Christ is God fully connected to the visible world, to which He offers peace beyond the civic peace that secularism continually defers, and points to salvation as the possibility of human harmony freed from the prevailing authorities of the political domain. That possibility is not an opiate, but a foundation for social formations fully rejecting bourgeois individualism, as Milbank makes clear in *Theology and Social Theory*.[17]

What we have called the third kind of post-secular thought argues for an adjustment of our view of modernity in the face of the persistent, indeed the increasing, relevance of religion in large segments of civil society. Given that relevance, the principle of equality requires secular citizens to engage, as Habermas describes it, in 'a self-reflective transcending of a secularist self-understanding of Modernity.'[18] No longer can it be expected that all publicly legitimate discourse be expressed in secular language; to do so is to impose a cognitive burden upon religious citizens and to deprive them of the full rights of citizenship. Also to be abandoned is the modern secular state's aspiration of training a citizenry of freely reasoning subjects, which views religion as a vestige of pre-modern irrationality.

As we saw in introducing Badiou, secularism's claim to a monopoly on reason may not hold up to scrutiny. When that claim occurs at the level of politics, it can be an instrument of power deployed to harass religious minorities. A recent example is Switzerland's December 2009 referendum banning the construction of minarets, first conceived as an openly bigoted gimmick of the right-wing Swiss People's Party and ultimately passing by a popular vote of 57 percent—hardly a rational turn of events in a nation with a 4 percent Muslim population and exactly four minarets.[19] Daniel Pipes, a U.S. Republican thinker and Taube Visiting Fellow at Stanford's Hoover Institution, sees the referendum as legitimizing Europe's widespread and justifiable resistance to 'Islamisation,' citing newspaper polls conducted in France, Germany, and Spain all with 73 to 93 percent support of a minaret ban. That irrational fear and majoritarian bullying can masquerade as enlightened defense of liberal values does indeed demand that we re-evaluate the aggressive form secularity can take in its domination of public discourse.

∽

We shall seek in the following chapters a mutually critiquing dialogue between Milton's pre-secular thought and current post-secular formulations. Along the way we shall also explore the ways in which language is made to represent the existence of absolute truth. The first chapter deals with an epistemology where belief requires no dialectical engagement of empirical knowledge. We find the myth believed as truth in moments of plain style in *Paradise Lost*, where Milton displays precisely the epic tendency that Badiou associates with Brecht: 'The epic is what it exhibits . . . the *courage* of truth. For Brecht, art produces no truth, but is instead an elucidation—based on the supposition that the true exists—of the conditions of a courage of truth.'[20] Though Milton's epic has famously been described as grand in its style, we can see that the poet circumscribes limits upon literary sumptuousness by speaking truth in the plain voice of such characters as God the Father, Abdiel—the poem's most courageous truth warrior—and Michael. In those moments we learn that revelation is not to be modified through a rationalist thrust and parry of contending claims, and is neither generated by nor circumscribed within the poem as aesthetic object. The plain style of Milton's revealed truth is considered in this chapter alongside Badiou's appreciation of Saint Paul's adherence to the fable of the Resurrection, which, he claims, embraces plainness and dispenses with languages of received knowledge, whether Hebrew law or Greek philosophy.

The second chapter focuses on the ethics of reading suggested in Milton's *Areopagitica* and on recent engagements of ethics, which has been described as the most contentious branch of current philosophy. The occasion of *Areopagitica* is the Licensing Order of 1643, a law reviving a system of pre-publication censorship. Milton goes well beyond the immediate demands of responding to that order, dazzling us with claims on the nature of knowledge in his most beautiful prose tract by far. The rhetoric of *Areopagitica* thus shows an excess quite at odds with the plainness that we emphasize in chapter one.[21] The sometimes conflicting statements of that excess can be likened to the Freudian 'kettle logic' that Slavoj Žižek has discerned in the justification of the Iraq War, where the 'too many reasons' given for the war served as cover for imperialist ideology. That parallel suggests the presence of the political in the ethical determination of the good, which has been explored in a 2007 dialogue on *Areopagitica* by Marshall Grossman and Sharon Achinstein, and that is also silently at work in recent formulations of ethics by Jacques Derrida, Simon Critchley, and Alain Badiou. This chapter finds promise in Gayatri Spivak's ethics of responsiveness to human others—rather than the more infinite, Levinasian Other adopted by Derrida—a responsiveness foreclosed by the privileged ethos with which we are presented in Milton's tract and which resurfaces in Žižek's attempts to defend the flirtations with radical politics of Heidegger, De Man, and Foucault.

Turning to political theory's engagement of post-secularity, the third chapter concerns itself with the challenge to the secular state mounted in our time by religious communities. With such communitarian critique in view, several political theorists have presented ours as a post-liberal age—as in such titles as Paul Edward Gottfried's *After Liberalism* (1999) and Robert B. Talisse's *Democracy after Liberalism* (2005). As Paul W. Kahn suggests in *Putting Liberalism in Its Place* (2004), we might distinguish between 'liberalism of speech,' where the state secures an arena of free expression to which all have equal access, and 'liberalism of faith,' which constrains the state so that it does not interfere with the freedom to pursue the ultimate meaning that is beyond its bounds. We find that distinction dramatized in the development of Milton's politics: where the prose of the early 1640s casts the political realm as an expression of the nation's reforming spirit, the tracts of 1659–60 limit the authority of church and state so that the individual can follow divine promptings. We can again see this development present itself in Milton's language by charting the relationship between the form of political speech and its conception of the *polis*: where the literary flourishes of the early prose draw reforming energies into the political sphere, the plainness of 1659–60 expresses a politics of restraint where the state is perceived to be menacing to true reformation—the energy of reform is now separated from the government of externals with which the magistrate should be concerned. Contrary to Kahn, I argue that 'liberalism of faith' is not liberalism at all: it is a believing community's agitation for exceptional recognition that does not recognize the similar rights of other groups, as John Rawls recognizes in calling such groups 'free-riders' in the liberal state. With this in view, I turn to the compromise on religion in the public sphere recently proposed by Jürgen Habermas, which compromise I find generally congenial.

The final two chapters turn to the subject of religious violence, where belief most aggressively asserts its opposition to existing politics. Reading *Samson Agonistes* on its own terms and in light of relevant contexts—Milton's disgust with church and state in the Restoration; his plans for tragedies; his handling in the three major poems of the heroes of faith of Hebrews 11; and the writings of those close to Milton, such as Henry Lawrence and the younger Sir Henry Vane—it is quite clear that Samson's divinely inspired massacre of the Philistines was much more a source of comfort than distress for the poet. Distancing him from what we would now call an ethic of religious violence thus performs the ideological work of expurgating that ethic from the Western tradition, or of locating it in a distant and irrelevant past, so that it might be uncomplicatedly associated with a cultural Other. We might find the same ideological work performed in Milbank's partial reading of pre-modern Christian orthodoxy, particularly in the claim that such orthodoxy completely and uniquely embraces difference in its vision of divine order. Continuing this book's exploration of language in chapter five, and drawing on the insights of Talal Asad, I describe the self-immolation of the suicide bomber as a radical self-effacement. On the silence of the suicide bomber the order of narrative is imposed, whether hagiographical or demonizing, a tendency evident in Milton's handling of Samson and in literary representations of suicide bombers in our own moment, such as those of John Updike and Mohsin Hamid.

The thread running through this dialogue between post-secular thought and a pre-secular poet is the fundamentally asocial nature of the language of believed truth. Rather than participating in dialogue and seeking consensus, the language of strong belief stakes unassailable claims. With Ezekiel its truth drapes flesh over the dry bones of unbelief in the hope of raising an army of the faithful. Its ethical commitment is not primarily defined in terms of obligation to human dialogue and institutions; its politics not primarily defined as a contract securing the participation of the greatest number of citizens. At their best, those qualities can turn absolute principles of compassion and justice into a powerful critique of the given. At their worst, they produce the suicide attacker's terrifyingly complete disregard of the realm of the living.

II. On the present and the historical Other

Reading Milton in light of pressing political and intellectual concerns is a practice as old as reading Milton.[22] Shortly after being published, the republican spirit of *Paradise Lost* was praised by the parliamentarian Sir John Hobart, though received with mixed emotions by John Beale, a country minister in the national church who was also a Fellow of the Royal Society sympathetic to the epic's encyclopedic inclusion of new learning.[23] That 'villainous leading Incendiarie *John Milton*' was a bogey conveniently raised by Tories wishing to cast their Whig opponents as anti-monarchical during the Exclusion Crisis.[24] Toryism would find itself more conflicted in its view of monarchy during James II's reign, as signaled by conservative involvement in the 1688 folio edition of *Paradise Lost*. Following such sympathetic Tory response is Anthony à Wood, who embellishes the poet's connection to Oxford in the 1691 *Fasti Oxoniensis* though hardly endorses Milton's defense of the regicide styled the 'monstrous and unparallel'd height of profligate impudence.'[25]

In writing his 1698 biography, the freethinker John Toland clearly had applications to his own context in view, intentions made explicit in his discussion of the anti-Presbyterian sentiment of Milton's prose defense of tyrannicide, *The Tenure of Kings and Magistrates*. Having faithfully reproduced Milton's objections to Presbyterian hypocrisy, Toland turns his attention to those 'now cal'd *Presbyterians*,' who are as self-seeking and anti-tolerationist as ever.[26] The concerns of his own moment likewise explain his scorn for Milton's younger brother Christopher, who:

> more resembling his [Popish] Grandfather than his Father or Brother, was of a very superstitious nature, and a man of no parts or ability. . . . [T]he late King *James* [the Second], wanting a set of Judges that would declare his Will to be superior to our Legal Constitution, created him the same day a Serjeant and one of the Barons of the Exchequer, knighting him of course, and making him next one of the Judges of the Common Pleas: But he quickly had his *quietus est*, as his Master not long after was depos'd for his *Maladministration* by the People of *England*, represented in a Convention at *Westminster*.[27]

We do not know with certainty whether the younger Milton converted to Catholicism, though a group of seamen did storm his private chapel in the heat of the Glorious Revolution of 1688 and burn its 'Popish trinkets.'[28] Through this digression in his discussion of Milton's family, Toland vents hostility toward James II's favorites, along with the king's absolutism and religion.

Perhaps none were more emphatic about their application of Milton to their own concerns than the Romantics. William Wordsworth's 'Milton! thou shouldst be living at this hour' conveys an attitude shared by John Keats's ode on Milton's lock of hair and William Blake's illuminated poem *Milton*. The last of these certainly justifies Joseph Wittreich's observation on the Romantic reading of Milton not only in present but in 'future tense, so that poems emerging from one moment of crisis could reflect upon, and explain, another crisis in history when, once again, tyranny and terror ruled.'[29] That tendency persists into the twentieth century. During the Second World War, G. Wilson Knight's *Chariot of Wrath* associates

Milton's Satan with Adolf Hitler in its account of the values threatened by fascism; this despite Knight's earlier critique of *Paradise Lost*, 'The Frozen Labyrinth,' which scorns Milton in a way made fashionable for a time by Ezra Pound, F. R. Leavis, and T. S. Eliot.[30] In *'Paradise Lost' in Our Time*, a book arising from lectures delivered at Cornell in 1943–44, Douglas Bush notes the change in sentiment, cringing over Knight's tendentiousness:

> In 1942, having felt the impact of the war, Mr. Knight mounted the architect of the frozen labyrinth in a chariot of wrath as the great apostle of national liberty and destiny. One may respect the feeling behind the change while thinking that Milton might have preferred relatively intelligible criticism to a whirlwind apotheosis.[31]

A sophisticated poet, Bush rightly argues, certainly deserves a more sophisticated reading.

Though he is himself the finest of readers, Bush tends to turn Milton into the avatar of a tradition of Christian humanism threatened by fascism—and by the various forms of modern philistinism to which he objects in haughtier moments. In this vein he takes Milton's views on *recta ratio* apiece with those of Richard Hooker and Jeremy Taylor.[32] The war had made obsolete the skepticism, cynicism, and 'sensual irresponsibility' that made Donne seem relevant to 'defeatist intellectuals' of the Armistice period of 1918–39.[33] Milton's Christian humanism, by contrast, is a 'noble anachronism . . . in an increasingly modern and scientific world.'[34] That non-Christian forms of humanism are a sidelight in Bush's anachronism make it seem rather more anachronistic today—unless one feels with Milbank that Christianity opens vistas of human harmony unavailable in any other religion or philosophy. But one must note that his standard of Christian humanism allowed Bush to mount a strong critique of the moderns' flirtations with fascism and to remain skeptical of the New Humanism advocated by his Harvard professor Irving Babbitt, with its unabashed neo-roman elitism.[35] In ways that Bush is sometimes reluctant to acknowledge, Milton is more than a little sympathetic to such neo-roman meritocracy, and placing him in a tradition of Christian humanism can downplay his considerable heterodox energies. Bush's handling of the poet is a studied apotheosis, but an apotheosis nonetheless.

That kind of presentism was duplicated in the Cold War preparation of Milton's prose works by Don M. Wolfe, and has surfaced again in the context of the 'war on terror.'[36] Wittreich finds liberating energies especially in the ambiguity of Milton's poetry, which 'confronts the perils' of our time by impressing upon us 'the smallness of our understanding of them.'[37] Praising G. Wilson Knight's comprehension, Wittreich joins him in finding the final poems prophetic in their prefiguration of present-day global conflict, with Samson especially 'a weapon of mass destruction' whose brutality Milton deploys to arraign all those who would engage in divinely inspired slaughter. John Carey takes a similar view in his now infamous pronouncements on the first anniversary of 9/11. 'September 11 has changed *Samson Agonistes*,' he declares, 'because it has changed the readings we can derive from it while still celebrating it as an achievement of the human imagination.' It is the task of literary criticism, by this standard, to celebrate human imagination in a way untroubling to current political sensitivities and the casual bigotries they breed. One can only paraphrase Milton's response to the Remonstrant's defense of the English liturgy as being so wisely framed as to be inoffensive to the pope: O new and never-heard of Supererogative height of wisdom and charity in our criticism![38]

This brief survey suggests that the presentist reading of Milton has a long history though not an especially distinguished one. When deployed to read current concerns, Milton tends to take one of two shapes: an uncomplicated champion of liberty summoned to arraign unjust authority, or a demonized anti-monarchist representing the horrors of anarchy among defenders of order. The first of these tends to glide past those aspects of the poet's thought not entirely humane and democratic. The second tends to inflate those aspects of his thought. That Milton takes for granted the divine inspiration of Samson's mass slaughter is only one reason for the untenability of the poet's uncomplicated heroism, which feminist interpretation of his works should have made untenable some time ago. But sensitivity to that feminist interpretation should not take the form of Samuel Johnson's infamous charge of a 'Turkish contempt for women,' itself an alibi for politically motivated disparagement—its casual swipe at Turks now also given renewed relevance by a potential association of Milton with Muslim backwardness.

The shortcomings of presentism are no less apparent in Shakespeare studies, where the term has come increasingly to appear and where it has seemed at times like a facile rejection of the careful evaluation of works in their original contexts. Its privileging of the present moment tends blithely to claim, as Linda Charnes does, that it is 'fine' to 'use' Shakespeare in a 'pliable deployability' striving for 'timely/polemical intervention.'[39] Ewan Fernie legitimately asks what purpose the historical otherness of Shakespeare's oft-read and oft-staged plays serves in our moment, but proceeds in the process to describe as unnecessary that scholarly work providing any 'extra' historical account beyond this aura. His presentism ultimately rests on a textual 'presence' conceived as a transhistorical aesthetic response, a 'powerful *imminence* of sense' that is 'ineffably beyond thought.'[40] Though it spends much time setting itself against the ascendancy of New Historicism in studies of early modern drama, this presentism does retain one of the most dubious assumptions of that movement: the sloppy Habermasianism of the notion that literature shapes its political circumstances as much as it is shaped by them. It does, however, differ from New Historicism in seeking more fully to liberate that presupposition from the burden of proof.[41]

'Presentism' thus seems a term worth disowning, and I do not use it to describe the approach of this book. I accept the basic premise of historicism, namely that understanding contexts—artistic, intellectual, political, material—is necessary to understanding a written work, literary or non-literary, and that scholarship must strive for as rigorous and balanced an account of those contexts as is possible. (This is not to say that literary works are reducible to historical data, or that history as such is the agent of cultural production, or that the internal textures of literature should be overlooked; none of these is a principle fundamental to historicist criticism, though each can be implied in the blunders of critics.)

The necessity of careful attention to historical contexts might be demonstrated by the unsettling consequences of Wittreich's presentism, with its emphasis on ambiguity and its labile 'shifting contexts.' In the view advanced especially in his studies of *Samson Agonistes*, new contexts can unfurl a text's latent meanings. One of the most suggestive applications of that approach is his reading of the boy guide who leads Samson to the temple, which applies to Milton's dramatic poem questions raised by the character Body in Ralph Ellison's *Juneteenth*: '[Do] you remember in the Bible where it tells about Samson and it says he had him a boy to lead him up to the wall, so he could shake the building down? . . . Well answer me this, you think that little boy got killed?' That question alerts us to Milton's fleeting mention of Samson's guide:

> he his guide requested
> (For so from such as nearer stood we heard)
> As over-tir'd to let him lean a while
> With both his arms on those two massie Pillars
> That to the arched roof gave main support.
> He unsuspitious led him[.] (1630–35)

Wittreich takes the description of the guide as 'unsuspitious' as a 'telling emendation of the Judges story' by which Milton 'deepens the horror of the final catastrophe' and 'acknowledges as Ellison seems to comprehend, that Samson is a fixture within a culture of supposed heroes who, "killing multitudes," are themselves in need of the deliverer they sought to be.'[42] The Samson story teaches Milton that 'blood spilled in violence begets more violence,' making him in turn the teacher not only of Ellison, but also of Malcolm X, whose reading of *Paradise Lost* in prison planted the seed of his eventual turn away from an ethic of violence; and Toni Morrison, who in her novel *Paradise* evokes Milton's poetry as 'a model for mounting her own critiques of God and religion, theology and politics.'[43] In what Wittreich describes as 'Milton's (post)modernity,' poetic ambiguities liberate us from political absolutism and religious dogma supporting violence, liberating energies not lost on the African-American thinkers to whom he draws our attention.

Inviting. But much as I would like to imagine Milton marching on Washington, such reverie is quite at odds with the stubborn fact of his casual attitude toward the African slave trade. In *Paradise Lost* the Archangel Michael makes that trade an instance of divine justice in his account of the curse of Ham:

> Witness th'irreverent Son
> Of him who built the Ark, who for the shame
> Don to his Father, heard this heavie curse,
> *Servant of Servants*, on his vitious Race. (12.100–104)

Handling this biblical episode in her long poem on the book of Genesis, Milton's contemporary Lucy Hutchinson (1620–81) emphasizes the fault of Noah, whose actions hardly befit patriarchal dignity:

> Noah of the sparkling juice drunk deep,
> And, stupefied with liquor, fell asleep,
> Whom Ham, his scoffing son, in lewd plight found
> Immodestly incovered on the ground.[44]

In the *First Anniversary*, Andrew Marvell (1621–78) uses Ham as an emblem of ungrateful irreverence applied to those radicals opposing Cromwell's reign who celebrated the national crisis threatened by his overturned coach.[45]

Unlike Hutchinson, Milton places blame for the episode entirely on Ham, departing from form in not making this an instance of Noah resigning his manhood through intemperate indulgence. And unlike Marvell, Milton reads the Curse of Ham all too literally: he applies it to the Canaanites and by implication to their seventeenth-century descendants through Ham's son Cush, those sub-Saharan Africans whose abject servitude is justly imposed. The point is not lost on the eighteenth-century philologist James Paterson in his commentary on *Paradise Lost*: '[Ham's] *Curse* has lain heavy upon his *Posterity* to this Day: For the *Old Carthaginians*, *Grecians*, *Romans*, and all the *Nations of Europe*, made *Slaves* of the *Africans*: Let all Children take Care of *Disobedience* to their Parents.'[46] In this light, a program of reading Milton that would make him the great tutor of those black thinkers dismantling the vicious legacy of slavery is not only imprecise, it also imposes upon Ellison, Malcolm X, and Morrison the intellectual paternity of a poet blithely accepting precisely the racial attitudes that they resist. A presentist program of reading that would 'use' Milton according to the pliable deployability emerging from 'shifting contexts' covers up our knowledge of his participation in a culture of white supremacy.

If we read Milton's less appealing moments aright we will see that they are not exceptions to his eloquent demands for liberty but are corollaries of the brand of liberty to which he subscribes. Internal fitness is always a prerequisite in Milton's terms to outward liberty.[47] Milton's first *Defence* cites Aristotle and Cicero in claiming that 'the peoples of Asia readily endure slavery, while the Jews and Assyrians were born for it. I confess that those who long for liberty or can enjoy it are but few—only the wise, that is, and the brave; while most men prefer just masters so long as they are in fact just' (*YP* 4: 343). Such liberty assumes its enjoyment to be above the capacity of the common herd, whose inner servility takes naturally to outward servility.

A similar exclusivity operates in Milton's thought on Christian liberty. Critiquing the reading of *Samson Agonistes* that appears in chapter four of this book, Paul Stevens has described toleration and zeal as 'rival desires' in Milton's thought.[48] That strikes me as imprecise. Toleration of sectarian Protestantism—the only brand of toleration that Milton ever defends—resists those institutions interfering with individual seeking of a divinely appointed path, which path can in some cases lead one to righteous destruction of idolaters. Toleration is the condition by which zeal can find appropriate expression, and is never extended to those whom Milton identifies as enemies of truth. As with his neo-roman principles, his views on Christian liberty assume internal fitness as a prerequisite.

Any approach striving for clear-sighted reading—the only aim that matters in criticism—must make an accurate reckoning of Milton's thought and work with little heed for what inspires and what offends. Presentism tends to fall short of this measure, and to be prone to three pitfalls in particular: (1) the dead end of relevance; (2) the 'wisdom of the ancients' fallacy; and (3) rewriting an author to suit our interests. Relevance can serve as a barker's call when one wishes to enliven for a moment a room full of undergraduates in various stages of sleep. As an end in itself, it really cannot be deemed productive in any other way. And those who attempt to make relevance seem critically productive can often fall into the comfort of the 'wisdom of the ancients' fallacy, which holds not only that Milton (or Shakespeare, or Sophocles) is engaged by concerns like ours, but possesses by virtue of age the insights we so desperately need. That is a fine view of literature for Matthew Arnold or Lynne Cheney; those seeking engaging and nuanced criticism will not find it compelling. Which leads us to the height of critical hubris, draping an author in those fabrics fashionable in our own moment while covering the dated and unseemly attire of his or her own selection. The theoretical insight that all criticism is a form of re-writing should not lead us to view re-writing as our primary task.

We shall seek to avoid these traps, and to discern order and fundamental principles rather than to take the *a priori* road of presentism. Our approach will aim to offer, as the chapters on *Samson Agonistes* in this book hope to show, the strongest possible critique of a program of reading that would surround unscrutinized assumptions of our time with the *gravitas* of cultural heritage. Even though the launching point of this book's historicist inquiry is current concern, it must be mounted in a way that respects historical otherness insofar as criticism can. That is nothing new. More novel is allowing that historical Other to yield in turn an anachronism informing inquiry into the present, which might then also be explored with some of the rigor and critical distance that historicism lends to a study of the past, so that we might better perceive the limits of orthodoxies pervasive in our own moment.[49] Such an approach lends the historical otherness of the past an active charge in its critique of the present, rather than being ossified as part of a 'tradition' or obscured by the demands of polemical intervention.

I do not call this a dialectic between past and present because it is in fact an interruption of the progressivism implicit in a Hegelian view of history, a view suggesting that the new emerges as a synthesis retaining finer elements of the old. What I propose comes much closer to Benjamin's 'Theses on Historical Philosophy' in treating each historical moment as a monad: we might pick up two objects from the wreckage at the feet of Benjamin's Angel of History and ask what each one tells us about the other.[50] Comparison need not subscribe to—and can indeed provide a strong resistance of—the notion that one of these monads anticipates or is superseded by the other. Its concern with two temporally discrete moments remains largely agnostic on the big question of historical appearance, not necessarily subtending materialism or idealism, Whig historiography or absolute contingency. The focus of this book may be on literary criticism in light of intellectual history, but its approach will certainly lend itself to other kinds of focus. Properly conducted, such inquiry critiques historicism's tendency toward implicit progressivism, and presentism's tendency toward brazen partiality.

Rather than tossing a concern for evidence in the dustbin, we shall aim for precise handling of artifacts and careful questioning of historical narrativization. But we shall also view the present not as an obstacle to the 'scientific' study of the past, but as potentially fructifying—to say nothing of it being an inescapable fact to be confronted head on. The readings that follow will strive toward a mutual critique of past and present. While they worry about anti-humane and anti-democratic forces in both of those moments, they shall open, rather than foreclose, the complexities of the writers and thinkers under discussion, and explore pre-secularity and post-secularity on their own terms.

1

'Not but by the Spirit understood': Milton's Plain Style and Present-Day Messianism

Arguments for Milton's ability to speak to our moment seem increasingly to refer to the rationalist thrust and parry of contending ideas in his work. In a 2008 article in the *New Yorker,* Jonathan Rosen avers that '[in] America, where God and the Devil live alongside Western rationalism, Milton seems right at home.'[1] Milton scholars draw similar conclusions. Nigel Smith's fine introduction, *Is Milton Better than Shakespeare?*, objects to a reading of the poet that places God too firmly in the center of his vision, arguing especially against the views of Stanley Fish and claiming that Milton is 'both theistic and post-theistic, mono-theistic and polyglot.'[2] 'Milton *matters*,' Joseph Wittreich claims in more sanguine terms, because 'he forces us to reach beyond an axis of good and evil in the world . . . to a more ambiguous reality.'[3]

I am not persuaded by this view, but it does alert us to aspects of Milton that might be overlooked by too narrow an emphasis on his theism. Perhaps a term that might productively describe Milton is 'pre-secular.' We hear everywhere in his writings the footfalls of those modes of thought predominant in secularism, but these are contained within and measured by a fundamentally non-secular system of belief. Implicitly at issue is the value of reason as a category significant to discussion of secularization. Turning away from the dubiously productive distinction between faith and reason, current studies point to secularism's dissociation of belief and imagination.[4] When natural order is secured by myth rather than knowledge we are in a frame of mind at odds with secularism. Biblical narrative governs Milton's view of the world's creation, progress, and ultimate end, though he gives space to the language of geographical exploration and scientific discovery. We shall see how Alain Badiou finds in Saint Paul a similar faith in the 'pure fable' of the Resurrection that is the standard by which law and language are measured.

If Milton is 'pre-secular,' he might be brought into productive dialogue with our post-secular moment, the most obvious symptom of which is the *revanche de Dieu* that seems to be awakening zeal in all religions across the globe and producing increasingly un-liberal theologies claiming, like the Reformation sects before them, repristination of religious ideals: whether the rise of Wahhabism; or the Catholic Church's appointment of a pope decidedly of the global North and West; or the June 2008 assembly in Jerusalem of conservative Anglican divines threatening to split from the Communion in their ire over the openly gay American bishop Gene Robinson. Among these conservatives the Archbishop of Uganda, Henry Orombi, has articulated aims that will sound familiar to any student of the Reformation: 'I want that we go back to the first love that the early Church had in Jerusalem . . . that we go back to believing the word of God to be the word of God, as it is in the Bible.'[5] (These splitters, however, themselves are split over whether to adopt Saint Paul's anti-feminism with his anti-gay sentiments: the purest purists among them object to the ordination of women as bishops.)[6]

It is easy to object to a brand of religion that, like Spenser's Ignaro, is ever looking backward in its progress. But the post-secular turn equally pervades current philosophy. This is not a moral equivalence—the authors in which I am interested claim no victims and repair to no ancient bigotries—but a discursive equivalence. This chapter will explore Milton's primacy of belief alongside post-secular formulations, paying particular attention to the way in which the adoption of plain expression affirms that primacy—the dissociation of belief and imagination brings to mind Eliot's 'dissociation of sensibility' with its attack on poetry residing in the realm of thought more than feeling. That attack is mistaken in taking aim at Milton. The privilege accorded to the plain style in *Paradise Lost* is an immediate expression of a felt truth received by divine illumination, and seems in Milton's terms to represent poetry's highest strain. Milton himself critiques a poetry that dissociates thought and feeling, the kind of poetry where emotional and intellectual richness are only literary. A similar relationship between style and truth can be found in current models of immanence. We will explore especially Michael Hardt and Antonio Negri, as well as Alain Badiou, with respect to the nature of truth and especially the democratic and anti-democratic dynamics of truth-claims. Particularly relevant is the model of democratic universality in which Badiou enlists Saint Paul's fidelity to the 'event' of the Resurrection.

I. Plain style as epistemic ground in 'Paradise Lost'

With Donne, style *is* faith: a measure of delivery that confesses his own inordinacy while remaining in all things ordinate. To state this is to affirm one's recognition of his particular authority in having achieved the equation; one recognizes also such authority in Milton and Herbert. They are not, generally, otherwise to be equated.

—Geoffrey Hill, *Style and Faith* (2003)

There is a great deal to unpack in Geoffrey Hill's characteristically rich comment on Donne, Milton, and Herbert: it encapsulates each poet's relationship to language, which is also a relationship to faith ('style *is* faith'), and how poetic authority resides in having achieved this 'equation.'[7] We must also see immediately the good sense of not otherwise equating the three poets. Donne shows us time and again that ordinacy in language is *only* ordinacy in language, mastery over a limited and limiting human system ever falling short in its attempts to incorporate divine Truth. This style corresponds to a faith where soteriological self-assurance is a temptation to be resisted—the lesson of the third satire is that our eternal fate depends upon a necessary doctrinal commitment of which we cannot be certain and for which no worldly authority can equip us. For Herbert style and faith are a stripping away of human confusion so that we can arrive at a Truth reminding us of the divine order beyond our grasp. This is the lesson on style of the 'Jordan' poems.

For Milton the equation of style and faith is more complex, for we must first ask, 'Which style?' There is perhaps no other poet who has at his command so broad a range of styles, from grand to plain. It is the former that has always been taken as his hallmark, earning Addison's comment that Milton adopts the grand style 'to give his Verse the greater Sound, and throw it out of Prose'—an observation made more feline in T. S. Eliot's comment that Milton's 'poetry is poetry at the farthest possible remove from prose,' and that he is 'the greatest of all eccentrics. His work illustrates no general principles of good writing; the only principles of writing that it illustrates are such as are valid only for Milton himself to observe.'[8]

Leavis and Eliot tend to object to Milton's style as excessively ornamented and big-mouthed—that it is grand in the way of rococo's garish display rather than in the way of baroque sublimity. In his *Origin and Progress of Language* (1773–92), the Lord Monboddo more accurately observes that Milton's style is both lofty and 'chaste,' that it is characterized by its compactness of expression and that no device, it seems, is used without effect. His pet example is Satan's justification of his rule in book 2:

> Mee though just right, and the fixt Laws of Heav'n
> Did first create your Leader, next free choice,
> With what besides, in Counsel or in Fight,
> Hath bin achievd of merit, yet this loss
> Thus farr at least recover'd, hath much more
> Establisht in a safe unenvied Throne
> Yielded with full consent. (18–24)

Milton departs from 'natural' word order, 'taking advantage of the pronoun *I* having an accusative, and has placed it at the head of the sentence, at a great distance from its verb *established*.' In that distance are 'whole sentences concerning the laws of Heaven, the free choice of his subjects, the atchievements in battle and in council, and the recovery of their loss so far; and some of these are parentheses.' Monboddo finds precedent for such separation in Horace, and argues that the intervening statements are not 'idle words' but 'such as fill up the sense most properly, and give a solidity and compactness to the sentence, which it otherwise would not have.' Word order and syntax thus not only lend 'elegance and beauty' to the passage, but also a 'density of sense';[9] in his felicitous phrase, Milton's style is 'rounded, compact, and nervous,' a collocation that captures well its tightly and intricately interlaced energies.[10] That he connects these qualities especially to the oratory of Demosthenes—the measure of eloquence for Monboddo—and opposes them to the empty ornament that he locates in French influence on English prose style, qualifies the excessive ornamentation of which the moderns accuse Milton. As we use the term 'grand' style, it will be with awareness of Monboddo's insight on its 'chaste' qualities.

We must also raise some questions of Monboddo, however, when we find him identifying as the apex of Milton's style the speeches of Satan and the fallen angels in book 2, which he relates to the 'manly eloquence' and 'high republican spirit' of *Eikonoklastes*.[11] That Satan's republican spirit is so far from Milton's own should lead us to be skeptical of equating the style by which the two are expressed. Much as readers of *Paradise Lost* have long relished the twists and turns of diabolical eloquence, Milton himself seems strongly to value plainly expressed truth. The early prose suggests that ornament and opacity are modes of human expression opposed to the flawless clarity of God's word. By this standard *Of Reformation* declares that the 'very essence of Truth is plainnesse, and brightnes; the darknes and crookednesse is our own' (*YP* 1: 566); reform depends upon the casting off of the 'pamper'd metafors' of the Fathers in favor of the 'transparent streams of divine Truth' (*YP* 1: 568–69). *The Reason of Church Government* describes ornate poetry as appealing to those of a 'soft and delicious temper who will not so much as look upon Truth herselfe, unlesse they see her elegantly drest,' and who are distracted by 'libidinous and ignorant Poetasters' from 'that which is the main consistence of a true poem, the choys of persons as they ought to introduce, and what is morall and decent to each one' (*YP* 1: 817–18).

Plainness is of course central to *Paradise Regained*, which all but eliminates epic convention in Jesus' straightforward dismissals of Satan. This seems for Milton a long-standing model of resistance to temptation, equally discernible in the Lady's steadfastly moral, if also sententious, handling of Comus:

> swinish gluttony
> Ne're looks to Heav'n amidst his gorgeous feast,
> But with besotted base ingratitude
> Cramms, and blasphemes his feeder. Shall I go on? (776–79)[12]

'Please don't,' we might reply. This is Milton's language, as the Lady terms it, of 'sacred vehemence' (*Ludlow Mask* 795), which is not to be confused with emotional vehemence. The force of this locution derives from its expression of truth, rather than any stimulation of passion—as opposed to the temptingly infectious energy of Comus's brisk couplets: 'The Star that bids the Shepherd fold / Now the top of Heav'n doth hold, / And the gilded Car of Day . . .' (93–95).

The most infamous example in *Paradise Lost* of a character who speaks unadorned truth is of course God the Father, whose lines on the Fall are as elegantly dressed as a kick to the mid-section:

> ingrate, he had of mee
> All he could have; I made him just and right,
> Sufficient to have stood, though free to fall.
> Such I created all th' Ethereal Powers
> And Spirits, both them who stood and them who faild;
> Freely they stood who stood, and fell who fell.
> Not free, what proof could they have givn sincere
> Of true allegiance, constant Faith or Love,
> Where onely what they needs must do, appeard,
> Not what they would? what praise could they receive? (3.97–106)

It is easy to join William Blake in seeing this as Milton writing 'in fetters'—as Milton simply not being himself—but to do so is to sell this most careful poet short, as though he feels something akin to Woody Allen's character in *Stardust Memories*: 'How can I play God? I don't know what I'm doing, and I don't have the voice.'[13] We certainly see here an absence of those elements that Christopher Ricks has described as characteristic of Milton's grand style. The syntax is not at all what we would expect: rather than flowing periods, there are six independent clauses in under ten lines.

The reader who has grown accustomed to the style of books 1 and 2 is startled to find in this passage that each of these independent clauses begins with the main clause, which tends to adhere to subject-verb-object order: 'he had of mee / All he could have ... I made him ... Such I created all th'Ethereal Powers ... Freely they stood.' Though Ezra Pound's favorite example of Milton's 'Latinate' inversion derives from a speech of the Father—'him who disobeys / Mee disobeys' (5.611–12)—inversion in book 3, as in book 5, serves an important emphatic purpose.[14] In this case it establishes a series of questions demonstrating the pointlessness of forming a creature not endowed with free will, lent further emphasis still through alliteration of the qualities such creation would preclude: 'what *proof* could they have givn,' 'what *praise* could they receive,' 'what *pleasure* I from such obedience' (3.107; emphasis mine). As is typical of the Father's frequent use of rhetorical schemes of parallelism and repetition, the effect is not propositional but declarative. He is not advancing a case for why the fallen angels should be damned as much as he is revealing the nature of the universe in a way that demonstrates its government by divine clarity rather than chaotic uncertainty: 'Freely they stood who stood, and fell who fell.' The adverb 'freely' applies equally to standing and falling; the parallel construction and restrictive 'who' leave no doubt that obedience and rebellion are willed choices made by individual angels. Milton's ability to craft a divine voice articulating the most complex of theological topics in this way is central to his theodicy, and is no small literary achievement.[15]

We find a creaturely counterpart to this divine speech in Abdiel's resistance to Satan. When Satan appeals to liberty and the dignity of angelic nature, Abdiel responds with direct counter-claims on divine order. He begins with precise application of a term that the Father has already associated with fallenness, 'ingrate' (5.811). While his first speech to Satan aims to persuade by arguing from concession—'But to grant it thee unjust,/That equal over equals Monarch Reigne' (5.831–32)—persuasion turns more fully to righteous proclamation when Satan proves recalcitrant: 'O alienate from God, O spirit accurst,/Forsak'n of all good; I see thy fall/Determind' (5.877–79). Sustaining the plain style of Abdiel's pronouncement is the commentary immediately following it, made in this instance through the voice of Raphael:

> So spake the Seraph *Abdiel* faithful found,
> Among the faithless, faithful only hee;
> Among innumerable false, unmov'd,
> Unshak'n, unseduc'd, unterrifi'd
> His Loyaltie he kept, his Love, his Zeale;
> Nor number, nor example with him wrought
> To swerve from truth, or change his constant mind
> Though single. From amidst them forth he passd,
> Long way through hostile scorn, which he susteind
> Superior, nor of violence fear'd aught;
> And with retorted scorn his back he turn'd
> On those proud Towrs to swift destruction doom'd. (5.896–907)

This verse paragraph is in its own way as arresting as the most sumptuous passages in *Paradise Lost*. We see at every turn the sound devices that Milton typically uses to great effect—the assonance, sibilance, and alliteration of 'spake the Seraph . . . faithful found, faithless, faithful' and 'proud Tow'rs to swift destruction doom'd'; and enjambment into emphatic statement as in 'his constant mind/Though single' and 'which he sustain'd/Superior.' With the quickness of the latter enjambment Milton whisks away as negligible the difficulty emphasized in the opening spondee and long vowels of 'Long way through hostile scorn.'[16]

As with the speeches of God the Father, we can also notice that this passage is not in the grand style. There are five independent clauses in twelve lines, and we twice begin a thought with a main clause: 'So spake the Seraph *Abdiel*' and 'Nor number, nor example with him wrought.' The most notable syntactic ambiguity arrives in the second independent clause, where we might initially wonder if the catalogue of participles, 'unmov'd, / Unshak'n, unseduc'd, unterrifi'd,' is governed by 'found,' but see instead that these introduce the main clause 'His Loyaltie he kept, his Love, his Zeal.' In resolving the ambiguity Milton clarifies the distinction between virtue's causes and effects: heroism resides not in constancy, but in a constancy arising from religious zeal. In the same stroke Milton reveals as empty Satan's earlier self-congratulation for a 'mind not to be chang'd by Place or Time' (1.253); Abdiel's unshakeable loyalty is allowed the honorific task of exposing this Satanic error frequently displayed in the epic's first four books.

The passage similarly eschews the wordplay of the grand style, though John Leonard is certainly correct to note the play underlying 're-torted scorn,' with its reference to the Latin *retortus*, or 'turned back.'[17] One measure of this lack of wordplay is that Richard Bentley smells no rat in these lines, offering only one emendation ('proud Troops' rather than 'proud Towrs'), and even this he offers relatively tentatively and on the basis of Abdiel's having already traveled a 'long way' from the physical center of Satan's camp.[18] The tendency here is rather to fix meanings with absolute clarity. If Matthew Arnold finds problematic theology's taking in a 'fixed and rigid' manner those biblical words describing emotions in a 'fluid and passing way,' Milton is a great offender in this moment.[19] 'Loy-altie,' 'Love,' and 'Zeale' are removed from the realm of fluid and passing emotion and shown to have their true meaning in the posture toward God exemplified by Abdiel.

Milton as well here exposes the limits of Eliot's charge of eccentricity, for this is not at all poetry at the farthest possible remove from prose. The figures used are not simple ornament; they generate the terms of heroism of faith upon its first historical example. This is the purpose of the schemes of repetition—the anaphora of 'Among the faithless . . . / Among innumerable false'; the climax of 'His Loyalty he kept, his Love, his Zeal'; and the repetition of words with like prefixes—a sort of translation into English of *homoioptóton*, the repetition of case endings—seen in 'unmov'd,/Unshak'n, unseduc'd, unterrifi'd.' This last device Milton also uses in book 3 where the Son describes the operation of grace—which 'to all/Comes unprevented, unimplor'd unsought' (230–31)—and to emphasize the change of notes to tragic in the proem to book 9, a portion of the epic that Ricks identifies as deviating from grandness: 'foul distrust, and breach/Disloyal on the part of Man, revolt,/And disobedience: On the part of Heav'n now alienated, distance and distaste' (9.6–9).[20] Jesus also uses the device in his dismissal of the 'captive Tribes' in *Paradise Regained*: 'Unhumbl'd, unrepentant, unreform'd' (3.429).[21]

In noticing Milton's repetition of prefixes, one recalls a further example in Belial's masterful speech counseling inaction, used to emphasize the suffering that a renewed divine wrath could impose upon the fallen angels: 'for ever sunk/Under yon boyling Ocean, wrapt in Chains; . . ./ Unrespited, unpitied, unrepreev'd,/Ages of hopeless end' (2.182–86). This instance of the device, however, admits slippages of meaning that subtly betray Belial's fallen condition and his 'ignoble' argument (2.227). 'Respite' can mean both 'to relieve by an interval of rest,' the sense Belial apparently intends, and 'to grant a stay of execution.' As such it reminds us that the respite here recommended cannot offer release from the fallen angels' inevitable extirpation. The same implications are made more strongly with the term 'unrepreev'd,' which can also mean not to be granted a delay of execution.[22] 'Unpitied' is ambiguous in that 'pity' can mean in the period both to receive pity and to feel it—for the latter of these meanings the *OED* cites Pepys's entry for 20 July 1666, 'Old Mr. Hawly, whose condition pities me.'[23] Regardless of their response to Belial, the fallen angels will remain cut off from pity in both senses: like the 'hope' that has no place in Hell, and as implied in the parable of the debtors (Matt 18.23–35), 'pity' is an emotion with a divine source felt only by the upright soul. The ambiguities of these terms suggest the spiritual motions of which the fallen angels are incapable and the divine justice from which they cannot escape. Where their council skirts around these truths of their existence, heavenly 'council' is the mechanism by which the truths defining existence are unambiguously revealed. Belial's repetition of prefixes may appear to employ a figure of the plain style used by Abdiel or the Son, but it is in fact a corruption of that style whereby the speaker reveals his distance from divine truth. Belial's tongue, we are told, drops 'Manna' (2.113), a term that had become dislodged from its straightforward reference to the food supplied to the Israelites, and by extension to God's word, in being applied more figuratively to any food of value and associated with grains of frankincense.[24]

The same is true of the plainness affected by that fallen angel to whom Belial is responding, Moloch, who adopts the military man's opposition to florid speech, which is supposed also to reveal a lack of guile: 'My sentence is for open Warr: Of wiles / More unexpert, I boast not' (2.51–52). His plain speech is reminiscent of Lucan's Caesar, who claims a soldierly ethos in mocking his opponents and inspiring his troops to mount a civil war:

> Men who have fought and faced with me the peril of battle a thousand times, for ten years past you have been victorious. Is this your reward for blood shed on the fields of the North, for wounds and death, and for winters passed beside the Alps? . . . As it is, when Fate deals kindly with me and the gods summon me to the highest place, my foes challenge me. Let their leader, enervated by long peace, come forth to war with his hasty levies and unwarlike partisans—Marcellus, that man of words, and Cato, that empty name.[25]

Thus Caesar presents Pompey as an ambitious usurper and himself as a courageous restorer of order. Moloch similarly opposes those political minds who 'contrive' rather than act (2.53), argues that the 'Millions that stand in Arms' deserve better than the 'Den of Shame' appointed by the 'Tyranny' of him 'who Reigns / By [their] delay' (2.55–60), and claims that in their 'proper motion' the fallen angels 'ascend / Up to [their] native seat' (2.75–76). In both Caesar and Moloch, the appearance of directness is used as a persuasive form of equivocation. It is a device advancing their contriving, rather than a true opposition to rhetoric divorced from truth. The hollowness of Moloch's call to arms is signaled before he utters a word, when we are told that his fierceness arises from 'despair' rather than courage, a fact revealed in his recommendation of a suicide mission: being reduced by God's wrath 'To nothing' is 'happier farr / Than miserable to have eternal being' (2.97–98).

Lucan's presentation of manipulative plainness recalls Cicero's praise of Caesar's rhetorical style in the *Brutus*. Caesar laid great emphasis on the 'choice of words,' and especially on a 'pure Latin' untainted by foreign influence.[26] His *Commentaries* are especially pure in that they lay aside oratorical ornament altogether in a spare narration of feats: 'they are like nude figures, straight and beautiful; stripped of all ornament of style as if they had laid aside a garment. . . . [In] history there is nothing more pleasing than brevity clear and correct.'[27] The *Orator* describes more fully the attributes of the plain style of rhetoric: it 'follows the ordinary usage' of language; it avoids 'cementing . . . words together too smoothly, for the hiatus and clash of vowels has something agreeable about it and shows a not unpleasant carelessness on the part of a man who is paying more attention to thought than to words'; and it expresses itself in 'pure Latin' with 'propriety' of diction being 'the chief aim.'[28] While minimizing the 'charm and richness of figurative ornament,' it does 'employ an abundance of apposite maxims' and can use metaphor 'because it is of the commonest occurrence in the language of townsman and rustic alike.'[29]

Though the Lady's speech quoted above draws on apposite maxim, the plainness of *Paradise Lost* and *Paradise Regained* seems characterized much more by a propriety of diction and by an absence of ornament, and in fact employs the syntactic parallelism and schemes of repetition against which Cicero warns:

> [T]his shrewd orator must avoid . . . clauses of equal length, with similar endings, or identical cadences. . . . Likewise if repetition of words requires some emphasis and a raising of the voice, it will be foreign to this plain style of oratory. Other figures of speech he will be able to use freely, provided only he breaks up and divides the periodic structure and uses the commonest words and the mildest of metaphors.[30]

These are standards hard to reconcile with the repetition of cadence and clauses punctuating the speeches of the Father—'but gráce in mé . . . Uphéld by mé . . . By mé uphéld . . . to nóne but mé' (3.174–82). Milton's retreat from some Ciceronian conventions of plain style reflects an impulse not to generate 'shrewd' oratory, but a style fitting, to use the language of the *Artis logicae*, the 'bare attestation' of divine testimony: '[D]ivine testimony does indeed affirm or deny that a thing is so, and it makes me believe; it does not prove, it does not teach, it does not make me know or understand why it is so, unless it also adds reasons' (*YP* 8: 318, 319). By these standards divine testimony is not subject to logic in that it is entirely unlike argument, which 'is relevant to something of which there is question' (*YP* 8: 220).

This participates in the Reformed view of scriptural plainness that Kenneth Graham has described as expressing the 'conviction' arising from direct revelation.[31] In Calvin's terms the certainty properly belonging to faith is an effect of 'the secret testimony of the Spirit,' which is a stay against the 'whirl of uncertainty' that would otherwise beset human conscience; '[T]hose who are inwardly taught by the Holy Spirit acquiesce implicitly in Scripture' and have a 'conviction which asks not for reasons.'[32] As has been well documented, such inspired plainness evinces itself throughout the period in the sermons and tracts of those on the left wing of Reformation.[33] Milton nods to this tradition in *A Treatise of Civil Power*, which concludes that 'in matters of religion he is learnedest who is planest' (*YP* 7: 272), and in the Archangel Michael's relatively unadorned biblical history, which tells us that the human corruption from which the visible church is far from immune leads the faithful few to rely upon 'those written Records pure, / Though not but by the Spirit understood' (12.513–14). Such is the inward testimony that guides Abel, Enoch, Abraham, Noah, and all others 'who in the worship persevere / Of Spirit and Truth' (12.532–33).

Our reading of the Father and Abdiel suggests that plainness is a standard to be met by Christian reader and poet. To put it another way, we can see Milton as adapting to his own project as poet-prophet the plain style of an earlier generation of seventeenth-century poets and of earlier Renaissance debates on Ciceronianism. We find plainness valued by Socrates in the *Gorgias* and *Phaedrus*, where it is associated with dialectic and opposed to the ornamentation of rhetoric. Diogenes of Babylon defines qualities of the plain style commensurate with Stoic values, where to speak well is to speak the truth: in his definition plain style is valued for clarity, brevity, and the precise appropriateness of its diction.[34] As Andrew Shifflett has shown, the plain style of Stoicism reflects self-knowledge and responsiveness to a 'greater Oracle,' seen in Lucan and which Milton seems especially to have in mind in *Paradise Regained*.[35] An opposition to florid language is equally taken up by the Roman satirists, Horace and especially Persius; and Horace's view of the plain style as the language of *urbanitas* would influence Ben Jonson and lead him to apply it beyond its traditional genres of comedy, satire, epigram, and epistle.[36] Milton eschews *urbanitas* in favor of the plain style's earlier association with self-knowledge and truth (or rather knowledge of the relationship between the self and divine Truth). Drawing on classical and biblical precedents, he develops a plain style rising above ornament in its direct expression of heavenly light.

Even in *Paradise Lost*, then, plainness seems to have a special relationship to faith: it is associated with God and with the Saint justified in his prophetic pronouncements against the iniquity with which he is surrounded. To return to Geoffrey Hill's terms, the sumptuousness of the grand style shows us an authority over language and only language; the plain style in Milton's handling is an expression of sanctifying faith. It is in achieving this equation between style and faith that Milton's claim to authority resides.

∽

If I emphasize the plain style, it is in part because its prominence occasions my departure from such recent studies as Wittreich's *Why Milton Matters* and Peter Herman's *Destabilizing Milton*. While these works subtly explore the contemplative aspects of Milton's poetry, its theodicy demands that it cast competing ideas in the scales and determine which side is 'light' and 'weak' (*PL* 4.1012). Milton's present-day Romantic readers would do well to recall that the finest of the Romantics saw him as a poet who 'Discord unconfoundest.'[37] As Nicholas von Maltzahn and Victoria Kahn persuasively claim, to see Milton as interested in creating a politically neutral aesthetic object is to impose upon him precisely the aesthetic ideology that he opposes, and to secularize his works in the spirit of those Restoration and eighteenth-century readers seeking to enlist him in a culture of civic religion. Milton is, as Kahn notes, 'one of the earliest critics of aesthetic ideology, that is, of the purely affective response to the work of art that places art in the service of the political status quo.'[38] Drawing on Walter Benjamin's theorization of *Trauerspiel*, she contrasts *Samson Agonistes* to baroque drama's departure from classical tragedy in detaching passion from meaningful action: 'Benjamin linked this dislocation to the Reformation, to a new focus on the individual believer, and to the priority of faith over works, which deprived human action of any immanent meaning or worth and thus provoked melancholy in the hero.'[39] *Hamlet* is thus the baroque play *par excellence*. That the martyr play becomes common in *Trauerspiel* reflects a shift of focus from action to passion, which also transforms passion into a 'stage-property' whose force exhibits 'a strange kind of externality.'[40] Reading the 'rousing motions' that prompt Samson to join the Messenger, she incisively finds the tragedy showing the insufficiency of mere pity and fear as an audience response: 'Unlike the hero of *Trauerspiel*, Samson has elevated *Spiel* or play or representation to the enabling condition of tragic action. For it is under the cover of play-acting that Samson transforms his servitude into an act of political resistance.'[41]

If there is an equivalent to Samson's rousing motions in *Paradise Lost*, it is those moments where plainspoken truth distances us from the aesthetic response invited by the poem's richly expressed passages. Just as *Samson Agonistes* invites consideration as *Trauerspiel* only to explode these conventions in its catastrophe, so too *Paradise Lost* flies above the Aonian mount when it eschews literary ornament and aligns itself with divine truth. Diminishing the authority of such high mimetic modes as epic and tragedy further still, Milton—who always expects us to be aware of his career—places in the Archangel Michael's mouth close paraphrases of *A Treatise of Civil Power*, privileging modes outside of epic, namely scripture and religious treatise, in guiding us to the paradise within.

II. Truth and the sign 'democracy'

> If something like political truth exists, that truth is an obligation for every rational mind, so freedom is absolutely limited. Conversely, if there is no such limitation, there is no political truth, but in that case there is no positive relationship between philosophy and politics. So the three terms, politics, democracy, and philosophy, are finally tied by the question of truth. The obscure knot is in fact determined by the proper obscurity of the category of truth. So the problem is, what is a democratic concept of truth? What is, against relativism and skepticism, a democratic universality? What is a political role that applies to all of us, but without the constraint of a transcendency?
>
> —Alain Badiou, 'Democracy, Politics and Philosophy'

Alain Badiou's comment on the knot of politics, democracy, and philosophy perceptively distances philosophy from a democracy making no claim of adherence to truth, and goes far in explaining the anti-democratic tradition in philosophy from Plato to Heidegger.[42] Against that tradition and a politics divorced from truth, Badiou and others seek to explore the possibility of a 'democratic universality' that can answer the nihilistic despondency they locate in liberal democracy's exclusive focus on deliberative procedures. To this end there is in current thought a turn to a new brand of democracy, one that mobilizes and unites humanity under a common cause, rather than resting on the overlapping consensus of individuals guided by unfettered reason. We will see how the language of such thought suggests privileged access to truth even as it makes claims of advancing democracy, and is thus quite opposed to the Rawlsean limits imposed upon comprehensive doctrines.

Michael Hardt and Antonio Negri speak in this language of 'democracy' in the opening paragraph of *Multitude*:

> The possibility of democracy on a global scale is emerging today for the very first time. This book is about that possibility, about what we call the project of the multitude. The project of the multitude not only expresses the desire for a world of equality and freedom, not only demands an open and inclusive democratic global society, but also provides the means for achieving it. That is how our book will end, but it cannot begin there.[43]

In the three paragraphs beginning this book, the words 'democracy' and 'democratic' appear eleven times. The word 'war' appears seven times and functions as the Anti-democracy frustrating the arrival of a moment when 'freedom' will be all in all. If we dismiss this as lame prose style, we miss the point: it is a prose style of affirmation rather than deliberation. In this regard, to compare small things with greatest, it resembles the stylistic qualities of *Paradise Lost* on which we have focused, where style reflects the giving over of open-ended contemplation so that principles above the realm of human strife can be declared with a clarity meant to reflect their status as truth.

The usage of 'democracy' here gropes for Whitman's 'pass-word primeval' much more than for anything found in political philosophy, though in Hardt and Negri's handling it falls far short of that measure and recalls instead Adorno's jargon of authenticity: 'While the jargon overflows with the pretense of deep human emotion, it is just as standardized as the world it officially negates. . . . The jargon has at its disposal a modest number of words which are received as promptly as signals.'[44] Given the cosmic aspirations of such language, it is not entirely surprising to find that Hardt and Negri's first installment on this subject, *Empire*, calls for a new chiliasm to defeat the Old Enemy of imperialism and concludes by turning to St. Francis of Assisi as a model of '*the future life of communist militancy*': 'Once again in postmodernity we find ourselves in Francis's situation, posing against the misery of power the joy of being . . . biopower and communism, cooperation and revolution remain together, in love, in simplicity, and also innocence. This is the irrepressible lightness and joy of being communist.'[45] This is not a party communism, but a universal condition of movement defined according to Bakhtinian principles of polyphonic narration and the carnivalesque: the '*logic of the multitude*' is '*a theory of organization based on the freedom of singularities that converge in the production of the common. Long live movement! Long live carnival! Long live the common!*'[46]

When Hardt and Negri descend from the mystic's Cloud of Unknowing their practical proposals are persuasive, indeed urgently necessary: they suggest that the migrant workers on whom global corporations depend be granted an immigration status that would allow them access to such vital social services as health care; and that human rights will be more than a language supporting imperialism only when a neutral, effective, and truly international judicial body tries cases on crimes against humanity. The final installment, *Commonwealth*, is the most lucid of their trilogy, exploring the foundations of modern political thought in the concept of property and seeking to re-invigorate the idea of the common. But the leap from practical proposals and analysis to a polyphonic and universal fact of human movement leads them to paper over differences among kinds of movement. As Paul Rabinow and Nikolas Rose observe, they advance a 'simplistic Manichean opposition of a mysterious global Empire to an even more phantom "multitude."'[47] The limits of their politics might arise in part from the limits of Deleuzean immanence, which takes affirmation and multiplicity as ends in themselves, rather than making discerning evaluations among various kinds of affirmation and negation.[48] For Hardt and Negri, globalization and all of its political and economic accoutrements reside in the realm of negation, while 'human movement' is affirmation; the division between the two is as unassailable as that between damnation and redemption in any other chiliasm.

Their category of 'biopolitical production' encompasses 'the production of material goods in a strictly economic sense,' and also production in 'all facets of social life, economic, cultural, and political,' a gesture that allows all to be producers.[49] But this is to lose sight of the hierarchies existing among these modes of production, and to do so in a way that ignores the privilege of cultural and political production. A strongly Western bias is perceptible in the claim that 'the contemporary scene of labor and production . . . is being transformed under the hegemony of immaterial labor, that is, labor that produces immaterial products, such as information, knowledges, ideas, images,' a bias imperfectly rectified in the next breath, where it is conceded that 'workers involved primarily in immaterial production are a small minority of the global whole.'[50] The same can be said of their perverse definition of the global poor as 'those who are inserted in the mechanisms of social production regardless of social order or property.'[51] Rather than a democratic universality, such moments reveal that those outside of America and Western Europe are of secondary concern, and thus confirms, rather than challenges, the primacy of global North over South.

Multiplicity as an end in itself seems quite at odds with democracy, which depends for its survival upon some form of consensus. A Franciscan joy rejecting the ennui of the world at large does not seem quite like the posture of a democratic subject, and is instead consistent with a sectarian mindset, of which Avishai Margalit has recently provided a productive definition: '[T]he general attitude of sectarians is undemocratic on several counts: in their elitist attitude to outsiders, in their hostile attitude to compromise, and in their disregard of numbers. . . . The sectarian claims a monopoly on all values. There is no good value outside the sect.'[52] We may thus see as sectarian what Tom Nairn describes as the 'metaphysical transports' of 'French universalism.'[53] In his trenchant critique of *Multitude*, Nairn unpacks the 'emerging Totality' anticipated by the authors' Spinozism—though we should bear in mind the distinction Slavoj Žižek draws between Spinoza's neutrality toward the good and bad effects of the multitude and the brand of popular movement that Hardt and Negri have in mind.[54] 'As in the 17th century,' Nairn writes, 'heresy underwrites faith. Disowning an orthodoxy makes for a purer belief, rather than its demolition. The heretic normally believes self-consciously that he has some new access to the secrets of the universal essence. . . . In this case, the people being fostered by prophecy are a "network," contemporary academese for those "born again."'[55] With their opposition of faith to globalization, Hardt and Negri are in the 'Redemption business' in a way that 'uncannily echoes the feigned panic of Washington anti-terrorists.'[56]

Nairn's critique of such universalism shades into a critique of internationalism. Rehearsing the arguments of his *Faces of Nationalism*, he claims that '"Internationalism" . . . was a part of the 1870–1989 nationalist world, not an answer to it.'[57] Like Hamlet's father, he claims, Internationalism is a ghost ever-present in the nationalist era, 'pouring out a familiar mixture of admonition, reproach, and prophecy,' a presence haunting socialists and capitalists equally.[58] The post-national world might just as soon become more particular rather than more global in a way the ghost would decry as 'Balkanization,' yielding not universals but a world of 'spiky exceptions';

globalization might prompt 'the boondocks and those multitudinous elsewheres . . . to be *more* themselves than previously.'[59]

These observations on the growing particularization of political communities seem astute if terrifying, raising as they do the prospect of a world of ancient tribalisms equipped with modern implements of war. In some ways, however, Nairn does not push his conclusions far enough. For the lesson we might learn from late Milton is that Messianism is the language of particularization, not a harkening after internationalism. It is after Milton has lost faith in the nation as a category significant to Reformation history that he most fully inhabits the role of poet-prophet revealing divine Truth to trees and stones. Because 'nor number, nor example' will prevail upon the sectarian who knows and relishes that 'his constant mind' is single, his justification lies beyond this world and his hopes reside in the promise of a Totality to come.

We thus hear the language of our moment in Milton's sense that the highest form of expression is declaration of transcendent truth justifying the speaker and a like-minded faithful few. It is a posture on language unconcerned with broad consensus destined to make every individual a sect of one.[60] Its promise of a distant future when the energies of the multitude will be all in all rings hollow, and seems to serve only to steel the righteous resolve of the alter-globalization sect.

I have argued elsewhere that digital media allow for the flourishing of that relationship to language by providing an outlet for unmediated individual speech while lending a sense of connection to co-sectarians through an abstracted network—thus it can produce the paradoxical cultural affiliations of a jihadist Briton feeling intimately involved with the plight of co-religionists on the other side of the globe and relegating to de-humanized infidel the fellow citizen living around the corner.[61] As Marshall McLuhan has suggested, each medium is an extension of a human faculty. Where the printed page is an extension of the eye, electricity is an extension of the central nervous system, an insight fueled by his knowledge of the cultural transformations of the sixteenth century—we often forget that he wrote his Cambridge dissertation on Thomas Nashe, in which he points to *grammatica* as a technology for interpreting the upheavals of the early modern period.[62] This distinction among faculties fundamentally alters the epistemology fostered by each medium—McLuhan would say that it fundamentally alters anthropology—so that the linear, rational mode of thinking fostered by literacy is replaced by impulse in the electronic age. Arianna Huffington confirms this view in commenting on the impact of blogging upon political speech. Unlike the op. ed. with its claim of expert interpretation and its dependence on at least a day or two of thinking, writing, and editing, the blog allows immediate response from anyone with access to the Internet and is a forum for sharing, in Huffington's terms, those 'first thoughts' that are 'our best thoughts.' (Those familiar with *Macbeth* will wonder if making the firstlings of our hearts the firstlings of our hands is the path to enlightened politics.) The Web, she claims, is a stay against the fear-mongering of a Karl Rove. It is in fact precisely the opposite: it is a medium where fears and desires hold unchecked authority, as she seems to imply in describing it as a democratic forum for 'passion' and 'enthusiasm.'[63] If, as she perhaps rightly observes, it is the medium that allowed Barack Obama to win the presidential election, it is as much for its fund-raising capacities as it is for its erotics: like Bush in 2004, Obama traded in the visceral much more effectively than did his opponent.

The new democratic vistas offered by the Web are not defined by deliberation and overlapping consensus. Rawls's ideal of liberal democracy would reduce such comprehensive doctrines as religion to the level of 'background culture' divorced from the forum of political speech. 'Ha, ha, ha,' replies the sectarian.[64] Donne comes close to a liberal theology in claiming that 'in strange way / To stand inquiring right, is not to stray; / To sleepe, or runne wrong, is' (*Sat III*, 77–79); it is precisely such open and ongoing inquiry that sectarianism forecloses.

∽

But against sectarian exclusivism, Badiou seeks a 'democratic universality' without 'the constraint of a transcendency.' We shall treat the ethical dimension of his thought in the next chapter. Here we are concerned with affirmations of truth and the extent to which they advance or frustrate democratic equality. A good measure of Badiou's motivation on the subject arises from his important and forceful leftist critique of the identitarianism informing post-1989 politics:

> The senescent collapse of the USSR, the paradigm of socialist States, provisionally suspended fear, unleashed empty abstraction, debased thought in general. And it is certainly not by renouncing the concrete universality of

truths in order to affirm the rights of 'minorities,' be they racial, religious, national, or sexual, that the devastation will be slowed down. No, we will not allow the rights of true-thought to have as their only instance monetarist free exchange and its mediocre political appendage, capitalist-parliamentarianism, whose squalor is ever more poorly dissimulated behind the fine word 'democracy.'[65]

Humanity finds its highest calling in truth seeking, so that resigning truth is also an abandonment of our most dignified endeavor (a statement made with particular force in the original French): 'Si, comme nous le pensons, seule les vérités (la pensée) permettent de distinguer l'homme de l'animal humain qui le sous-tend, il n'est pas exagéré de dire que ces énoncés "minoritaires" sont proprement *barbares*.'[66] Where minoritarianism is the conceptual ground of the *polis*, a politics grounded in truth cannot emerge and an anthropology of market demographics flourishes: 'What inexhaustible potential for mercantile investments in this upsurge—taking the form of communities demanding recognition and so-called cultural singularities—of women, homosexuals, the disabled, Arabs! . . . Each time, a social image authorizes new products, specialized magazines, improved shopping malls.'[67] Badiou's observations seem confirmed by the carefully tabulated identities of the market research firm Nielsen Claritas, from '16. Bohemian Mix'; to '51. Shotguns & Pickups'; to '65. Big City Blues,' a population that is 40 percent Latino but is also 'the multi-ethnic address for low-income Asian and African-American households occupying older inner-city apartments.' One glimpses in these enumerations a modernity reminiscent of the television cult classic *The Prisoner*, though in this case we know with certainty who is Number One: '1. Upper Crust,' those 1,742,531 households with a median income of $114, 343 that are predominantly white, watch the Golf Channel, and read the Washington *Post*.[68]

To this retreat from truth and blithe acceptance of consumer identity, Badiou opposes his figure of the militant adhering to the supernumary name, *'le nom surnuméraire,'* of the event existing outside knowledge but 'within the effect of an interventional nomination.' Fidelity to this event recognizes only two values, connection and non-connection to the 'field of effects entailed by the introduction into circulation of the supernumerary name.'[69] Thus Badiou's meditation on Saint Paul, whom he describes as adhering to the event of the Resurrection. It is of paramount importance in this analysis that the phrase repeated in the Pauline epistles is 'Jesus is Resurrected,' rather than Jesus was crucified, or was born, or spoke, or performed the miracles that would make him cognizable as a first-century holy man. The Resurrection resides entirely outside of our experience in the realm of a 'fable' whose authenticity cannot be verified by knowledge—though Roland Boer rightly suggests that the contact of the 'fable' with natural order in the form of the 'event' places it in the realm of myth.[70] Even the textual 'proof' of the Resurrection available in the gospels is absent as Paul preaches this new fidelity by which all law, human and biblical, will subsequently be measured. Validity is determined by a subjectivity 'devoid of all identity and suspended to an event whose only "proof" lies precisely in its having been declared by a subject.'[71] Paul thus does not recognize established institutions as legitimizing. After his moment of conversion on the road to Damascus, he does not travel to Jerusalem to join the 'institutional apostles,' but is sustained in his errand only by the 'personal event' that has made him an *apostolus*.[72]

This position of fidelity is reflected in Paul's language, which Badiou describes as eschewing both the Jewish language of the law and the Greek language of wisdom whose 'instrument is that of rhetorical superiority':

> The wisdom of men is opposed to the power of God. It is thus a question of intervening *ouk en sophai logou*, 'without the wisdom of language.' This maxim envelops a radical antiphilosophy; it is not a proposition capable of being supported by a *philosophia*. The essence of all this is that a subjective upsurge cannot be given as the rhetorical construction of a personal adjustment to the laws of the universe or nature.[73]

'What matters' in Paul's prose is 'the forceful extraction of an essential core of thought. Consequently, there will be no parables, no learned obscurities, no subjective indecision, no veiling of truth.'[74]

Who more than Milton resembles this view of Paul, with its iconoclastic sweeping away of laws and institutions conflicting with a truth secured by the declaration of an enlightened subject? Those moments of *Paradise Lost* trading in plain truth are also ones where the bard claims illumination beyond knowledge. The invocation to book 3 invites us to see its celestial dialogue between Father and Son, the 'things invisible to mortal sight' (3.55), as the expression of a divine inspiration lying beyond the order of nature. Milton exploits the ambiguity of the six days of creation, casting himself as 'Cut off' (47) from those things illumined by the physical light of the sun created on the fourth day, but invoking the light of the first day, 'off-spring of Heav'n first-born' (3.1), of which we have no guarantee in the natural world and for which our modes of knowledge cannot fully account—we see here an implicit critique of that tradition arising with Saint Augustine's *De Genesi ad litteram* that would attempt to contain this light within a literal history by claiming that it refers to the creation of the angels. The unveiled truth that we observe in this book is fundamental to the bard's self-construction as performing a subjective upsurge authenticated by fidelity and making no concession to worldly law. The force of the epic's militant statements on the laws of politics and worship rests on the eventual site of this inspiration requiring no external logic of justification.

In ways that Badiou handles too cursorily, that fidelity can also be the ground of its own juridical pronouncements and a means by which the militant advances a hierarchy of merit. With the bland indifference of unadorned truth, the Father pronounces both that his grace is dealt to all of humanity and that it is not dealt to any of the fallen angels. It is in the apostrophe on 'wedded Love' (4.750)—a reformist critique of those who would constrain its divine properties, or 'mysterious Law' (4.750), within corrupt human principles—that we find an implicit defense of polygamy and a masculinist emphasis on the 'Relations dear' of 'Father, Son, and Brother' that coincides with the gender hierarchy plainly stated in our first encounter with Adam and Eve: 'Hee for God only, shee for God in him' (4.299). In the performative speech whereby the bard enacts his vision of things invisible to mortal sight, he simultaneously establishes distance between himself and the sighted reader scanning his lines. As an afterthought to his reading of Paul, Badiou tetchily dismisses the apostle's anti-Jewish and anti-feminist remarks.[75] Those skeptical of conversion narratives will see these remarks as quite consistent with the persecutory impulse prominent in Paul before his bout of heat stroke on the road to Damascus (Acts 9.1-2). Early modern formulations of the egalitarian dimensions of a priesthood of believers—to which priesthood Badiou would return in forming a more inclusive democracy—tend to generate an anti-democratic superiority of the faithful.

Badiou would seem to answer this anti-democratic implication in his fundamentally un-Christian and un-Platonic ontology. Rather than decreasing multiplicity as we approach a One, or a Godhead, he offers a realm of Being that has no less multiplicity than the realm of matter. 'Mathematics is ontology,' in Badiou's terms, for mathematics, and particularly set theory, provides a model of self-contained multiplicity with no dependence upon an outside referent. This is not a universe governed by a single Truth, but one where an infinite number of discrete and equally authentic truths are made available through events to which militants adhere. The multiplicity of truths answers those elements of monotheism that Regina Schwartz identifies as the ground of violence against non-adherents: 'The One suggests both single and All. . . . The danger of a universal monotheism is asserting that its truth is *the* Truth. . . . What needs to be imagined is neither a circle that includes everyone—a whole that submerges and subjects all individuality to itself, a totality that closes possibility—nor a part that reviles other parts.'[76] Badiou's lively intellect fills that imaginative need. But one also discerns certain limits in his thought: his emphasis on truth as an 'immanent break' distinguishes him from those whose immanence rests upon multiplicity as such, but the sheer number of events potentially qualifying as truths renders that distinction nugatory—everything from a revolutionary cause to falling in love.[77] Rather than the deliberative procedures of capitalist-parliamentarianism we are left with a procedural activism contingent upon a posture of belief more than on its content.

Reminiscent of such placement of mathematics above matter, Peter Berek observes of the plain style deployed by God the Father that 'language is stripped of emotion, stripped of connotations, and used as though it was an abstract and precise mathematical notation.'[78] But that linguistic achievement is not its own end in *Paradise Lost*. The content of belief matters a good deal to Milton, and it would not be amiss to read his epic as a thoroughgoing assault on the wrong-headed activisms that falsehood inspires. Perhaps the most relevant aspect of that critique occurs immediately after the event of the fall, when Adam joins Eve in experiencing a Knowledge above their existing modes of knowledge:

> As with new Wine intoxicated both
> They swim in mirth, and fansie that they feel
> Divinitie within them breeding wings
> Wherewith to scorne the Earth: but that false Fruit
> Farr other operation first displaid,
> Carnal desire enflaming[.] (9.1008-13)

This seems to me Milton's greatest insight on human nature in the poem: in the first movement of our fallen condition—at the moment when we become fully human, as it were—we take physical desire to be divinization, the urgings of libido to be the dawning of insight. At those times when humanity feels itself to be ascending the divine *scala*, it is all too often moved by its basest motives—there is no certain measure by which the experience of the embrace of truth can be distinguished from the satisfaction of the passions. Our command of our faculties is so vitiated that we are entirely incapable of authoritatively distinguishing between those callings above reason—perception of the good through *noûs*—and the bestial impulses below it. For Milton this moment is a parody of the truly divine inner promptings of grace. As I take it, it calls into question all militant adherence to personally experienced truth.

It is in his strident assertion of his own access to truth that Milton can resemble elements of current thought. Arguing for Milton's relevance in 1939, Douglas Bush was given to criticize both the focus on 'musical beauties' encouraged by Sir Walter Raleigh and the moderns' affection for Donne: 'Instead of Milton, who expounds a lofty faith in God and human reason,' Bush lamented, 'we prefer a smaller poet like Donne, whose sceptical uncertainties and staccato realism are more congenial to a generation which has lost its way. Milton is too big, too sternly strenuous, to allow us to feel at ease in his presence.'[79] Bush's estimation of the two poetic personae seems just, though the Christian Humanism by which he measures his contemporaries is a rather more conflicted tradition than he allows. The sternly strenuous do indeed make skeptics ill at ease, their language of unadorned truth piercing through the decorous hubbub of uncertainty. But the challenge they pose might in the end be one that we should not readily dismiss, as we wonder especially if truly emancipatory thought can do without truth and without the commitment afforded by belief.

2

Areopagitica and the Ethics of Reading

In the previous chapter we explored truths held by belief and eschewing the value of external verification, and how plain language is deployed as expression of that epistemic posture. Now truth shall sally forth to meet her adversaries and aim to triumph in the advancement of the good. Milton gives most lively expression to that endeavor in *Areopagitica*, where he goes much further than is strictly necessary in responding to the Licensing Order of June 1643, making arguments on the nature of knowledge, of human discovery, and of political order consonant with divine will.

We will first take some account of the terms of *Areopagitica* in the hope that it might then ask questions of our moment—ethics has been debated frequently in the past decade, and has been described as 'the most controversial field of contemporary philosophy.'[1] In his important intervention, Alain Badiou takes aim at those who would found ethics upon respect for human others, a tendency that he locates in the pragmatism of Richard Rorty, the cultural studies approach of Seyla Benhabib, or, more generally, in current thought on human rights.

Where the previous chapter focused on moments of plain style in *Paradise Lost*, this chapter will look at the rhetorical excess of *Areopagitica*. In its several discrete arguments against pre-publication censorship we find contained several approaches to ethics, as well as the anxieties underwriting any attempt to produce ethically motivated speech. Its 'too many reasons,' a phrase to which we will return, for abolishing the Licensing

Order are made consistent by the ideological commitment directing its somewhat conflicted ethical statements. We are thus led to an engagement of the relationship between ethics and politics explored in the recent dialogue on *Areopagitica* between Sharon Achinstein and Marshall Grossman. As opposed to an Aristotelian ideal where politics is an expression of ethics, we shall see that ethics is consistently an attempt to elevate political commitment to the level of the good, a tendency apparent in Milton, in Badiou, and in late Jacques Derrida. Though equally informed by political commitment, we shall find some promise in Gayatri Spivak's ethics of reading, which presents a habit of literary reading as the foundation of ethical action in its ability to prompt imagination of the subjectivities of others. The subaltern as she figures it lends a human dynamic to Wittgenstein's making sense of nonsense, the process in which ethical reading must engage.

I. 'Areopagitica,' reading, and the good

It seems an apt time to re-address the ethics of reading, to borrow J. Hillis Miller's 1987 title, all the more apt given our critical distance now from the categories of deconstruction central to engagements of this topic appearing in the last twenty years. Miller is strongly indebted to de Man's theorization, where ethics is an entirely linguistic category. '[E]thics,' says de Man, 'has nothing to do with the will (thwarted or free) of a subject, nor (a *fortiori*), with a relationship between subjects. . . . Morality is a version of the same language aporia that gave rise to such concepts as "man" or "love" or "self," and not the cause or consequence of such concepts.'[2] Reading this passage Miller avers that 'for de Man ethical obligations, demands and judgments work in the same way as the court system in [Kafka's] *Trial* works . . . as one perpetually unverifiable referential dimension of an irresistible law, in de Man's case a law of language.'[3]

This limits significantly an Aristotelian view of the ethics of reading, which would see it leading to the exercise of the intellect that is our highest happiness and the means by which human life approximates the divine.[4] Deconstruction tends to distance language from contemplation, and with Plato to see text as a particularly empty form of linguistic exchange. To provide an example from early Derrida, the reading of the *Phaedrus* offered in 'Plato's Pharmacy' associates text with Freudian dream logic. In analyzing one of his dreams, Freud tells us that contradictory explanations exist side by side, as in the self-defense of a man returning a broken kettle to his neighbor: 1. The kettle I am returning is undamaged; 2. The holes were there when you lent it to me; and 3. You never lent me a kettle.[5] The act of writing, says Derrida, likewise excuses its simultaneous exteriority to and pollution of living speech: 1. Writing is exterior and inferior to living speech, which is undamaged by it; 2. Writing is harmful to living speech because it puts it to sleep; and 3. One resorts to writing because living speech has holes in it already.[6] In these dynamics writing is an obstacle to living speech at best, and thus distanced from knowledge.

The approach to pre-publication censorship in *Areopagitica* is deeply concerned with the ethics of reading and of writing, and offers something resembling its own kettle logic on the nature of text—though they are not strictly self-contradicting, the claims Milton provides are more discrete than one expects to find in a single piece of deliberative rhetoric. We might enumerate these claims as follows. 1. Books have an inherent life and must be accorded the respect of citizens in a well-governed state: 'as good almost kill a Man as kill a good Book: who kills a Man kills a reasonable creature, Gods Image; but hee who destroyes a good Book, kills reason it selfe' (*YP* 2: 492).[7] We shall return to the qualifier 'good' twice applied to books in this passage. 2. Agency resides with the reader, who either can or cannot benefit from both good and bad books: '[A] wise man like a good refiner can gather gold out of the drossiest volume[;] . . . a fool will be a fool with the best book, yea or without book, [so] there is no reason that we should deprive a wise man of any advantage to his wisdome' (*YP* 2: 521). And 3. Neither books nor human agents can fully discover Truth, which appears in God's time: 'Truth indeed came once into the world with her divine Master, and was a perfect shape most glorious to look on. . . . From that time ever since, the sad friends of Truth . . . went up and down gathering up limb by limb still as they could find them. We have not yet found them all, Lords and Commons, nor ever shal doe, till her Masters second comming' (*YP* 2: 549).

In this kettle logic, good books approach the realm of Form—they are associated with 'reason itself'—only to be diminished in the face of their human readers and the divine embodiment of Truth. One can detect in Milton's impulse to invest books with inherent virtue the oft-theorized paternal anxiety at the heart of the act of writing.[8] *Areopagitica* is strongly influenced by the reception of his divorce tracts, such as Herbert Palmer's attack of them as the horrifying result of unregulated printing: 'If any plead Conscience for the Lawfulnesse of *Polygamy* (or for divorce for other causes then Christ and His Apostles mention; Of which a *wicked booke* is abroad and *uncensured*, though *deserving to be burnt*, whose *Author* hath been so *impudent* as to *set his Name* to it, and *dedicate it to your selves*,) or for Liberty to *marry incestuously*, will you grant a *Toleration* for all *this?*'[9] The divorce tracts had argued only for the relaxation of divorce laws, but Palmer is incisive in one respect: early and late Milton is sympathetic to polygamy, from the Commonplace Book to the *Christian Doctrine*, and implicitly in *Paradise Lost* as the brand of wedded love by 'Saints and Patriarchs us'd' (*YP* 6: 355–68; *PL* 4.762).[10]

Just as such hostile reception strongly informs the composition of *Areopagitica*, so we might also recognize that the divorce tracts' sexual anxieties mirror its view of authorship. *The Doctrine and Discipline of Divorce* in particular is distressed by a human sexuality that is only physical, with its famous sentence on the 'perversness' of being forced by a Christian magistrate to 'grind in the mill of an undelighted and servil copulation . . . oft times with such a yokefellow, from whom both love and peace, both nature and Religion mourns to be separated' (*YP* 2: 258). *Paradise Lost* provides a straightforward apostrophe on the 'Relations dear' arising from wedded love, but registers its own fantasy of asexual reproduction in the exclusively male focus on 'Father, Son, and Brother' that imagines procreation as akin to Cadmus's casting of dragon's teeth (*PL* 4.756–57). *Areopagitica* analogously opposes viewing books as mere physical objects: 'Books are not absolutely dead things, but doe contain a potencie of life in them to be as active as that soule was whose *progeny* they are' (*YP* 2: 492; my italics).

The paternal anxiety at the heart of writing is also the paternal anxiety at the heart of ethical commitment: ethics is that system of thought providing regulation and sanction of the libidinal. The equation of writing with paternity seeks a purer ethics released from the law of physical desire, but cannot eliminate the threat to order posed by brutish impulse. Paternity is an act with a profound wish for ethical significance—one wants it to be born of a desire for the good and to effect a greater proximity to it—that can be dismissed, as Stephen Dedalus does in *Ulysses*, with a withering statement: 'What links [father and son] in nature? An instant of blind rut.'[11] If ethics, as Lacan describes it, 'begins at the moment when the subject poses the question of that good he had unconsciously sought in the social structures,' then ethical writing impelled by the reality principle seeks to stretch what is articulable toward that Other, or *das Ding*, which can never fully be discovered.[12] Paternity is anxious of the charge of being driven only by libidinal pleasure; ethics is anxious in turn of the charge of moving only within the regulation of the libidinal provided by existing social structures and of not stretching the articulable toward the good—the accusation that it trades only in conventional wisdom rather than wisdom itself, that it seeks civility more than the good. Milton shows this anxiety in (too) frequently opposing in the 1640s stale 'custom' to the progressive, iconoclastic 'reason' of which he is the avatar and that he presents as necessary to a thoroughgoing reformation of knowledge—we find statements to this effect in *The Reason of Church-Government* (*YP* 1: 749), *An Apology against a Pamphlet* (*YP* 1: 868–69), and especially *The Doctrine and Discipline* and *The Tenure of Kings and Magistrates* (*YP* 2: 222–23, 3: 190).

More fully revealing the masculinist terms of such a figuring of ethical subjectivity are Milton's statements on the consequences of licensing. In depriving an author of the father-function, licensing reduces him to pre-pubescence; he is 'a punie with his guardian' (*YP* 2: 532) who cannot exercise the independence that Milton figures in terms of intellectual mobility: 'When a man writes to the world, he summons up all his reason and deliberation to assist him; he searches, meditats, is industrious, and likely consults and confers with his judicious friends' (*YP* 2: 532). By associating them with the spiritual exercise of manly liberty—which is always a tautology in his terms[13]—Milton makes books much more than physical artifacts arising from the act of writing. Such psychosexual dynamics are also at play in the tract's statements on reception—and indeed, as Lana Cable shows, pervade a good deal of the tract's language.[14] Just as the best sort of man can try and fail in the selection of a suitable mate in *The Doctrine and Discipline of Divorce*, so the best sort of reader is the one who enters the arena of ideas and rejects evils known. Simple retreat avoids worthier purification by trial. Better to be a Guyon who travels 'with his palmer through the cave of Mammon and the bowr of earthly blisse that he might see and know, and yet abstain' (*YP* 2: 515–16). Though, as we well know, Milton gets Spenser wrong in stating that the Palmer is with Guyon in the Cave of Mammon, it is perhaps because the image most on his mind in this passage—the image that makes most sense of the passage—is the Bower of Bliss, where the Palmer seeing in Guyon 'signes of kindled lust' sharply directs his 'wandring eyes' away from the bathing damsels, and where we learn unequivocally that the active virtue of Temperance is not to be confused with abstemiousness.[15]

It is here, in the second turn of our kettle logic, that we get to the heart of the tract's statement on reading ethically. If the first turn emphasizes books as repositories of manly force, the second turn empties books of inherent power in arguing against pusillanimous fear of printed sheets: flying far from the famous Cadmus image, Milton now makes absurd any apprehension over 'suspected *typography*' and challenges his audience not 'to fear each book, and the shaking of every leaf' (*YP* 2: 529, 539; italics in original). Aristotle tells us that 'acts done in conformity with the virtues . . . must spring from a fixed and permanent disposition of character' (85 [II.iv.3]); Milton likewise makes clear that the virtue of reading is contingent upon the ethos of the reader—the difference with Aristotle being Milton's sense that the finest human reasoning is still vitiated and requires constant exercise. This is not entirely at odds with the statement that *good* books have an inherent life, nor does it reduce text to a dead language; it carefully qualifies the influence of text in a way that recognizes writing and reading as two separate processes. If we think of this in Wittgenstein's terms, text is a public language having distinct relationships with the two private languages of writer and reader.[16] The more confining the rules of public language, the more likely that it cannot be made to reflect or to impact those private languages, engaging instead in insipid re-circulation of that which is already accepted. When strait-jacketed in tightly controlled permissibility, text loses any relationship to the *ethos* of reader or writer and cannot be deemed ethical. Hence simply accepting the view of a text offered by the state, or a hired divine, is equivalent to abandoning learning altogether.[17]

The act of *writing* can invest public language with thought that would otherwise remain exclusively private—it can, in Milton's terms, be an extension of the author's soul—but the discernment and acceptance of that thought depends upon the capacities of the reader. The act of *reading* is a confrontation with public language that re-shapes the terms of private language in a way not directly related to content. In the right hands, Milton tells us, a debased text can have a salutary effect: 'Bad meats will scarce breed good nourishment in the healthiest concoction; but herein the difference is of bad books, that they to a discreet and judicious Reader serve in many respects to discover, to confute, to forewarn, and to illustrate' (*YP* 2: 512).

Though the occasion of *Areopagitica* demands that Milton argue for the lack of harm caused by bad books, one senses that his real hopes are revealed in the image of London as a 'mansion house of liberty' with 'pens and heads there, sitting by their studious lamps, musing, searching, revolving new notions and idea's wherewith to present, as with their homage and their fealty the approaching Reformation: others as fast reading, trying all things, assenting to the force of reason and convincement' (*YP* 2: 554). Text connects the thought-action of active writers and active readers; its generation and consumption are ethical in allowing for the formation of intellectual communities carried by a common rational enterprise toward a perceived good. To put it in more explicitly Aristotelian terms, writing and reading allow the ethos of a community of fit souls to become a politics in mediating their reformation of the public sphere. Or, in Lacan's terms, Milton describes as fundamental to the reformation of social structures the unfettered activity of a community of right-thinking readers and writers developing through textual exchange ideas approaching *das Ding*.

The final turn of *Areopagitica*'s kettle logic, however, diminishes the significance of this community in a way that runs counter to an Aristotelian relationship between ethics and politics. Much as even the fittest element of humanity might be invested in the intellectual exercise of Reformation, it is ultimately an event in divine control. Immediately before the mansion house of liberty passage, we learn that 'God is decreeing to begin some new and great period in his Church' (*YP* 2: 553), making His the hand guiding our community of writers and readers toward liberty. This does not entirely nullify the agency of books or of readers, but it does claim that humanity cannot on its own rightly conceive of or effect the good. Where Aristotle claims that a virtuous act must be chosen for its own sake (85 [II.iv.3]), Milton defines the virtuous act as one performed in conformity with the will of a transcendent being.

We must thus be skeptical of Thomas Fulton's recent association of the tract with an emerging liberal epistemology, and of his critique of the careful corrections of Whig historicism of Quentin Skinner, Blair Worden, J. C. Davis, and John Coffey.[18] Fulton finds support for his claims in the tract's debt to natural law, which he describes as offering 'process-based models of reason.'[19] Milton thus draws on 'the unchangeable nature of reason itself' in presenting licensing as a 'violation of human nature' preventing individuals from knowing the good,[20] making his position in *Areopagitica* like Henry Robinson's and William Walwyn's essentially secularist resistance to Presbyterian control of matters religious.[21] Fulton sees in *Areopagitica* a 'metaphysical explanation of the process of gaining moral knowledge' to be 'the first sustained treatment of a subject that would distinguish the fields of ethics and epistemology in the Enlightenment, finding perhaps a full expression in Kant's *Metaphysics of Morals*.'[22]

Such findings contribute to our understanding of the immediate historical context and language of this tract, building on our awareness of its appeal to Erastians and natural lawyers for which Ernest Sirluck and, more recently, Nigel Smith have argued. It is certainly true that Milton saw the Erastians as the parliamentary group most likely to be alarmed by the Presbyterians' growing influence and to have the numbers to thwart it. Milton not only refers to Selden's works but uses Selden's language, along with that of Henry Parker.[23] He is in part providing a theory of human epistemology that, if accepted, necessitates toleration and an associated view of the public arena as a forum where seekers can exchange insights for mutual benefit, and in this respect situates himself in a dialogue with Hugo Grotius, Henry Robinson, and William Walwyn.[24]

To see *Areopagitica* as a 'sustained' treatment of the ethical and epistemological concerns of the Enlightenment, however, is to misrepresent the role of reason in the text. As Phillip Donnelly has incisively observed, Milton's is not an instrumental rationality in that it does not separate reason 'from the biblical narrative contexts that he invokes and which make it clear that he does not view "reason" as merely a calculative capacity.'[25] Overlooking the presence of biblical narrative, Fulton's argument for liberal epistemology in *Areopagitica* rests on an infelicitous reading of the tract's definition of truth: '[T]he posture of the believer in conceiving the truth is more important than the belief professed: what matters is how well the believer knows what he or she professes.'[26] This might be concluded from the emphasis on fit reading in the second turn of the tract's kettle logic, but such a conclusion is frustrated by its third turn, which identifies truth with its divine source. The process of seeking matters—without it one becomes a 'heretick in the truth' (*YP* 2: 543)—but not all postures of belief can be associated with truth, which is why Milton cannot endure 'tolerated Popery, and open superstition,' another tautology in his thought (*YP* 2: 565). Smith and Sirluck are sensitive to such conflicts in the logic of Milton's tract, rightly presenting it as a revolutionary polemic rather than a philosophical treatise. Part of Milton's polemical method is, to use a term from present-day political speech, to 'dog-whistle' to various groups in language with which they sympathize without necessarily joining their cause—it is a tactic also at work in his handling of the Presbyterians in the anti-prelatical tracts.

If *Areopagitica* continues somewhat to perplex, it is perhaps because it contains two competing languages of ethics: one based on a posture of affirming truths appearing phenomenologically, and the other guided noumenally by a transcendent Other. Those two modes of thought are represented recently in Alain Badiou, who describes ethics as a posture of militant fidelity to an 'event,' and in late Derrida, who emphasizes an undischargeable debt to a quasi-divine Other. In Badiou's terms, fidelity attaches itself to the 'truth' embodied in an 'event' that is a matter of historical occurrence for which no 'encyclopedic determinant,' or existing category of knowledge, can account—as examples of such events Badiou cites 'the French Revolution of 1792, the meeting of Héloïse and Abélard, Galileo's creation of physics, Haydn's invention of the classical musical style.'[27] It is the militant commitment to such an event that constitutes an ethic of the Real, 'and consistency, which is the content of the ethical maxim "Keep going! [*il faut continuer*]," keeps going only by following this thread of the Real.'[28] The counterpart to that sentiment in *Areopagitica* is the image of the sad friends of the 'virgin Truth' gathering up her torn and scattered limbs as they find them, an image suggesting that ethics resides in commitment to those truths that have presented themselves in the natural order (549). For Badiou, however, these are not parts of a single body emblematizing truth itself, but rather individual truths giving rise to discrete ethical commitments—in his terms there is no universal truth and thus no universal ethics.[29]

In his engagement of ethics, Derrida expands the category of 'performance' typical of his earlier statements on text and language, and describes it as neutralizing the ability of the event to stand apart from conventional knowledge.[30] The ethical arises when both performative and constative language are 'in the service of another language,' namely a sense of infinite responsibility to the 'sovereign without power.'[31] Elucidating Derrida's ethics, Simon Critchley describes this sovereign, or 'other,' as justice in its formal universality, which is not a 'regulative principle like the Moral Law in Kant' but a making explicit of what is implicit in 'the performative structure of speech acts'[32]—to use the distinction offered by French, it is *justice* rather than *justesse*. It does not imply a Kantian sense of civil society as containing glimpses of and tending teleologically toward fulfillment of a regulative Idea; to Derrida the call of the Other constitutes a possibility 'that is infinitely deferred' yet also in 'the *here and now*'—it is '*the memory of that which carries the future, the to-come, here and now.*' As such 'the expression "democracy to come [*la démocratie à venir*]" translates, to be sure, or calls for a militant and interminable political critique. A weapon aimed at the enemies of democracy, it protests against all naiveté and every political abuse, every rhetoric that would present as a present or existing democracy, as a de facto democracy, what remains inadequate to the democratic demand.'[33] The call of the Other which for Derrida constitutes a 'messianicity without messianism'—a demand from the beyond that does not promise arrival, retribution, or reward—borrows from Emmanuel Lévinas's turn away from Greek metaphysics and to the Hebrew Bible, where overriding responsibility to the Law of the divine Other forces constant awareness of the subject's limitations.[34] Milton's God, of course, is a sovereign with a good deal of power and one whose return is eagerly anticipated, but we can nonetheless discern echoes here between the conformity of ethical speech to a transcendent truth rather than to the demands of forces wishing to exercise legitimizing power over language, be they prelatical or presbyterian.

II. The Challenge of a pre-political ethics

We might shed most light on the contending ethics contained in Milton's tract by turning to the issue vexed in Grossman and Sharon Achinstein's recent 'Exchange Passing through the *Areopagitica*': the relationship between ethics and politics. Achinstein's initial comment in this dialogue is rightly skeptical in its claim that 'the conditions in which we are able to do ethics . . . to "determine what the good is," are indeed political conditions.'[35] Our distance from Milton's time should allow us to see relatively clearly how closely involved are his politics and his ethics. In disclosing this inevitable intertwining of ideology and ethics, we might at the same time notice the ideological underpinnings of the current ethics that we have touched on, those of Badiou and Derrida. With those underpinnings in view, we might find most compelling an ethics grounded in an ideology of human equality, toward which Gayatri Spivak has gestured in her engagement of a Derridean 'democracy to come.'

As a first step in this direction, we can see the self-exculpating tendency of any kettle logic as potential cover for political motives. This is certainly true of the kettle logic that Žižek discerns in the justification of the Iraq War: 1. Saddam Hussein possesses weapons of mass destruction; 2. Even if he does not, he was involved in the 9/11 attacks; and 3. Even if there is no proven link between Saddam and al-Qaeda, his is a ruthless regime and that alone is reason to topple it. The problem, he observes, is not that there was no reason given for the war, but that there were '*too many reasons*'; what 'imposed a semblance of consistency upon this multitude of reasons' was the underlying ideology of asserting U.S. hegemony and controlling global oil reserves.[36] In this way rhetorical excess masks ideologically motivated interests. If ideology is the ground of its contending claims, we must revise the way in which we see *Areopagitica* as a text on the vanguard of revolution whose conflicted nature is to be associated with a pre-political language.[37] To use Terry Eagleton's recent definition, 'elites are self-perpetuating whereas vanguards are self-abolishing. Vanguards arise in conditions of uneven cultural and political development.'[38] Milton in the 1640s is on the vanguard of a culturally and materially privileged class that finds itself deprived of self-determination in affairs of church and state and seeks to remedy the situation by securing its own power. It desires not simply to overturn existing structures and make itself irrelevant in the way of a true vanguard, but rather to replace the hegemony of one elite with the hegemony of another. Milton does not extend inherent life to all books, but, as we have seen, states that 'he who destroys a *good* book, kills reason itself,' implicitly claiming for himself and those who think like him the authority to determine the good. The argument consistent in Milton's ethos-based rhetoric of the early 1640s—the anti-prelatical tracts, the divorce tracts, and *Areopagitica*—is that the nation had gone astray in interfering with the political agency of the class of individuals like Milton's rhetor.

Ethics in this sense becomes not the reasoned acceptance of a positive course of action open to the contributions of all, but, as Christopher

Kendrick describes it in his indispensable reading of *Areopagitica*, the 'monistic ethos' is itself a 'discrete and unassimilable level of ethical feeling.'[39] *The Tenure of Kings and Magistrates* shows how quickly Milton can close the door on an argument for open political process when he himself becomes an agent of political authority: where the first edition is at pains to demonstrate the right of a private citizen to tyrannicide, the second, written after the Rump had settled into power with Milton among its spokesmen, concludes with the statement that 'to doe justice on a lawless King, is to a private man unlawful, to an inferior Magistrate lawfull' (*YP* 3: 257).[40] Lest we see Milton's endorsement of post-publication censorship in *Areopagitica* as only a concession to his immediate audience, we know on the evidence of the 1650 warrant issued to him by John Bradshawe that he could be called upon to perform the task of search and seizure: 'These are to will & require you forthwith to make your repairs to the studdy & chamber of William Prynne Esquire . . . which you are dilligently to search . . . for all writings, letters or papers by him written, or in his custody of dangerous nature against the Commonwealth.'[41] In the absence of evidence that Milton refused the charge, we can only suppose that he was not entirely displeased to take such action against that 'Apostate Scarcrowe' Prynne (*YP* 3: 194). *Areopagitica* may use the language of natural law and appeal to the Erastian element in Parliament, but its kettle logic resists doctrinaire commitment to either of these as a cover for its ideology of the hegemony of an emerging reforming class—Milton tends to recommend openness at those moments when such a class seems on the verge of coming to power, and to recommend force when it is threatened. The '*too many* reasons' in its argument for the relaxation of constraint are made consistent by the ideological primacy of the ethos articulating them with dizzying display of the cultural weaponry at his disposal.

If we detect an anticipation of the liberal tradition here it is in the tract's participation in a doctrine of possessive individualism, which, as Marxian intellectual historians consistently argue, is at the core of liberalism and fundamentally at odds with socialism. In C. B. Macpherson's terms, articulations of individualism in the seventeenth century contain the 'central difficulty' of liberal-democratic theory in their 'possessive quality,' which is found in 'its conception of the individual as essentially the proprietor of his own person or capacities, owing nothing to society for them. . . . Society consists of relations of exchange between proprietors.

Political society becomes a calculated device for the protection of this property and for the maintenance of an orderly relation of exchange.'[42] Milton's approach is more consistent with the neo-roman principles that Skinner has described partly as a corrective to Macpherson: we see in *Areopagitica* concern that an intellectual and material elite is frustrated in its proprietorship by the licensing that has placed limits on it. The tract does not emphasize the obligation of this elite to the nation as a whole, but it does view the liberty of the meritorious as necessary to the progress of national enlightenment. It would thus be imprecise to call Milton's a 'bourgeois' view—he could praise both Sir Henry Vane, born into privilege, and Samuel Hartlib, the self-fashioning son of a self-fashioning father—and he does not see possession as fundamental to his anthropology in the way of Thomas Hobbes.

Nevertheless, the interest of a class of proprietors is suggested by Milton's casting of *Areopagitica* alongside the divorce tracts and *Of Education* as his contributions to the cause of 'domestic' liberty (*YP* 4: 624). Sir Walter Raleigh observes that this is 'a strange conception of domestic liberty which makes it rest on a threefold support—divorce at will, an unrestrained printing-press, and the encyclopædic education of polyglot children. But the truth is that Milton's classification is an after-thought.'[43] Perhaps it is an afterthought, but the three arguments are united in their concern for the male authority exercised in possessing private property to be married to virtue and extended to the public sphere. The imagery of commodity exchange in *Areopagitica* has been frequently noted, and has been associated with Milton's concern over the monopolization of printing under the aegis of the Stationers' Company.[44] But it is important also to notice that Milton's argument in such figuration is that knowledge is not a 'dividuall moveable' as other commodities are: 'We must not think to make a staple commodity of all the knowledge in the Land, to mark and licence it like our broad cloath, and our wooll packs. What is it but a servitude like that impos'd by the Philistims, not to be allow'd the sharpening of our own axes and coulters, but we must repair from all quarters to twenty licensing forges' (*YP* 2: 536). Such imagery is not at all invested in a marketplace of ideas; it is, rather, concerned with the free movement of that elect part of the nation that is a *de facto* Israel. Over and again Milton signals his concern with the liberty of 'wise men.'[45]

Indeed the largest share of figurative language in *Areopagitica* concerns itself in some measure with a tension between the mobility of the enlightened and the futile confinement promoted by the foolish, between 'manly' openness and cringing retreat: the satirical portrait of the complimenting and ducking Imprimaturs places them in the open 'Piatza of one Title page' while the author is consigned to the 'foot of his Epistle' (*YP* 2: 504); unpraised is a 'fugitive and cloister'd vertue' (515); licensing domestic books while allowing unfettered import of foreign ones is likened to 'that gallant man who thought to pound up the crows by shutting his Parkgate' (520); controlling books and leaving such other influences as music and dance unregulated is to 'shut and fortifie one gate against corruption, and be necessitated to leave others round about wide open' (523); even 'dettors and delinquents may walk abroad without a keeper, unoffensive books must not stirre forth without a visible jaylor in thir title' (536); under licensing 'the freedom of learning must groan again, and to her old fetters' (541–42); the suppression of dissent will 'starch' the nation into a conformity in as 'stanch and solid peece of frame-work, as any January could freeze together,' and will produce a 'conforming stupidity, a stark and dead congealment of *wood and hay and stubble* forc't and frozen together' (545, 564); in gathering scattered remains, Isis and the friends of Truth move 'up and down gathering . . . limb by limb' (549). In a similar spirit the imprisonment of 'the famous *Galileo*' is used to illustrate the injustice of the Inquisition (538). Such language consistently associates licensing with a confinement that is ridiculous at best and destructive at worst, and figures the liberty of the press as allowing bodily movement. In his pervasive concern with the mobility of 'wise men,' Milton reveals that what truly exercises him about the Order is its creation of a system of thought control not coinciding with his aristocracy of merit: licensing will allow 'the Pastor of a small unlearned Parish' to become 'Archbishop over a large dioces of books' (*YP* 2: 540). That he endorses the portion of the Licensing Order preserving authorial copyright, that he recommends post-publication censorship, and that he sees no problem with divisions of property and state control of the means of production all suggest the desire for increased influence of an already existing elite at the core of his ethics of reading and writing.

Recognizing such ideological dynamics in *Areopagitica* can allow us to re-approach some present-day formulations of ethics. Derrida's *démocratie à venir* is closely bound to his view that 'there is no Enlightenment other than the one to be thought.'⁴⁶ His transcendent 'sovereign without power' thus seems very much like a confirmation of the liberal tradition's politically neutral abstract absolutes—justice, democracy, liberty—though he eschews progressivism and teleology by describing these terms as always in the mode of 'to come.'⁴⁷ Such ideological underpinnings are further suggested by Critchley's adumbration of real-world movements that coincide with Derrida's ethics:

> [F]or me, democracy should not be understood as a fixed political form of society, but rather as a process or, better, processes of democratization. Such processes of *democratization*, evidenced in numerous examples (the new social movements, NGOs, Greenpeace, Amnesty International, *médecins sans frontières*, the battle in Seattle), work within, across, above, beneath, and within the territory of the democratic state, not in the vain hope of achieving some sort of 'society without the state,' but rather as providing constant critical pressure upon the state[.]⁴⁸

Derrida himself identifies the alter-globalization movement with his 'messianicity without messianism.' In its heterogeneous, unformed quality, the movement gathers 'together the weak of the earth, all those who feel themselves crushed by the economic hegemonies.'⁴⁹

Derridean ethics is thus consonant with a critical pressure from the political left that is primarily a critical pressure, rather than a radical politics seeking to harness the revolutionary potential of unformed resistance. It is a revealing slip in the passage quoted above that Critchley describes 'processes of democratization' as working '*within*, across, above, beneath, and *within*' the territory of the state. One can imagine Badiou gnashing his teeth at the processes Critchley derives from Derrida, with the objection that applying 'critical pressure upon the state' accedes to the primacy of capitalist parliamentarianism. His thought on ethics is born of his own impatience with liberal acceptance of capitalism, as well as his long career of Maoist activism and affiliation with the movement for recognizing the rights of undocumented workers: in writing his brief book on ethics he claims to have been 'driven by a genuine fury. . . . The intellectual counter-revolution, in the form of moral terrorism, was imposing the infamies of Western capitalism as the new universal model. The presumed "rights of man" were serving at every point to annihilate any attempt to invent forms of free thought.'⁵⁰ He especially objects to the anthropology implied in ethics arising from cultural studies, claiming that feeling for a suffering

Other reduces humanity to the status of victim—to a 'suffering beast' and thus to our 'animal substructure'[51]—rather than pointing to the ways in which we can aspire to immortality through fidelity to a cause larger than ourselves. An anthropology of victimhood is consistent with the 'democratic materialism' of capitalist parliamentarianism, with its axiom that 'the law protects all bodies'; for Badiou, the statement 'there are truths' is the 'initial empirical evidence.'[52] In this sense he is as opposed as Milton is to a 'liberal epistemology' founded on rational process alone.

But it is nonetheless not just any militant fidelity that Badiou seeks to endorse: the 'return to the old doctrine of the natural rights of man,' he opines, is 'linked to the collapse of revolutionary Marxism'; 'humanitarian individualism and the liberal defence of rights against the constraints imposed by organized political engagement' stand in the way of 'a new politics of collective liberation.'[53] Žižek's *Defense of Lost Causes*, a book dedicated to Badiou, shares this concern, and seeks to interrogate the blanket condemnation of 'revolutionary intellectuals' arising from Heidegger and De Man's flirtations with Nazism. In this spirit he defends Michel Foucault's praise of the Iranian Revolution against those detractors who measure such praise against the brutal theocracy of the ayatollahs, and draws distinctions between Iran's true event and the pseudo-event of Nazism: '[It] was an authentic Event, a momentary *opening* that unleashed unprecedented forces of social transformation, a moment in which "everything seemed possible." . . . There was nothing comparable to the effervescent first months after the shah's fall—the constant frantic activity, debates, utopian plans, etc.—in Germany after the Nazi takeover.'[54] Hardt and Negri also apologize for Foucault's position on Iran, stating that he 'of course does not endorse political Islam, and he clearly insists that there is nothing revolutionary about the Shiite clergy or Islam as such.'[55]

The record suggests otherwise. Such apology for Foucault's journalism on Iran is transparently untenable after Janet Afary and Kevin B. Anderson's archive and analysis, *Foucault and the Iranian Revolution*. They show a tunnel vision in Foucault's support of Khomeini that is alarming, to say the least. Though Žižek might value the unleashing of 'forces of social transformation' emerging after the fall of the shah, Foucault was excited by quite a different possibility: he overlooked various dissenting voices of the Iranian left in favor of identifying Khomeini with an emerging 'political spirituality' rejecting Enlightenment truth regimes, including

Marxism. The 'utopic' possibilities in Iran lay in the wish to return to Islam's originary moment. 'What Are the Iranians Dreaming About?' he wonders in a 1978 essay:

> 'A utopia,' some told me without any pejorative implication. 'An ideal,' most of them said to me. At any rate it is something very old and also very far into the future, a notion of coming back to what Islam was at the time of the Prophet, but also of advancing toward a luminous and distant point where it would be possible to renew fidelity rather than maintain obedience. In pursuit of this ideal, the distrust of legalism seemed to me to be essential, along with a faith in the creativity of Islam.[56]

Anyone with cursory knowledge of the *Qur'an* will scoff at the possibility of a return to 'the time of the Prophet' that is simultaneously a rejection of 'obedience' and 'legalism.' The brilliant satire of *The Satanic Verses*—a novel in which Khomeini took some interest—exposes a religious text positively 'obsessed by law,' with 'rules, rules, rules . . . rules about every damn thing, if a man farts let him turn his face to the wind, a rule about which hand to use for the purpose of cleaning one's behind. It was as if no aspect of human existence was to be left unregulated, free. The revelation—the *recitation*—told the faithful how much to eat, how deeply they should sleep, and which sexual positions had received divine sanction.'[57]

Foucault had his limited knowledge of Islam thrust upon him in a 1978 conversation with Iranian sociologist Ehsan Naraghi, when he casually assumed that an Oriental religion would be tolerant of homosexuality. Naraghi's wife, Angel Arabshaybani, promptly enlightened her guest on the punishment described in the *Qur'an*: 'She got up and brought a French translation of a Quranic verse, placed it in front of Michel Foucault, and said, "Execution!" Foucault was dumb-founded.'[58] Leftists and experts on Iran were sounding warnings from the start about Khomeini, and exposing the real divisions within the movement against the shah.[59] Foucault was nonetheless inveterate in his idealization of 'this almost mythical figure' whom he took to embody the collective will of Iranians: '*Khomeini is not a politician*. There will not be a Khomeini party; there will not be a Khomeini government. Khomeini is the focal point of a collective will' (italics in original).[60]

Perhaps most alarming of all is Foucault's whisking away of concerns over the ayatollahs' assault on women's rights—alarming, but not entirely surprising given his consistent inattention to gender issues in his analyses of knowledge and power.⁶¹ In praising the ideals of the revolution, Foucault casually takes at face value the theocrats' arguments on the separate rights of the sexes: '[B]etween men and women there will not be inequality with respect to rights, but difference, since there is a natural difference.'⁶² This seems not only a naive acceptance of the terms of religious zealots, but also an indifference to the retrenchment of those equal rights that had emerged in Iran's rare moments of mixed monarchy: under social democrat prime minister Muhammad Mossadeq, women earned the right to vote in local elections in 1952; undeterred by protests led by Khomeini in the 1960s, the Iranian regime continued to extend suffrage; and the 1967 Family Protection Law made it possible for women to initiate divorce, a law further revised in 1975 to allow some rights of child custody.⁶³

Responding to Foucault's idealization of Khomeini's movement, an Iranian expatriate calling herself 'Atoussa H.' wrote a letter to *Le Nouvel Observateur* calling attention to the repressive stance toward women in the mullahs' interpretation of the *Qur'an*: '[So] the Iranian people have no other choice than that between SAVAK [the shah's intelligence agency] and religious fanaticism? . . . Today unveiled women are often insulted, and young Muslim men do not themselves hide the fact that, in the regime they wish for, women should behave or else be punished.'⁶⁴ Foucault would respond to this letter in the 13 November issue of *Le Nouvel Observateur* without expending a single word on the plight of women, charging 'Atoussa H.' instead with the 'intolerable' errors of branding all 'the potentialities of Islam' as fanatical.⁶⁵ He would later become hostile to the demonstrations against the forced wearing of the veil that were led by men and women of the Iranian left in March 1979. Khomeini's order compelling the veil was issued on 8 March, International Women's Day, and was met with organized demonstrations at Tehran University that continued intermittently over the remainder of the month. Responding to the support of this cause by such intellectuals as Kate Millett, Claudine Moullard, Simone de Baeuvoir, and Raya Dunayaevskaya, Foucault wrote an open letter to Prime Minister Mehdi Bazargan in April 1979 dismissive of such 'noisy objections' and associating them with Western support of the shah's human-rights abuses.⁶⁶

Such is the tunnel vision of fidelity to an 'event' taking itself to be outside of the truth regimes of existing knowledge. To see 'utopian activity' in the 'political spirituality' of Iran is to overlook the retrograde ideas of the ayatollahs that were apparent from the start and especially obvious on the subject of women's rights. Rather than endorsing with Badiou and Žižek the possibility of an 'evental site' standing apart from knowledge, then, we might more accurately refer to an 'evental claim,' which points to an event enabling fidelity and making more forceful the injunction '*il faut continuer.*' Though the militants adhering to this 'truth' seek to accord it ontological significance beyond the realm of contingent occurrences, that claim is itself made within the terms of an already existing ideology that it is meant to confirm. Critchley recognizes this in arguing that Badiou's use of the term 'truth' is simply 'a way of talking about the justification of moral claims. It just sounds more impressive than justification.'[67] But it is also more than a justification, for the ethos claiming privileged expression of truth, as we have learned from our reading of Milton, deems itself innately qualified to determine political authority.

In this way Derrida, Badiou, and Žižek all reproduce the ideological grounds of determining the good apparent in the ethics of *Areopagitica*. In the midst of his amour for the ayatollah, Foucault shows a glimmer of his usual insight in his comparison of that revolution with England's: 'In England, during the bourgeois revolution of the seventeenth century, underneath the bourgeois and parliamentary revolutions as such, we have a complete series of religious-political struggles. . . . I therefore think that the history of religions, and their deep connections to politics, ought to be thought anew.'[68] In taking up this invitation, we might see that religious truth is often used in Milton's milieu as cover for the aspirations of an elite—whether the bishops under the monarch, or a Presbyterian assembly, or an oligarchy of Independents.

It is for this reason that Derrida likens the call of the Other to a *democracy* to come, for democracy is 'the only paradigm that is universalizable.'[69] Badiou shows sensitivity to this standard in claiming that a 'truth' must be potentially accessible to all—thus Nazism is not a truth to which one can ethically adhere. But does this go far enough? It seems that the stronger corrective to this ideology aspiring to be ethics arises from precisely those approaches to which Badiou objects in being founded upon an anthropology where 'man is *the being who is capable of recognizing himself as a victim.*'[70] Gayatri Spivak's introduction of the subaltern as the ground of ethical concern is a critique of the tendency of political commitment to overlook the humanity of the disenfranchised. In the 'descriptive-culturalist' or 'ideology-critical' work of 'literary folk in the United States,' even of 'feminists with a transnational consciousness,' one can find that 'the very civil structure *here* that they seek to shore up for gender justice can continue to participate in providing alibis for the operation of the major and definitive transnational activity, the financialization of the globe, and thus the suppression of the possibility of decolonization.'[71] In Spivak's terms ethics must not ventriloquize the aspirations of those who cannot articulate them from beyond the pale of subjectivity, those who are disenfranchised by class, race, gender, and global locale. The call of the subaltern Other does not prompt acknowledgment of victimization, but acknowledgment of the aporia of a not-yet realized subjectivity.

Spivak's trenchant critique of the politics of elite leftist intellectuals is persuasive, but also has been taken as a warning against political intervention initiated by a global elite *per se*—precisely the paralysis in Western thought that Badiou sees himself as correcting. She has more recently engaged the topic of human rights as an 'enabling violation' of the sort producing the colonial subject. Though the imperatives of human rights activism are too often determined by elites in the global North and South, this is not a reason to discard human rights altogether. Fundamental to the view of human rights she advances is the broadened availability of a brand of reading that can be deemed an ethical practice, which she sees as the benefit of the humanities' approach to learning: 'As long as real equalization through recovering and training the long-ignored ethical imagination—not necessarily an operative script—of the rural poor and indeed, all species of sub-proletarians on their own terms—is not part of the agenda to come, s/he has no chance of becoming the subject of Human Rights as part of a collectivity, but must remain, forever, its object of benevolence.'[72]

Bearing in mind the capacity of text to re-shape private language, we might see potential in Spivak's sanguine claim that the global elite, too, can benefit from a 'habit of literary reading' that will challenge the dominant ethics of corporate citizenship and will train the 'suspending [of] oneself into the text of the other—for which the first condition and effect is a suspension of the conviction that I am necessarily better, I am necessarily indispensable, I am necessarily the one to right wrongs, I am necessarily the end-product for which history has happened, and that New York is necessarily the capital of the world.'[73]

There is a great deal of merit in Spivak's reconsideration of human rights, a category upon which Badiou heaps Heideggerian scorn, particularly in that it is clearly not predicated upon a view of humanity as potential victim. And she brings stronger global awareness to Derrida's *démocratie à venir*. Her proximity to Derrida also suggests the ideological underpinnings of her comments on ethical reading, which are apparent in her stated aim of 're-activating cultural axiomatics' to be sutured into the principles of Enlightenment. Such suturing requires a certain degree of compatibility between donor and recipient, and cannot be read as endorsing a revolutionary sweeping away of Enlightenment axiomatics. It inherently presumes a re-activation of those ideas and practices reconcilable with Enlightenment principles, not to mention the principles of a moderately left intellectual seeking through adjustment of existing political structures the equitable distribution of resources and the elimination of class and gender bigotries in the rural margin and metropolitan center.[74] This is, I think, a view of humanities education well worth embracing; but intellectual honesty requires that one disclose the ideological dynamics that humanist first principles have taken on in becoming a program of action. Spivak frequently describes humanities education as an uncoercive re-arrangement of desires. Perhaps it is more precise to call it a non-revolutionary re-arrangement of desires toward humane ends. The brand of education Spivak promotes, as I read her, would broaden the franchise of liberal democracy and move it toward social democracy. Reading is not only an ethical activity, it is the ground of ethical activity in its initiation of the call by which positive political change can occur, because it is only through the kind of reading sometimes fostered in the humanities that we are invited to imagine alien subjectivities.

But the problem remains that in an ethics of reading the desire for the good that prompts entry into the arena of public discourse immediately confronts, like Satan entering Chaos in *Paradise Lost*, 'a universal hubbub wilde / Of stunning sounds and voices all confus'd' (2.951–52). In its most persuasive moments, *Areopagitica* describes the necessity of that confusion to ethical reading and recognizes as repressive those political orders that so limit public discourse as to deprive the individual of being able to seek the good. This occurs in an economy circulating only the self-perpetuating claims of the sovereign itself. In such a context, the only truly ethical act is resistance, which is shaped by a more promising politics.

Considering *Areopagitica* also reminds us, however, that arguments for 'openness' are underwritten by a teleology determining the truths toward which intellectual exercise should tend. This might seem to return us to De Man's ethics of reading—where we are always caught in allegory, moving from one symbolic level to the next in the economy of signs—but not entirely so. It does leave room for what Marshall Grossman, influenced by Lacan, has described as the desire for the good that is the ground of ethics. In the realm of text we are aware that such desire will attach itself to ideologically determined pronouncements of the good, but it can also make demands of those pronouncements. And it can provide, of course, moments where we feel the pleasure of encountering the refined thoughts of a master-spirit, for which pleasure the rational delight of discovery cannot fully account. At its best that confrontation between reader and text can stretch the boundaries of an existing ideology toward greater inclusivity and humanity.

Anticipating Spivak's claims was Wittgenstein's insight in the *Tractatus Logico-Philosophicus* and in his 'Lecture on Ethics' that consciousness of the limits of language should prompt an exercise of the imagination where we try in good faith to make sense of nonsense.[75] In Wittgenstein's terms the ethical impulse is above the realm of proposition. The attempt to articulate the transcendent, which must fail, is distinguished from the desire producing that doomed attempt, which is a noble aspect of human nature: unsuccessful articulations of ethics are in his terms 'a document of a tendency in the human mind which I personally cannot help respecting deeply and I would not for my life ridicule it.'[76] It is for this reason that the *Tractatus*, which shows us the limits of our perceived knowledge, concludes with an invitation that is best described as mystical flight:

> 6.54 My propositions serve as elucidations in the following way: anyone who understands me eventually recognizes them as nonsensical, when he has used them—as steps—to climb up beyond them. (He must, so to speak, throw away the ladder after he has climbed up it.)
> 7 What we cannot speak about we must pass over in silence.[77]

This is strongly reminiscent of the Pseudo-Dionysian tradition in mysticism, whether Bonaventure's scaling heavenward on the wings of angels in the *Six Steps* or that of the author of *The Cloud of Unknowing*. Unlike the mystic, however, Wittgenstein does not describe the conditions whereby that flight might be achieved and its insights conveyed. It remains an entirely transcendent possibility that cannot be described, and thus frustrates definition as an 'event'—that we can articulate the nature of an event presupposes that it has become governed by a logic: 'It is as impossible to represent in language anything that "contradicts logic" as it is in geometry to represent by its co-ordinates a figure that contradicts the laws of space, or to give the co-ordinates of a point that does not exist.'[78]

We might apply these principles to an articulation of the human rather than the transcendent: though we can never fully succeed in describing in its full dynamics another human subjectivity, and especially the subaltern, the ethical impulse resides in the attempt to do so. If it is made in good faith, that attempt will involve the mystic's stripping away of one's material and ideological concerns—which is also impossible. The ethical impulse is thus as fraught as the literary habit of reading that can serve as its inspiration. But its imagining of other subjects challenges a logic of the instrumentality of others, recognizes its limitations as an imagining, and serves as reminder of the infinite subjectivities of which we have not yet taken account.

3

Liberty before and after Liberalism: Milton's Politics and the Post-secular State

Political theorists currently exercise themselves a good deal in confronting the stubborn persistence of human irrationality. Despite the liberal tradition's ability in the West to secure basic rights and broad political participation its ideal citizenry has yet to emerge: even the most liberal states frequently divide themselves along religious and ethnic fault lines and are thus a far cry from achieving a civil society where individuals select their affiliations with unfettered reason. Indeed we seem, at the dawn of the twenty-first century, to be retreating from that Whiggish end: Western states consistently grapple with the demands of those bound by the inherited and primordial qualities of race, gender, sexual orientation, and faith.

All of this seems to be much more than the communitarianism that Michael Walzer described some twenty years ago as a vogue providing intermittent critique of liberal individualism. Recent monographs in political theory advertise ours as a post-liberal age and negotiate a middle ground between liberalism and cultural pluralism—in this vein are Richard Bellamy's *Liberalism and Pluralism* (1999), Paul Edward Gottfried's *After Liberalism* (1999), and Robert B. Talisse's *Democracy after Liberalism* (2005). Walzer himself recently argues in a similar spirit that if liberalism is to survive in any form, it should concern itself less with the 'construction of dispassionate deliberative procedures' and more with countering the 'bad' passions of religiosity with 'good' passions of activism advancing the cause of equality.[1] The challenges to liberalism are similarly engaged by

Paul Kahn's work, beginning especially with his 2005 book *Putting Liberalism in Its Place,* which describes cultural pluralism as forcing us 'constantly [to] confront the question of whether some of the practices supported by these values are beyond the limits of our own commitment to a liberal moral philosophy and a political practice of tolerance.'[2]

Seeking fuller understanding of this philosophy and practice, Kahn turns to an exploration of American liberalism that seeks not only to anatomize its institutionalization of collective reason, but also to account for those claims of the popular sovereign reaching beyond reason, particularly its demands of self-sacrifice and its embodiment of national will, concluding that the popular sovereign of the American tradition 'draws as much upon the Christian tradition of love and will as on the Enlightenment tradition of reason.'[3] If, as Slavoj Žižek describes it, the Jacobins' version of democracy sought to empty the locus of power and to preserve this vacancy through the Terror, American democracy might be described as installing an elected sovereign in the seat of power who is taken to embody consensus along with national identity and aspiration—the authority of the body that voices the law derives not only from liberalism's contractual notion of the will, but also from the 'erotic character of the political' for which liberalism cannot account.[4]

That character of American politics was apparent on the night of Barack Obama's presidential victory, when the newly elected official was greeted with an outpouring of tears.[5] The confession of lachrymony became a common trope in reportage of that election night, adopted by figures as diverse as Sean Penn and Michael Walzer.[6] Several of my friends and colleagues reported the same reaction. This was the culmination of a political campaign that consistently claimed to operate in a realm above politics—for much of his political career Obama has been wont to end his stump speeches with those three little words that mean so much, 'I love you.'[7] Walzer justifies tears such as political scientists weep: 'I wept with relief when it became clear that Obama had won—because of the high hopes riding on his candidacy and the sense of desolation and demoralization that would have followed on his defeat.'[8] Nowhere is the paradox of the liberal state—and especially the American state—more amply illustrated: though political liberalism calls for public discourse and institutions to be governed by reason alone, it also summons such emotions as hope. Despite the stability of state institutions, that hope can seem to have great fragility—another four years of Republican rule and the 2004 election might be seen not as an anomaly, but as a grim foretaste of the end of the American experiment.

With conflicting expressions of liberalism in view, and drawing on the checkered history of America's practice of tolerance, Kahn identifies as competing a 'liberalism of faith' and a 'liberalism of speech.' Where the former 'constrains the state in order to preserve a domain, or domains, of ultimate meaning beyond the state,' the latter 'builds a conception of legitimate political order from the ground up[.] . . . [P]olitical order gains its meaning not from something beyond politics—religion—but from an internal, discursive practice among citizens.'[9] Where a liberalism of faith imagines the state as living 'in the shadow of the church' in limiting the claims it can make on individuals, a liberalism of speech demands that all religion, like all legitimate public acts, 'be tested in the forum of reason.'[10]

We should keep these two 'liberalisms' in mind as we turn to Milton, for they hold in several respects the key to important distinctions between his conception of political order in the prose addressed to the Long Parliament in the early 1640s and the prose of 1659–60. Where the earlier prose envisions a new national order encompassing both church and state and more fully reflecting national desire than the corrupt institutions of episcopacy and absolute monarchy, the later prose limits the authority of the state in order to allow independent religious determination of ultimate meaning. As in previous chapters, we will examine this development through Milton's use of language, in this case the kinds of language Milton employs in addressing the constitution of church and state. In the 1640s we can notice Milton developing a political language expressive of the dynamic reforming energies that he hopes will rise to the fore in the years following the first sitting of the Long Parliament, and participates in a language presenting that sitting as eschatologically significant. In 1659–60, he exhibits a plainness that we must distinguish from the plain style of *Paradise Lost* that we explored in chapter one: rather than epic plainness delivering truth, we find a style of political speech that constrains the political arena by removing from it the energies of religious zeal animating the earlier prose. Approaching Milton's prose with this distinction in mind will allow us not only to explore underappreciated developments in the style and arguments of his political tracts, but also to evaluate the status of Kahn's two 'liberalisms' in our own political moment. We shall trouble these two categories with reference to Jürgen Habermas's recent assessment of the role of religion in the public sphere.

I. Milton's shifting politics

A significant shift in Milton's sense of political order is revealed by comparison of apocalyptic history in *Of Reformation* (1641) and *A Treatise of Civil Power* (1659). Typifying his earlier presentation of the end of time is the famous peroration in *Of Reformation*, with its lively imagining of the justification of energetic English reformers and damnation of the bishops:

> [T]his great and Warlike Nation . . . may presse on hard to that *high* and *happy* emulation to be found the *soberest, wisest*, and *most Christian People* at that day when thou the Eternall and shortly-expected King shalt open the Clouds to judge the severall Kingdomes of the World, and distributing *Nationall Honours* and *Rewards* to Religious and just *Common-wealths*, shalt put an end to all Earthly Tyrannies[.] . . . But they that by the impairing and diminution of the true *Faith*, the distresses and servitude of their *Countrey* aspire to high *Dignity, Rule* and *Promotion* here, after a shamefull end in this *Life* (which God grant them) shall be thrown down eternally into the *darkest* and *deepest Gulfe* of HELL. (*YP* 1: 616–17)

The nationalist character of the divine judgment here envisioned could not be more explicit: the eternal king distributes national honors and rewards to those commonwealths excelling in truth and righteousness, a status, Milton argues, filled by an England reclaiming its rightful place on the vanguard of Reformation.[11] In her magisterial article on Milton's apocalyptic thought, Stella Revard illumines significantly the political resonance of this statement, placing it in the context of the 'advent of the Long Parliament' that everywhere occasioned 'the cries that Babylon was falling'; '[T]he commentaries by Mede, Alsted, Brightman, Napier, and Pareus, which were Englished by order of the Long Parliament, stood alongside controversial millenarian tracts, such as Thomas Goodwin's *A Glimpse of Sion's Glory* (1641) and [Henry] Archer's *The Personall Reigne of Christ upon Earth* (1642).'[12] The closing words in *Of Reformation* thus participate in a common figuring of the Long Parliament's rise in influence as an event significant in God's time.

Milton generates, by contrast, a strict separation of divine and human time in *A Treatise of Civil Power*. Unlike in the anti-prelatical tracts, he here drives a wedge between justified Saints and worldly political institutions. A Protestant state is one allowing individuals freely to interpret Scripture and to follow inner light:

> First, it cannot be deni'd, being the main foundation of our protestant religion, that we *of these ages*, having no other divine rule or autoritie from without us warrantable to one another as a common ground but the holy scripture, and no other within us but the illumination of the Holy Spirit so interpreting that scripture ... can have no other ground in matter of religion but only from the scriptures. And these being not possible to be understood without this divine illumination, which no man can know at all times to be in himself, much lesse to be at any time for certain in any other, it follows cleerly, that no man or body of men *in these times* can be the infallible judges or determiners in matters of religion to any other mens consciences but thir own. (*YP* 7: 242–43; emphasis mine)

In this, the third paragraph of the tract proper, Milton twice draws our attention to the applicability of his arguments to a specific moment in biblical history—'we of these ages' must rely on Scripture; no 'body of men in these times' can judge religious matters infallibly—emphasizing the consequences of the human fall, which occupies a good deal of his attention at the moment, and anticipating that time when the human darkness necessitating reliance on Scripture will cease to exist and God will be 'all in all.'

But this remains only a vague anticipation, and Milton avoids the lively imagery of Judgment developed in *Of Reformation*. He seeks now to bracket that kind of inspired religious speculation from the public arena, which must limit itself to basic principles of religion as revealed in the Christian Bible. The oft-noted stylistic sparingness of *Civil Power* is thus fundamental to its rhetorical purpose: working only from straightforward demonstration 'drawn from the scripture only,' it provides an object lesson in the self-restraint urged upon the public officials it addresses (*YP* 7: 241). Where *The Reason of Church Government* claims a *sola Scriptura* argument urging state institution of a (small-p) presbyterian church—and famously does not deliver the biblical proof-texts it promises, relying instead on *ethos* and *dispositio*—*Civil Power* draws much more heavily on inartificial evidence gathered from Scripture in advocating the state's disengagement from matters religious.

This approach is also attributable to the fact that in a way unlike the Providential sitting of the Long Parliament in 1640, apocalyptic prophecy had become in 1659 a mode of resistance to Parliament and the army. The Quakers especially took to the presses in what seems in retrospect like well orchestrated political lobbying, with regular news reports on their persecution;[13] practical-minded proposals to Parliament and the Council of State to defend liberty of conscience; and strongly hortative, divinely inspired appeals from prophets and prophetesses for the nation's leaders to return to God's path. The advice was less than appreciated: several leading Friends, including John Crook, were paraded before Parliament on 16 April 1659, forced to remove their hats, and advised to 'submit themselves to the Laws of this Nation, and the Magistracy they live under.'[14]

Among the Quakers, George Fox and Edward Burrough are both conspicuously active in this critical year. In *This is for You Who Are Called the Comon-Wealths-Men* (1659), Fox provides a straightforward recommendation that Parliament be chary of Presbyterian 'covetousness, and self-ends' and that the army act in the national interest rather than in its own.[15] In a tract of May 1659 addressing the army as it restores the Rump, he more fully reveals the eschatology underpinning such demands. In the absence of force in religion, '[T]hose that are in the spirit of truth, will assuredly prevail over them that be in the spirit of deceit, and this will be manifested soon,' a statement that resonates with the tract's closing chiliastic remark that those who trust '*in the wisdome or arm of flesh, they shall be broken.*'[16] Like Milton, Fox agitates against hire as well as force, arguing that tithing cannot be justified in a Christian church on the precedent of Levi and that the practice has resulted in persecution in England: the 'Priests' have 'robbed and spoyled both the fatherless, Widows, & others; & hath prisoned several unto death by a Law made by the Popish Kings.'[17] This view receives more extended treatment in George Fox the Younger's *Answer to Doctor Burgess his Book* (1659), which, like Milton's *Hirelings* (1659)—a companion tract to *Civil Power*—claims in its argument for de-institutionalization of the church that devotion is the *sine qua non* of a ministry rather than university-trained orthodoxy: 'Orthodox men which are called the Pillars of the Church, she suffered them to live, this false church, this Whore which hath drunk the blood of the Martyrs, Prophets, and Saints; so killed the true Ministers, and so these are them that have set up their Schools and Colledges, to make Ministers, and their Tenths.'[18]

Burrough makes many of the same claims with greater force and frequency, calling for liberty of conscience and describing the proper jurisdiction of the magistrate as the 'outward man.'[19] He joins several Quaker pamphleteers who make frequent use of the derisive terms 'hire' and 'hireling' in 1659, a list including *To All Friends and People in the Whole Christendome*, William Bayley's *Blood of Righteous Abel*, John Crook's *Tythes No Property*, the elder George Fox's *Paper Sent Forth into the World*, Francis Gawler's *Record of Some Persecutions*, and Thomas Greene's *Alarm to the False Shepheards*.[20] Though the terms carry a strong association with the Book of Job and especially with John 10.13, and Milton had used them before in the anti-prelatical tracts, he surely must have been aware of this resonance with Quaker agitation when he published *Hirelings*.[21] Burrough's *Faithful Testimony* (1659) laments the persecution of the Friends at the hands of the Presbyterians, likening them to 'the Papists and Prelates.' Here again he criticizes the forced payment of tithes and maintenance of an unfit ministry, attacking along the way the university training of English divines: 'Are not they made Ministers now by natural learning, receiving ordination from man, through the attainments of such Arts, and Sciences, & Degrees, through natural learning and humane policy, not having their ministry by the gift of the Holy Ghost.'[22] In a broadside addressed to Parliament that year, the elimination of tithes is urged in apocalyptic language: '[If] you do it not, but will be the imposers of unrighteous things upon the people under you, and will *carry the Whore*, and yet drink her cup, and *compel* others to drink it, then the Lord will break you to pieces, and bring freedom to this Nation some other way.'[23] In his lengthier *Message to the Present Rulers of England* (1659), the point is made with the mixed biblical metaphors of clumsy prophesying:

> Behold ye men; ye are verily as the dust before the winde [Ps 18.42], so are ye to him soon blown away, and your place not found, as the Grasse before the Mower [Ps 37.2], so are ye before him, soon cut down and withered, and your beauty utterly extinguished, as a Potters vessel under an iron Rod [Ps 2.9], even so are you to him, he can immediately break you, never to be bound up, as a drop to the Fountain [Isa 40.15], so are you to him, soon dried up, and made nothing; wherefore ye men, ye mortal creatures, ye ignorant persons, sons of a transgressor, ye dust and ashes [Isa 40.15]; for thus you are in comparison of him this mighty Prince; Hearken to this message which cometh to you from him.[24]

The menacing allusions here repeatedly present the prophetic voice as that of a David or an Isaiah called to announce divine retribution upon an ungodly nation harassing the chosen. Burrough is certainly not the only Quaker advising the national leadership at this moment of its impending doom; he is joined by John Anderson, William Bayley, Ester Biddle, John Chandler, and Dorothy White, to name a few.[25]

Milton's twin tracts on deinstitutionalization of the church thus share a good deal of the Quakers' concerns, but express them in a style distancing itself from prophetic resistance. The preface to *Civil Power*, addressed to Richard Cromwell's Parliament, presents its argument as completing the task that the Council of State had previously envisioned for itself:

> *I shall write to many eminent persons of your number, alreadie perfet and resolvd in this important article of Christianitie. Some of whom I remember to have heard often for several years, at a councel next in autoritie to your own, so well joining religion with civil prudence, and yet so well distinguishing the different power of either . . . that if any there present had bin before of an opinion contrary, he might doubtless have departed thence a convert in that point, and have confessd, that then both commonwealth and religion will at length, if ever, flourish in Christendom, when either they who govern discern between civil and religious, or they only who so discern shall be admitted to govern.* (*YP* 7: 240; italics in original)

Rather than urging reform, the tract thus presents itself as rehearsing the heurism of members of the assembly in the English republic's heyday of 1649–51. Milton adopts in *Hirelings* a similar *topos* of loyalty to an assembly of the wise; his exordium praises Parliament and calls attention to his achievements on behalf of the Cause: 'Owing to your protection, supream Senat, this libertie of writing which I have us'd these 18 years on al occasions to assert the just rights and freedoms both of church and state, and so far approv'd as to have been trusted with the representment and defence of your actions to all Christendom against an adversarie of no mean repute' (*YP* 7: 274). These passages also show that Milton is not necessarily advancing the Quaker cause; he seems to refer here to that champion of Root and Branch extirpation of episcopacy Sir Henry Vane, who had mixed feelings about the Society of Friends, consistently objecting to their overemphasis of external moral conduct rather than internal seeking—damning criticism in enthusiast circles.[26] Vane and his disciple Henry Stubbe did, however, share the Quakers' animosity toward *hire*, as evinced in the latter's *Light Shining out of Darkness* (1659), a tract that, as David Hawkes observes, is frequently described as influencing Milton's statements on tithing.[27]

Despite his praise for the 'supream Senat,' Milton's arguments at this point diminish Parliament's role in leading England on the path of truth and righteousness. This may be an entirely natural position in *Civil Power*, which addresses an especially ineffective body of legislators in Richard's Parliament—in its brief sitting it occupied itself almost entirely with disputes over recognition of the new Protector, election returns and matters of privilege, and declarations of the dismal state of public revenue.[28] Even in *Hirelings*, addressed to the much more promising reconvened Rump in August 1659, Milton does not revive the nationalist apocalyptism of 1640–41, choosing instead to continue his divorce of biblical and national histories, especially revealed in his presentation of the beginnings of Reformation. The reader of Milton's prose will know that this is a history always pregnant with polemical intent. The anti-prelatical tracts turn consistently to Wycliffe as founder of reformation, and argue that his revelation of truth was stifled by the prelates—collapsing along the way the distinction between Catholic and Protestant bishops. In this vein Milton claims in *Of Reformation* that it is '*Wicklefs* preaching, at which all the succeding *Reformers* more effectually lighted their *Tapers*,' showing the '*Precedencie* which God gave this *Iland*, to be the first *Restorer of buried Truth*' (*YP* 1: 525–26).[29] *The Doctrine and Discipline of Divorce* locates the beginning of the English Reformation in Henry VIII's breach with Rome: '[It] pleas'd God to make [Henry] see all the tyranny of *Rome*, by discovering this which they exercis'd over divorce; and to make him the beginner of a reformation to this whole Kingdom' (*YP* 2: 347–48). This, of course, advances the tract's argument that canon law proscriptions on divorce frustrate the progress of Reformation and are opposed to Protestant liberty. That *terminus a quo* of Reformation is adjusted later in the divorce tracts when the need arises: in *The Judgement of Martin Bucer*, the reformer's credentials are secured with inclusion of Foxe's account of his life in the prefatory 'testimonies' and association with '*the first reformation of England*' under Edward VI (*YP* 2: 424, 437).

Hirelings, by contrast, looks outside of the English heroes of Reformation important to the Foxean tradition in its presentation of the Waldenses as the first Protestants. Yes, this is consistent with Milton's concern, and English concern more generally, in the later 1650s over the massacre in Piedmont; it is also consistent with this tract's removal of the task of Reformation from the hands of the magistrate. Immediately after showing that 'those ancientest reformed churches of the *Waldenses*, if they rather continu'd not pure since the apostles, deni'd that tithes were to be given,' Milton associates the idea of a 'national church' with the '*Jewes*' and points to the universality of the Christian church: '[T]he Christian church is universal; not ti'd to nation, dioces or parish, but consisting of many particular churches complete in themselves' (7: 291–92). Where the antiprelatical tracts' nationalist view of Reformation participates in the Long Parliament's self-styled sainthood, England is here denied a privileged role in the history of Protestantism and its magistrates reduced to one of a number of worldly officers potentially menacing to the Saints.

This alteration of Milton's approach to Reformation history is all the more striking when read alongside the Quaker John Crook's *Tythes no Property* (1659), a tract that strongly evokes Foxean martyrology in a juristic assault on tithes. Crook quotes several reformers out of Foxe, including Wycliffe, William Swindersby, Walter Brute, William Thorpe, and especially John Hus, who has 'by way of prophesie foretold . . . of a deliverance that *shall* come to the Church and people of God, as it is recorded in the book of Martyrs.'[30] The promise of English Protestantism to prevent, rather than to duplicate, further religious persecution is used to decry the practice of forcing payment of tithes against an individual's conscience.[31] In Crook's argument, Sir Edward Coke is just as heroic a figure as Foxe is: the nationalist religious language by which tithes are condemned reinforces his account of English law, which does not secure a positive claim to property but rather prevents others from encroaching upon an acquisition:

> [No] man can have a property but by descent, purchase, or gift, the law it self, not creating a property, but onely conserving to every man his just right and interest . . . and those laws for Tything made in the time both of *Hen.* 8. & *Edw.* 6. (there being no law before made by Parliaments, onely the Statute of *Ric.* 2. 15. & 6. confirmed by *Hen.* the 4. by which it appears that Tythes were but a free gift or alms[.)][32]

In this light the claim of the church to any part of a citizen's property has no legal basis, for no individual or institution can impinge upon a legal acquisition. Crook's is thus an appeal to English self-identification as a

Christian Commonwealth repealing those practices that neither are 'consonant to the law of God' nor advance the 'peoples weal.'[33] If his argument recalls Milton's prose, it is the harmonizing of Christian liberty and British legal tradition in *Eikonoklastes*.[34] *Hirelings* arraigns English law for its history of acquiescence to Rome (*YP* 7: 294).

Even in advancing a model republic in *The Readie and Easie Way* Milton is reluctant to invoke England's legal and constitutional tradition, preferring instead to focus on securing liberty of conscience and adopting quietist political measures.[35] Many of the practical proposals provided in this tract seem intended to redress grievances with which the various occupants of Westminster Hall were beset in the tumultuous years between the death of Oliver Cromwell and the Restoration. The state of public revenue, Milton claims, will turn from bad to worse with the additional expense of maintaining the sumptuous courts that monarchs demand, and no longer will the Commonwealth be able to turn to the sale of royal and episcopal lands in its duress. What's more, Milton is prescient in predicting that those loyalists to the Cause who had acquired such lands would be forced to relinquish them without compensation. A government wishing to be stable must stanch the influence of those 'ambitious leaders of the army' meddling in political affairs and preventing peaceful settlement of the 'army itself.' Many Rumpers surely felt the same way: in their 1659–60 sitting they consistently have army officers appear before them to receive their commissions directly from Parliament; they had also installed a good many of their own members in prominent posts. These measures may have made them overly confident in the support of the army. They vacated on 12 October the posts of the Lambert circle and attempted to establish an Army Commission—which are usually taken to be their fatal errors—and more self-destructively voted on the same day not to appoint a guard for the House that night.[36] Though consistent with the spirit of many of his writings, even Milton's frequent anti-populism in *The Readie and Easie Way* is illumined by concerns especially pressing at the moment: the London 'tumults' that are the period's surest barometer of impending political events had turned against Parliament, which moved to outlaw such popular entertainments as cockfights, bull-baiting, and horse-racing as hotbeds of royalist rabble-rousing.[37]

If scholars of the present day have difficulty in discerning how much of this tract and of Milton's thought at this juncture more generally constitute a rejection of Cromwell, how much is stop-gap measure and how much part of a long-standing oligarchism, we are in the company of at least one of Milton's contemporaries.[38] Moses Wall lauded Milton in a personal letter for adhering to the ideals of the Cause in *Civil Power*, taking the tract as a return to 'Liberty and Spiritual Truths' in its departure from the Cromwellian 'court'—unlike Milton, Cromwell's fellow Independents of the Center, who were prominent in the restored Rump, retained the Protector's reluctance to dispense with tithes. Though Wall is right thus to read *Civil Power*, he wrongly sees the tract as a sign that Milton might also oppose the 'Norman' feudalism by which the people 'are far more enslaved to the Lord: of the Manor, than the rest of the nation is to a King or supreme Magistrate' (*YP* 7: 511). *The Readie and Easie Way* significantly does not share the anti-feudalism of James Harrington's republicanism. Under the tract's proposals, local gentry would settle civil disputes and have suitable estates built at the public expense, which is less a Harringtonean, or Machiavellian, balancing of the Few and the Many than it is a pacifying measure meant to fix the privilege of the wealthiest landowners, sating their greed so that they are less inclined to resist the national authority—it renders the judiciary an arm of privilege in precisely the way that the Levellers had decried and sought to reform, and eschews the generation of a class of citizen landowners emphasized in Harrington's agrarianism. If there is a rejection of Cromwell at this point, it is only insofar as the Lord Protector had not advanced liberty of conscience as much as Milton would have wished; that this concern is much more constant than his labile republican values is indicated most explicitly by his desire for Monck to exert monarchical authority.

In brief, one of the great ironies of Milton's prose that the modern liberal reader must bear in mind is that he turns to practical proposals on the separation of church and state and the shape of an English republic at the point when he is least concerned with the nature of civil society as a whole. Taken together, his three tracts of 1659–60 show that his primary interest is in readily available means of securing liberty for a religiously enlightened minority in the hope that in God's time they would rightly rise to their due prominence. Harrington argues at this point that the privileging of liberty of conscience would frustrate civil liberty: 'The distinction of liberty into civil and spiritual is not ancient, but of a latter date, there being indeed no such distinction; for the liberty of conscience once granted separable from civil liberty, civil liberty can have no security.'[39] Milton's recommendations justify the claim. What little democratic rotation is proposed in *The Readie and Easie Way* is conceded grudgingly to an audience of adherents to the Cause sympathetic to Harrington's idealism. In his projected reformation of the nation's 'faulty education,' the Ciceronian sentiments of training greatness of spirit (*magnitudo animi*) found in *Of Education* take on a decidedly coercive, even Hobbesean, aim of promoting acquiescence to political authority: 'to teach the people faith not without vertue, temperance, modestie, sobrietie, parsimonie, justice; not to admire wealth or honour; to hate turbulence and ambition; to place every one his privat welfare and happiness in the public peace, liberty and safetie. They shall not then need to be much mistrustfull of thir chosen Patriots in the Grand Council' (*YP* 7: 443).[40] The advanced education imagined for the nation's nobility will allow them to travel to the capital to learn 'all liberal arts and exercises,' not necessarily to earn greater political agency in the affairs of the Grand Council, but to return to the country 'communicating the natural heat of government and culture more distributively to all extreme parts' (7: 460).

Such emphasis on stability and permanence marks a significant departure from the trenchant defense of the individual's right of resistance in the first edition of *The Tenure* and, more generally, the concern in much of Milton's prose with the sweeping away of institutions stultifying to the active and civic-minded. This shift is partly explicable within the terms of his classical republicanism. Those favoring a return to Stuart rule mark themselves in Milton's terms as *servili*, and are thus disqualified, no matter how numerous they may be, from deciding the affairs of the commonwealth.[41] In a sentiment recalling the *Second Defense* and repeated with tetchy frequency in the *Readie and Easie Way*, Milton declares that the greater virtue outweighs the greater number.[42] Unaccountable in terms of his classical republicanism, however, is how Milton's position is a consequence of the increasing priority he grants liberty of conscience. Though *The Readie and Easie Way* treats both religious and civil liberty, it rehearses the argument of, and refers overtly to, *Civil Power*, averring that 'liberty of conscience . . . above all other things ought to be to all men dearest and most precious' (*YP* 7: 456), showing—as we should expect—how closely related are Milton's ecclesiological and political statements at this juncture. The civil liberty that Milton describes is notably much more limited and is confined to local government. As with others who give priority to liberty of conscience, Milton has come increasingly to see political institutions as bearing the mark of worldly iniquity and to anticipate God's liberation of the Saints from this burden. Vane, like Milton, casts his lot with those willing to defend liberty of conscience by the sword: he betrays the Rump and Council of State of which he was the most prominent member in 1659 by working with the Committee of Safety, for which action he is expelled from the Rump upon its recall in December and forced once more into country retirement.[43] It is no accident that Milton adds to the 1658 edition of the *Defence* Augustine's sentiment from *De civitate Dei* that 'in the house of a just man who lives in accordance with the faith, even he who commands serves those he seems to command' (*YP* 4: 419).[44] In strictly neo-roman terms, such a view undermines the principle of a free state by subordinating the magistrate to the influence of an external power, in this case God and His faithful servants.

II. Liberty of conscience and overlapping consensus

To return to the two liberalisms Paul Kahn has identified as contending forces in the American tradition, it will be relatively clear that the earlier prose resembles a 'liberalism of speech' where *Civil Power, Hirelings*, and the *Readie and Easie Way* do a 'liberalism of faith.' In making this claim one must of course announce certain qualifiers: Milton nowhere envisions a liberal state based upon equal consensus and protection of all citizens, and nowhere locates absolute meaning in an exclusively political realm. Insofar, however, as texts like *Of Reformation* render a climate of religious and intellectual liberty as actuating political speech-acts moving the nation toward its destiny of truth and righteousness—and place Parliament at the helm of such progress—they do express something like the reification of political progressivism in the liberal tradition: Milton tells us in *Of Reformation* that 'a Commonwealth ought to be but as one huge Christian personage, one mighty growth, and stature of an honest man, as big, and compact in vertue as in body' (*YP* 1: 572). In the emotionally charged language and lively imagery of these earlier tracts we see that tendency Kahn notes of the state as erotic object, satisfying national desire for fulfillment in a way that cannot be accounted for by reason alone.

That the later tracts present us with a 'liberalism of faith' is much more straightforward. Unlike the earlier prose, Milton here locates ultimate meaning in a religious realm defined against worldly politics, urging public officials not to encroach upon an individual's prior spiritual obligations. As he puts it in *Civil Power*, it is 'the will of God & his Holy Spirit within us, which we ought to follow much rather then any law of man' (*YP* 7: 242). Absolute meaning in *Civil Power* is located in Scripture and in a divine illumination that cannot be discerned by the magistrate. The state is no longer an agent, or even a handmaiden, to national destiny, but finds its highest calling in non-interference with the righteous few who are the beneficiaries of cosmic destiny—no matter how much the national will must be ignored to institute such protection. Indeed, the account of the Waldenses as the beginners of Reformation undercuts entirely England's privileged status in biblical history, calling into question the very notion of national destiny. If the prose at the outset of the civil wars lends religious significance to the Commonwealth, the prose on the eve of Restoration strongly denies the state such significance.

With this tendency of Milton's later prose in mind, we may reevaluate the category 'liberalism of faith,' and perhaps wonder if it can be called liberalism at all. It might more precisely be termed a liberty of conscience quite at odds with liberal notions of freedom of religious expression. While Kahn likens this to John Rawls's 'liberalism as *modus vivendi*,' it is important to note that Rawls does not consider mere recognition of various modes of living a *bona fide* political liberalism.[45] He instead likens such recognition to the condition of two states that have agreed only not to engage in open war, such as that obtaining between 'Catholics and Protestants in the sixteenth century': 'In such a case the acceptance of the principle of toleration would indeed be a mere *modus vivendi*, because if either faith becomes dominant, the principle of toleration would no longer be followed.'[46] Rawls distinguishes between this temporarily expedient toleration and a more tenable overlapping consensus based on the commitment of various groups to 'the political conception of justice.'[47] Intolerant groups are fundamentally opposed to such consensus; they are 'free-riders' in a liberal state 'who seek the advantages of just institutions while not doing their share to uphold them.'[48]

The Rawlsean solution is a 'rational pluralism' that does not 'impose the unrealistic—indeed, the utopian—requirement that all citizens can affirm the same comprehensive doctrine,' but only the same conception of political order and justice.[49] In his recent interventions on religion in the public sphere, Habermas describes the undue psychological pressure that such a requirement can place upon the believing subject if the determination of political order is mounted in exclusively secular terms. The 'new, hitherto unexpected political importance' of 'religious traditions and communities of faith,' he claims, demands that we not simply treat believers as unenlightened—as the equivalent of children who have not yet reached the maturity rewarded with full enfranchisement—a tendency enshrined in the liberal insistence on secular public discourse.[50] If the public sphere excludes religious expression, it necessarily denies full access to those individuals motivated by beliefs for which they cannot articulate non-religious justification: 'In the liberal view, the state guarantees citizens freedom of religion only on the condition that religious communities . . . accept not only the separation of church and state, but also the restrictive definition of the public use of reason.'[51]

In seeking a compromise that does not make the strong believer a second-class citizen in the secular state, Habermas distinguishes the realm of political speech from the state's core institutions. A purely contractual notion of the liberal polity insists upon the formation of 'public arguments to which supposedly *all* persons have *equal access*.'[52] The conditions of the 'post-secular society' make that insistence itself a violation of the principle of equality. Secular citizens cannot justifiably view religion as a relic of pre-modern superstition, and must engage in a 'cognitive act of adaption' that goes beyond 'the political virtue of mere tolerance' in its 'self-reflective transcending of a secularist self-understanding of Modernity.'[53] If the secularist must relinquish a proprietary claim to Modernity, the believer must recognize that the test of equal access for all citizens must be applied as public discourse becomes policy. Habermas calls this the 'institutional translation requirement,' which demands that believing communities recognize the secular state's role in implementing policy before which all subjects receive equal treatment. He argues that this is something that religious citizens already 'assume anyway';[54] that claim rather optimistically ignores roiling controversies over abortion, creationism, and gay marriage.

With those controversies in mind, we must wonder if the dyke between public discourse and core institutions can hold: will removing the test of equal access in public discourse produce inequalities in everyday political life that will inevitably infect core institutions? Responding to

Habermas, Cristina Lafont endorses Rawls's claim that what separates political engagement from 'background culture' is the proviso that it be mounted for reasons that all citizens can reasonably accept. Simply moving the proviso of equal access 'up one step' from the 'informal public sphere' to the 'institutional framework,' she argues, does not solve the problem that Habermas seeks to address. The argument for undue cognitive burden on the believing citizen rests upon the difficulty, if not impossibility, for the strong believer to transform positions derived from belief into a rationalist justification to which all fellow citizens will have equal access. In light of the principle that 'ought' implies 'can,' that difficulty suggests a burden that is fundamentally unjust. And if this difficulty is as profound as Habermas suggests, she argues, then believers cannot occupy positions of institutional authority, since 'officials would not be able to fulfil their translation obligation.'[55]

This both is and is not a reasonable objection to Habermas. It is true that Habermas does not entirely solve the problem he seeks to address in that the strong believer he describes cannot be guided by personal ethics while occupying a position in the core institutions of the secular state, re-affirming the marginalization of the believer in the *polis*. It is not reasonable to the extent that the individual acting in an official capacity within a state institution is governed in that capacity by institutional codes of conduct. We expect that all such individuals set personal ethics aside in favor of professional ethics. Champion of *de jure* republicanism that he is, Harrington recognizes that aspect of constitutional government in telling of an Italian carnival pageant:

> [At] Rome I saw one which represented a kitchen, with all the proper utensils in use and action. The cooks were all cats and kitlings, set in such frames, so tied and ordered, that the poor creatures could make no motion to get loose, but the same caused one to turn the spit, another to baste the meat, a third to skim the pot and a fourth to make green sauce. If the frame of your commonwealth be not such as causeth everyone to perform his certain function as necessarily as this did the cat to make green sauce, it is not right.[56]

No self-respecting cat would cheerfully abide such indignity, but the green sauce gets made all the same. In state officials such constraint is a cognitive burden consciously and voluntarily borne in their public service, which is quite different than a requirement imposed upon all individuals accepted as members of civil society. Lafont's re-introduction of the Rawlsean translation proviso into the informal public sphere engages in precisely the *telos* of secularizing modernity against which Habermas argues: '[It] is not clear to me that trying to avoid cognitive dissonances is wiser than trying to resolve them, and whereas democratic deliberation may not contribute to the former, its *transformative power* can surely contribute to the latter' (emphasis mine).[57] The evangelical mission of democratic deliberation here described is precisely the quality of a liberal politics hostile to the personal ethics of the believing subject. And while Habermas is the thinker often associated with claims for the transformative power of the public sphere, his inclusion of religion in that forum of exchange yields a politics less assuredly progressive—and perhaps a shade more wise for that.[58]

It seems to me that Habermas goes as far as one can in providing a productive reconciliation of two ultimately irreconcilable givens: the given of a post-secular society and the given of a secular state. Lafont's more resolutely Rawlsean liberalism does not fully acknowledge the former given; any further introduction of belief into the core institutions of the state would alter the fundamental character of the latter given. It is important to emphasize that the compromise that Habermas strikes is more than simply a grudging concession to the rising currency of hoodoo, as one can see in his claim that 'religious traditions have a special power to articulate moral intuitions,' a power that can contribute to public discourse. The debate over human cloning provides an example: we might object to cloning on technical grounds founded in our imperfect abilities to generate viable organisms from genetic material, but something valuable is lost if no discussant wishing to be taken seriously is permitted to say that cloning violates the dignity of the human soul. While scientific language skirts around the issue by hunting for technicalities, a religious idiom pinpoints precisely what makes us recoil. Reasons seem in this case much more impoverished than moral intuitions.[59]

The kind of public sphere that Habermas now envisions can also serve as a corrective to that tendency in liberal democracy that Marx identifies in his essay on the Jewish Question as 'the perfection of the state.' The removal of faith claims from public language leads to what Marx describes as a subject's double life, 'a heavenly one and an earthly one'; such subject formation occurs in the 'complete state' that no longer needs the external approval of religious institutions.[60] In this completion the state effects a political emancipation only insofar as the political life of the individual is freed from religious expression. This is not to be confused with human emancipation in Marx's terms—we rather become slaves with two masters—which would depend upon liberation from the demands of religion and state, the formation of collectives not bound to these bodies in the cause of a freedom based on 'the union of man with man' rather than the freedom 'of a man treated as an isolated monad.'[61] There is justice in the Marxian recognition that the reduction of religion to private identity promotes the creation of a state no longer answerable to forces outside of itself.

So let us pinpoint the danger of the two extremes. If comprehensive doctrines are allowed too much latitude in public discourse and institutions, then arises the society of mere *modus vivendi* toleration that political liberalism fears and, worse still, the specter of a majoritarian imposition of an inegalitarian doctrine. Constitutionalism's securing of equality erodes as the secret resentments of those magisterial cats slowly taint the green sauce. Civil society is no longer bound by a common conception of justice. If, at the other extreme, all levels of political discourse are cleansed of comprehensive doctrines, then potentially salutary challenges to the liberal state might be suppressed. That is an especial danger when officials deploy the supposed neutrality of the secular state as cover for an aggressive brand of conformism.

We must also recognize that the groups strenuously objecting to the removal of religion from the public sphere have little regard for a common conception of justice. The demand for the state to recognize the primacy of God's law is not equivalent to a demand for the freedom of association central to 'liberalism of speech'; it is an effort to claim an exceptional status that objects to the extension of similar privileges to other groups. Thus many Christian conservatives felt betrayed by the Bush administration's 2001 support of 'faith-based initiatives,' objecting to the lack of distinction made between their truly godly institutions and charities organized by the Hare Krishna and Nation of Islam.[62] That Kahn is not entirely clear on this point is entirely fitting for an American jurist, for it reflects the nation's conflicted legal tradition—most obviously displayed in the Supreme Court's wonderfully inconsistent First Amendment rulings, which at various points in the latter half of the twentieth century have declared it unconstitutional for a nine-year-old to sell issues of the *Watch Tower*, though constitutional for the Amish to deprive their children of secondary education; unconstitutional for Oregon Native Americans to be allowed to use peyote in religious ceremonies, though constitutional for Florida Santerîans to perform animal sacrifices.[63]

The emphasis on free exercise of conscience is the real heart of the First Amendment—which is often misread as effecting a separation of church and state, a much later achievement of the Supreme Court's 1947 decision in *Everson v. Board of Education*. As Akhil Reid Amar has shown, the Amendment's statement that '*Congress* shall make no law respecting an establishment of religion' intentionally leaves room for the states to do so—several of them did, after all, have official religions in its 1791 context.[64] It is only the reciprocity of state and federal rights enacted by the Fourteenth Amendment (1868) that nullifies this provision. Franklyn S. Haiman has claimed that the carefully chosen phrasing of the First Amendment, moving as it does from non-interference with religion to freedom of expression, suggests 'that the freedom to speak or to commit one's thoughts to print presumes that one first has ideas to express. That requires a freedom of *conscience* that underlies *all* parts of the amendment.'[65]

America's is thus more aware than most other Western legal systems of the competing demands of individual conscience and judicial proceduralism. Any self-respecting secularist will be able to adumbrate retrograde tendencies of that awareness—as I have done above in my impatience with the intrusion of religion in the medical issue of reproductive rights, the civil issue of the right to marry, and the educational issue of determining science curricula. But the American tradition also has strengths reflecting its proximity to the Habermasian compromise. While the Swiss outlaw the construction of minarets and the British surveil mosques, the government of the United States, with its keen sense of freedom of conscience, has largely left Muslims within its borders to believe as they see fit, despite the excesses of the so-called war on terror.

At the same time, judicial emphasis on free exercise of conscience can itself impose inequality. The Supreme Court of Canada's 2007 decision in *Bruker v. Marcovitz* recognizes this in explicitly declaring the primacy of gender equality over religious freedom, restoring damages a lower court had awarded a wife whose husband refused to grant her a Jewish divorce, or *get*.[66] For all that it limits the free exercise of conscience, that strikes one as a precedent preventing the kind of intrusive claims prominently made by believers in the United States—even as it is also a self-conflicting precedent: it recognizes the special hold of religion on the believer by recognizing that a woman cannot simply abandon a faith that does not grant her equal rights, but at the same time imposes itself on sacred ground in measuring religious practices by the standards of civil justice. The Habermasian compromise would not seem to support this particular defense of equality in that there is no preservation of core institutions at stake.

Will our post-secular modernity come to resemble the pre-secular modernity of Milton? It already does in some respects. The secular state seems more and more nakedly invested in the self-preserving political stability that comes with conformity. Like the conformism of the English Church under Elizabeth I and James I, states advance that aim by speaking in a language of inclusivity while deploying their might against those branded as religious radicals. At the same time, the liberal tradition has provided a heritage of just procedures limiting state power and securing individual liberties, a heritage with which we should not dispense lightly in a too-casual acceptance of our post-secular condition. There is an exceedingly delicate balance to be struck between liberal values and liberty of conscience, which is exactly why one fears that state apparatuses are not up to the task. The religious violence of our time, to which we shall presently turn, poses a strong challenge to striking that balance in that memory of its terrors can be raised by the state presenting its own violence as a necessity.

4

Samson, the Peacemaker:
Enlightened Slaughter in *Samson Agonistes*

> [T]he relationship of the Biblical narratives to the pagan myths is necessarily asymmetric: the former could not be *critically* read through the latter because it belongs to the mythic grammar to conceal and not to expose arbitrary and fundamental violence. The latter can be critically read through the former because the Biblical narratives constitute and renew themselves through a breaking with sacrificial violence which exposes its social reality.
>
> —John Milbank, 'An Essay against Secular Order'[1]

Milbank's claim on biblical narratives seems on the surface a partial one. Though Adam and Eve enjoy the unadulterated gift of creation (if under the threat of death), humanity's full entry into the world in being cast out of Eden carries with it a divinely implanted promise-cum-obligation of violent retribution: 'I will put enmity between thee and the woman, and between thy seed and her seed; it shall bruise thy head, and thou shalt bruise his heel' (Gen 3.15). Abraham must prove himself through his willingness to sacrifice Isaac, making the potential of God's demand for arbitrary violence fundamental to the foundation of Israel. Even if we see such violence as abrogated by the gospel, we must acknowledge the existence in the Christian Bible of a foreboding divine justice. There are dire consequences to deviating from the rule of charity, as Jesus makes clear in the parable of the unforgiving servant, who is delivered 'to the tormentors . . . So likewise shall my heavenly Father do also unto you, if ye from your hearts forgive not every one his brother their trespasses' (Matt 18.34–35). The pronouncement that 'the last shall be first' is also a promise to the disciples that those who are marginalized in this world will have the satisfac-

tion of judging their fellow human beings: '[Ye] which have followed me
. . . ye also shall sit upon twelve thrones, judging the twelve tribes of Israel'
(Matt 19.28). The Bible's narrative unity demands that we accept Christ as
Alpha and as Omega, intertwining the gift of creation with the violence of
the world's dissolution.

To separate the two is to free the promise of an order of peace from
the terms of that narrative. That is precisely what Milbank does in a postmodern reading of the Augustinian *societas perfecta*. Whereas Augustine argues that 'all earthly cities are built upon the foundation of a primal crime'
and that it is only 'the Church's real, historical existence' that makes possible a 'social order based on love and forgiveness,' Milbank rightly claims
that we are now less certain that the visible church has a 'particular history
which has constantly run "counter" to the general run of human political
life.'[2] He concedes that for much of its history Christianity strays from its
own principles and becomes a force of exclusion, though its true promise
lies in the hope for perfect community. The Christian vision of cosmic
order is uniquely poised to embrace difference; it is peculiar in its attempt
to make 'differential additions a harmony "in the body of Christ."'[3] While
the anti-political order of love, Milbank avers, may not directly coincide
with the visible church, it may be thought of in more abstract terms where
the 'history of Christ . . . gives the universal pattern for reconciliation.
This mode of peace has its own separate origin, and although (for us)
inextricably entangled in the city of this world, it is nonetheless in itself a
completely self-sufficient *societas perfecta*.'[4]

Within Milbank's 'Essay against Secular Order' we learn just how
entangling that inextricable entanglement can be—or, perhaps more precisely, how the perception of participation in the invisible *societas perfecta*
can paper over such entanglement with the self-assurance of righteousness.
Appearing as an epigraph to his essay is a passage from Marvell's *Horatian
Ode*, meant presumably to point to the foundational violence of Roman
order:

So when they did design
The Capitol's first line,
A bleeding head where they begun,
Did fright the architects to run:
And yet in that the State
Foresaw its happy fate. (67–72)[5]

Marvell is drawing on this Roman precedent in celebrating an English Republic that first 'forcèd' its way to power with the execution of the king and shamed the Irish who find themselves 'in one year tamed' by a Cromwell who 'does both act and know' (73–76). That legitimation takes on more biblical terms in Marvell's *First Anniversary of the Government under His Highness the Lord Protector*, which casts some doubt on Fifth Monarchist over-confidence in the imminence of the Apocalypse even as its argument on Cromwell's concentration of time suggests that he may well be bringing the world into greater conformity with heaven in anticipation of the last day, if only nettlesome political interests would cooperate: 'Sure, the mysterious work, where none withstand, / Would forthwith finish under such a hand' (137–38). Cromwell's activity reconciles the fallen world with heaven's will, tuning 'this lower to that higher sphere' (47–48).

Heaven guides both war and peace. If Cromwell had gone well beyond his role as parliamentary general, it was 'heaven would not that his pow'r should cease,' a point reinforced with reference to the godly general Gideon who 'on the peace extends a warlike power' (243–56). That reconciliation with heavenly will could include violent subjection of the stubborn and ungodly is equally argued by Henry Lawrence, the president of Cromwell's Council of State. The role of his *societas perfecta*, the Saints, is to avoid worldly snares and to rely on 'God and his holy Spirit' who 'has married us to himself in holiness and righteousnes,' and thus to embrace the spiritual peace offered by the gospel. Inner peace will paradoxically—although this paradox exists in the modern secularist mind rather than in the seventeenth-century one—allow the Saints to be justified in their militarism: 'Let the world know that warre is but the Vizard, but there is peace within, underneath.'[6]

This view informs Lawrence's exegesis of Matthew 5.9: 'Blessed are the peacemakers, for they shall be called the children of God.' In Lawrence's terms the peace found by the Saints is internal and justifies outward war. 'Experience tells us,' Lawrence concludes, 'that it is the fate of some warres, not onely to be the meanes by which peace is gotten, and procur'd, but by which it is nourisht, and maintayn'd, and we know some countryes, which injoy the greatest benefites of peace in the midst of a confirm'd warre.'[7] Militarism is not a necessary entanglement at odds with the teachings of Christ, but is rather an expression of the spiritual peace bestowed upon the elect by the Mediator.

Lawrence might be described in Milbank's terms as displaying the Protestant tendency to read events as signs of a teleological history, where Milbank's own 'radical orthodoxy' argues for the pure contingency of events. The only escape from the post-modern nihilism attending awareness of that contingency is a countervailing awareness of divine gift uniquely emphasized in Christianity. In this way 'radical orthodoxy' offers a strong critique of those acts of terrestrial war claiming to express spiritual peace and cosmic harmony, acts as much a part of the seventeenth century as they are a part of our own time.

Milbank's sense of biblical narrative might equally critique a too-casual reading of present-day religious violence in biblical terms, found in Norman Mailer's account of the 9/11 attacks: 'A horror had come upon us. There were people on earth so eager to destroy us that they were ready to immolate themselves. That went right to the biblical root. Samson had pulled down the pillars of the Temple. Now there were all these Muslim Samsons.'[8] Gilbert Achcar similarly likens these suicide attackers to Samson in their 'hatred of the enemy and thirst for vengeance,' adding that their violence is just as 'pointless' and self-destructive as their biblical counterpart's.[9] Such likening is imprecise in one obvious respect. Even an atheist Muslim feels compelled to point out that despite his appearance in the Hebrew Bible and the Christian Bible, Samson receives no mention in the *Qur'an*: he's one of yours, not one of ours. Turning to this biblical story to explain Islamic religious violence thus reveals how the impulse to impose order upon events is governed by narratives at the 'root' of Western culture, rather than by the nature of the events themselves.

We shall return to that point in our exploration of the silence of the suicide bomber in the next chapter. For now we will be most interested in showing how *Samson Agonistes* exposes the limits of Milbank's view of biblical narrative, and especially how that narrative inherently operates in a grammar imposing order upon arbitrary violence. Occluding the violence of biblical narrative, or of Milton's tragedy, shields elements of a given tradition so that an ethic of violence can be attributed to the Other.

I. The discomforting certainty of 'Samson Agonistes'

Samson points to unsettling elements of biblical narrative that Milbank, and many of Milton's modern readers, prefer to ignore. *Samson Agonistes* has been described as a tragedy showing us the contingency of worldly events and opposed to a religious ethic of violent retribution, an argument expressed in John Carey's brief article in the issue of the *Times Literary Supplement* marking the anniversary of 9/11. In a manner like that of Mailer and Achcar, Carey remarks that 'the similarities between the biblical Samson and the hijackers are obvious. Like them he destroys many innocent victims, whose lives, hopes and loves are all quite unknown to him personally. He is, in effect, a suicide bomber, and like the suicide bombers he believes that his massacre is an expression of God's will.'[10]

Carey strives to dismiss the suggestion that Milton's dramatic poem looks favorably upon such actions, an argument that he attributes to Stanley Fish's *How Milton Works*. In Fish's comment that Milton's Samson bases his actions on a reading of divine will, Carey finds a 'monstrous . . . licence for any fanatic to commit atrocity.' The events of 9/11, he claims, 'seem like a devilish implementation of [Fish's] arguments.' If this is the message of *Samson Agonistes*, 'should it not be withdrawn from schools and colleges and, indeed, banned more generally as an incitement to terrorism?' Any person with a sense of 'common humanity' would be repulsed by Samson's actions, and since Milton is a 'subtle-minded poet' and not a 'murderous bigot,' we can safely attribute to him such repulsion (15). Milton holds up for our excoriation the Danite Chorus celebrating Samson's murder of the Philistine lords, an image Carey likens to 'the pictures screened on British television in the immediate aftermath of September 11, which showed people in Arab dress dancing for joy in the streets' (16).

Such an alarmist reading of Milton is truly frightening, though not in ways that Carey intends. Though ironic, his comment on withdrawing Milton's dramatic poem from schools and colleges implies that educational curricula might justifiably suppress dissenting views on terrorism. More significantly, he states that a right-thinking community cannot attribute literary value to a work that would condone Samson's actions: 'September 11 has changed *Samson Agonistes*, because it has changed the readings we *can* derive from it while still celebrating it as an achievement of the human imagination' (16, emphasis mine).[11] The status of Milton's dramatic poem as achievement of the imagination is, in this view, contingent upon eliminating readings that would associate the poet with religious violence. Such a view paradoxically empties the work of complexity by making a narrowed field of interpretation prerequisite to literary merit. Rarely has the complicity with the political dominant underpinning categories of literary value been so explicitly affirmed. Such views would sit rather well with the jingoists and paranoiacs sponsored by the Defense of Civilization Fund of the American Council of Trustees and Alumni, who lamented academic reluctance to reflect public endorsement of the 'war on terror' in their February 2002 report, *Defending Civilization: How Our Universities Are Failing America and What Can Be Done About It*.[12]

Rescuing Milton from an implied association with terrorism, moreover, has less to do with genuine horror over *How Milton Works* than it does with a certain history of interpreting the poet and his dramatic poem. Presenting Milton as a 'subtle-minded poet' rather than a 'murderous bigot' is not a response to Stanley Fish so much as it is a comment on the tradition exemplified by T. S. Eliot's remark that 'of no other poet is it so difficult to consider the poetry simply as poetry, without our theological and political dispositions . . . making unlawful entry'; and by Ezra Pound's famous 'disgust' with Milton's 'asinine bigotry, his beastly hebraism, [and] the coarseness of his mentality'—a comment proving slander to be strongest in the recoil.[13] Carey seems to see this tradition continued by 'the modern view of Milton as primarily interested in politics and only incidentally a poet' (15). More specifically, he is buttressing the claim of his 1969 book *Milton* that Samson is an 'outmoded' Jewish hero denounced in a Christian poem, and taking aim at those who deviate from his brand of close reading.[14] In this light, his vituperative warnings of the dangers of accepting a positive reading of Milton's Samson are less an expression of humanistic horror over the tragic fallout of fanaticism than they are a rather histrionic repetition of his previous arguments.

Also worth noting is that Carey's comments distort significantly Fish's reading of *Samson Agonistes*. It is true that in the passage cited by Carey, Fish declares that 'the only value we can put on Samson's action is the value he gives it in context. Within the situation, it is an expression, however provisional, of his reading of the divine will; and insofar as it represents his desire to conform to that will, it is a virtuous action. *No other standard for evaluating it exists.*'[15] Fish's qualifications here carry a weight in his argument for which Carey only marginally allows: Samson's is a '*provisional*' reading of divine will, and '*insofar as* it represents a desire to conform to that will it is a virtuous action.'[16] Milton's version of the biblical story, Fish claims, forces us to grant 'the Philistines the status of human beings,' and in the process evinces a 'disinclination to allow us a comfortable perspective on Samson's action.'[17] The human cost of Samson's 'triumph,' in other words, forces us to question his ostensible motive of obedience to God and thus to contemplate the inscrutability of divine will and the fallibility of human interpretation of it.

In *How Milton Works*, Fish argues that two plots are resolved at the end of the tragedy—Samson's internal regeneration and his external vengeance on the Philistines—and although it is 'tempting . . . to assume an intimate connection between these two plots, especially at those points where they coincide temporally. . . to do so would be to mistake contiguity for causality.' Samson is praiseworthy because he 'intends' his actions to be conformable to the divine will, but Milton's text is skeptical of such intentions, teaching us that 'he cannot know [that will], nor can we.'[18] Opposed to readings suggesting that Samson develops during his *agons*, Fish revives Dr. Johnson's remark that the dramatic poem 'must be allowed to want a middle,' arguing that Samson's final illumination 'is not the end of a linear and chartable progression or the conclusion to a chain of inferences.'[19]

This point is an important one: the view most influentially voiced by John M. Steadman and Mary Ann Radzinowicz that the middle of *Samson Agonistes* constitutes progressive, stepwise sanctification and regeneration tends, as several critics have recognized, to misrepresent the text.[20] If taken too far, however, Fish's reading paints a rather disjointed portrait of Milton's dramatic poem; it leaves us, ultimately, with a work that has no middle and two unrelated resolutions. What I argue here comes much closer to the approach that John Carey accused Fish of taking. If *How Milton Works* is to be faulted, it is not for being too strenuous in asserting that *Samson Agonistes* is a work that looks favorably upon Samson's final action, but rather for not being strenuous enough in doing so. The internal attributes of Milton's dramatic poem and the historical context that both Carey and Fish are reluctant to acknowledge provide a preponderance of evidence pointing to Samson's heroic status.

The middle of the dramatic poem does not, it is true, develop linearly toward its conclusion in a manner that allows for assertion of causality. Each of Samson's three major dialogues—with his father, Manoa; with Dalila; and with the Philistine giant, Harapha—rather operates to develop a framework for proper interpretation of the climax. As John Shawcross observes, 'Samson doesn't "grow" with each episode so much as he eradicates a negative aspect of himself with each episode.'[21] In Samson's refutations of these characters we see a collection of negative definitions delineating boundaries for interpreting his final triumph.

From the first encounter with Manoa we gain a sense of the insufficiency of relying exclusively on the Old Law. Manoa's hope resides solely in the physical and legal. He suggests that his son return home and visit God's 'sacred house,' where he can 'bring . . . off'rings, to avert / His further ire' (518–20), which, possibly, might lead to the restoration of Samson's eyesight. This jars with Milton's suggestion in the autobiographical portion of the *Second Defence* that it is 'not blindness but the inability to endure blindness [that] is a source of misery' (*YP* 4: 584). Samson feels in his early lament that his loss of 'light' is a loss 'almost [of] life it self' (90–91), which contrasts directly with the recompense of internal illumination emphasized by the bard in *Paradise Lost*: though light 'Revisit'st not these eyes, that rowle in vain / . . . / So much the rather thou Celestial light / Shine inward' (3.22, 51–52). Manoa's offered hope of restored eyesight leaves Samson in the 'swounings of despair' (631). The remedies suggested by Manoa—his legalistic notion of ransom and devotion via physical offering—make no impact upon his son's spiritual condition, which requires, as the Chorus recognizes, 'Some sourse of consolation from above' (664).

If Samson does not embrace the promise of the Old Law offered to him by his father, it should be no surprise that he spurns the rekindled romance offered by Dalila. Her betrayal, she claims, was motivated by the human foibles of jealousy and possessiveness (739–95), an argument for which Samson has little patience: 'Love constrain'd thee; call it furious rage / To satisfie thy lust: Love seeks to have Love' (836–37). After failing to convince Samson to rekindle the romantic spark that first drew him to her, she declares finally that 'civil Duty' and 'Religion' prompted her to 'entrap / A common enemy' (853–56). This episode, pointing as it does to competing political and religious ideologies and definitions of marital duty, would seem to speak to a very modern 'clash of civilizations,' to employ Samuel Huntington's catchy though unproductive phrase.

While some current commentary has seen the Dalila episode as pointing to the irreconcilability of competing value systems—Dalila voices her allegiance to her nation and her gods while Samson retains allegiance to his own—there is a very important difference between these two declarations of allegiance: Dalila's marks her as a confirmed idolater while

Samson's is a commitment to God. More importantly, and as Alan Rudrum has astutely observed, we see important differences between idolatry, a belief system that is the creature of princes and priests, and faith in the living God.[22] Though Samson's arguments are superior in kind, we are far too aware of his physical passion, of his lust for Dalila and her ability to rouse in him the desire to 'tear [her] joint by joint' (953), for him to be said to provide here a normative view of godly marriage and duty. The dialogue serves most strongly as a reminder of Samson's sins, a point brought home in his summation of the encounter: 'So let her go, God sent her to debase me, / And aggravate my folly who committed / To such a viper his most sacred trust' (999–1001).

Politico-religious ideologies clash especially in the dialogue with Harapha. That Milton departs completely from his biblical sources in introducing the Giant of Gath suggests that this portion of the drama might especially reveal his view of the Samson story. Those who see the final slaughter of the Philistines as negatively presented tend to look to the confrontation with Harapha as a precedent of Samson's error. His challenge to Harapha is indeed striking in its trial of God:

> . . . I to be the power of *Israel's* God
> Avow, and challenge *Dagon* to the test . . .
> Then thou shalt see, or rather thy sorrow
> Soon feel, whose God is strongest, thine or mine. (1150–55)

Samson seems very much here like a classical warrior pitting his gods against those of his opponent. His statements are in the spirit of Seneca's Hercules calling on Athena's and Phoebus' assistance to thwart Juno's attempts to destroy him, or of Euripides' Iolaus entering a seemingly hopeless battle against the Argives: 'Hera may be their patron but we have / Athena; and what counts in the long run / Is having stronger gods upon your side.'[23]

This attitude is opposite to the calm defiance exemplified by Christ in *Paradise Regained*: '[It] is written, / Tempt not the Lord thy God, he said and stood' (4. 560–61). Where Jesus' faith is unshakable, Samson's sense of godliness resides in heroic deeds. In the exchange of taunts with Harapha we are most aware of his history as Danite champion: Harapha has 'come to see of whom such noise / Hath walk'd about, and each limb to survey' (1088–89), he wishes 'that fortune / Had brought [him] to the field where' Samson 'wrought such wonders with an Asses Jaw' (1093–95), and he criticizes Samson's murder and robbery of 'those thirty men/At *Askalon*' (1186–87). As the earlier description of the victory at Ramath-lechi suggests—when with 'The Jaw of a dead Ass, his sword of bone,/A thousand fore-skins fell' (143–44)—these are conflicts fought under the terms of the Law. Samson carries with him, as Harapha describes it, 'The highest name for valiant Acts' among 'the unforeskinn'd race' (1100–101), a heroism defined in tribal, legalistic terms contrary to the universality of the gospel. We are reminded in this waving of circumcised and uncircumcised members that Samson's achievements are those of the flesh rather than the spirit, and that he is thinking here in terms of justification by works rather than justification by faith. He is, to use the terminology of Philippians, a mutilator of flesh rather than one circumcised in the Spirit of God (Phil 3.2–3).

Such are the nets of despair, sin, and vengeance in which we find Samson entangled in the middle of Milton's dramatic poem. As those who question the spiritual justification of his final action would point out, these nets leave him looking more like a washed-out strongman than they do a hero of faith. If we are to see Samson's final act as positive, it must transcend the fleshly, legalistic terms of his previous heroics; it must show valuation of internal illumination over physical sight and show recovery from the hubris that led him to marry Dalila. If Milton's Samson is indeed the hero of faith recorded in Hebrews 11, the final slaughter of the Philistines must be different in kind from the three encounters of the tragedy's middle: he will be a hero under the terms of the gospel if and only if he is not avenging his loss of eyesight, not succumbing to fleshly lust, and not settling a tribal blood feud.

Before moving from these negative definitions to a positive definition of Samson's role at the end of Milton's dramatic poem, we should note some seventeenth-century readings of Samson and justifications of divinely sanctioned violence. Many exegetes of the period sustained the traditional typological association between Samson and Christ, a tradition rooted in Augustine's *Sermo de Samsone*.[24] To provide just a few examples, John Diodati, nephew of the scholar with whom Milton proudly reports he 'conversed daily' in his stay in Geneva (*YP* 4: 620), provides in his *Annotations* the view that Samson's final action is 'a figure of the efficacie of Christs death, by which he finished all his combats and victories against the Devil and Sin.' In *Biathanatos* John Donne describes Samson as a 'man so exemplar, that ... the tymes before, had him in prophecy ... and the tymes after him more consummately in *Christ*, of Whome he was a figure' (135 [3.5.4]). George Herbert similarly evokes this typological tradition in his poem 'Sunday': 'As Samson bore the doors away,/ Christ's hands, though nailed wrought our salvation,/ And did unhinge that day.'[25] Clearly, to recall John Carey's terminology, many of Milton's contemporaries saw the biblical Samson as much more than a 'suicide bomber,' and this group includes such 'subtle-minded poets' as Donne and Herbert.

Milton's departure from this typology, however, is much more substantial than his adherence to it. Joseph Wittreich has recently described Milton's engagement of this tradition as a 'typology of difference' where 'Samson's slaying ... sets him at odds with Christ's saving' and even from the 'moral bearing' and 'heroic character' of Hercules.[26] As such, Wittreich continues, Milton engages in the interrogation of Samson's heroism evident in such contemporaries as John Trapp. While it is true that Trapp and others raise questions about Samson's heroism, the questions raised are typically not whether Samson is the hero of faith of Hebrews 11, but rather how he can be both this hero and the vengeful lecher of Judges. Such questionings, as Trapp's commentary evinces, raise objections so that they can be quelled and, in the process, illustrate God's patience with His people: '*Sampson* fell so farre ... that we should hardly take him for a godly man, did we not find his name in the list of those Worthies, *Heb.* 11. But, like a tame Hawke, though he flew farre, yet he came to hand again. So will all that belong to God: recover they shall of their relapses, though with difficulty, yet sometimes with advantage.'[27] This portrait of Samson is similar to Heinrich Bullinger's in the *Sermonum decades quinque*, which states that while Samson 'fuerit peccatum' in betraying the source of his might, the strength on which he draws in his final act is of divine origin: 'nomen domini inuocauit ... redijt robur, id est, redijt spiritus Domini' ('[He] invoked the name of God ... [and] his strength returned, that is the Spirit of God returned').[28]

The 'interrogations' to which Wittreich draws our attention, then, tend to explain the complexities of this biblical character while maintaining the heroism for which Scripture provides sanction. Similarly, the 'typology of difference' generated by Milton does not preclude Samson's heroism but argues instead for a heroism different from that of Christ or Hercules. Samson is not the perfect man that Jesus is in *Paradise Regained*;

his actions do not show a godlike impeccability. Nor is Samson's heroism legal or moral in the spirit of Euripides' Heracles. If the comparison of Hercules and Jesus in *Paradise Regained* is of 'Small things with greatest' (4.564), the terms by which Milton relates Samson to these two heroes instantiates a middle value between mere humanity and inimitable divinity. Milton presents, as Norman T. Burns has argued, a rare literary example of a hero of faith directed by spirit rather than bound by law.[29] The interrogations of typology in Milton's brief tragedy generate a neither/nor dialectic where such a hero is rendered ontologically inferior to Christ and, simultaneously, spiritually superior to such pagan counterparts as Hercules.

More pertinent than the typological tradition are definitions of the hero of faith. We have already seen how Henry Lawrence, who is immortalized as the 'vertuous Father' in Milton's twentieth sonnet, maintains that physical war can be an outward expression of spiritual peace. Sir Henry Vane the Younger, who knows 'Both spirituall powre & civill, what each meanes' (Sonnet 17, 10), soteriologically privileges the 'spiritual seed' on whom the 'living, unwritten Word of God' has been imprinted.[30] Because the Son is the Mediator from the beginning of time, the existence of these spiritual men precedes the physical arrival of Jesus. In this way Vane can describe such figures of the Hebrew Bible as Abraham as among the spiritual elect, and, more relevant for present purposes, look favorably upon Gideon. Like 'Gideon and his three hundred,' the Saints are justified in their militarism because they hold '*the sword of the Lord*' and have 'been taught the practice and use of it in the greatest purity and most exact subserviencie unto Christ it is capable of.'[31] Though introduced in the 1655 tract *The Retired Mans Meditations*, Vane's spiritualist views would enjoy their greatest currency after his 1662 execution as a regicide made him a martyr of the Good Old Cause: they were rehearsed in George Sikes's hagiography *The Life and Death of Sir Henry Vane* (1662) and in Vane's posthumous *Pilgrimage into the Land of Promise* (1664).

The discourse of the cause in which Milton was engaged thus frequently assumes that God's justice expresses itself in worldly violence. To see Milton adhering to the supposedly Christian principle of non-violence is not only to divorce him from his seventeenth-century context, but also to ignore his increasing sympathy with radical spiritualism after the Restoration.[32] As a good deal of recent criticism has shown, Milton's sympathies with the far left wing of Reformed religion grew a good deal stronger with the imposition of uniformity under the aegis of the national church that accompanied the restoration of monarchy. Janel Mueller and Sharon Achinstein associate resistance elements of *Samson Agonistes* with Restoration Nonconformity. David Loewenstein explores parallels between Milton's hero and the Quaker polemics of such figures as Thomas Ellwood, George Fox, and Edward Burrough, arguing for Milton's growing sympathy with the sect most harassed and persecuted by Restoration authorities. Barbara Lewalski has placed *Samson Agonistes* in the context of an overriding project of resistance evident throughout Milton's post-Restoration activity, showing how the supposed 'retirement' from politics that was long associated with his late religious poetry has been overstated.[33] In her recent, careful edition Laura Lunger Knoppers describes the indices prepared by one of the first readers of Milton's 1671 volume, which identify 'England's case' with that of Israel gone astray, underscore the faults of priests, and point to the themes of 'waiting upon the spirit of God, receiving divine impulse, and knowing when the time to act is right,' which are 'crucial in both of Milton's poems[,] and of major concern for Dissenters in Restoration England.'[34] Most relevant to present discussion is Blair Worden's argument that Milton's Samson is partly a tribute to Sir Henry Vane. That Milton was affected by his longtime comrade's execution is suggested not only by the great affinity between his late thought and Vane's, but also by the inclusion of Sonnet Seventeen in George Sikes's surreptitiously published *Life and Death*, a work that rehearses the major principles of Vane's spiritualism.[35]

If we see Samson as a hero of faith inspired by God in his slaughter of the Philistines, then we would expect him to conform to the brand of sainthood defined in the spiritualist discourse especially important to Milton in his later years. The options Samson faces over the middle of the dramatic poem do not open this spiritual path, but Milton also shows us early in the work a precedent for such spiritual illumination in Samson's account of his marriages:

> The first I saw at *Timna*, and she pleas'd
> Mee, not my Parents, that I sought to wed,
> The daughter of an Infidel: they knew not
> That *what I motion'd was of God; I knew*
> *From intimate impulse* . . .
> She proving false, the next I took to Wife [Dalila] . . .
> That specious Monster, my accomplisht snare.
> *I thought it lawful from my former act* . . . (219–31; my emphasis)

Milton here adapts Judges—which states that Samson's desire to marry the woman of Timnath was 'of the Lord' (14.4)—to his purposes. Samson's fulfillment of his divine promise is contingent upon his ability to decipher the 'intimate impulses' received directly from God. It is when he is not 'motion'd of God' and when he instead relies on rationality and legalistic precedent—he thinks the marriage to Dalila is 'lawful' from his 'former act'—that his actions are those of corrupt humanity rather than the spiritually justified Saint.[36]

The 'rouzing motions' felt by Samson as he is escorted to the Philistine arena recall these 'intimate impulses' from God—and hearken further back in the 1671 edition to the 'strong motion' leading Jesus into the desert of *Paradise Regained* (1.290–91). Samson, like Jesus, is not fully aware of why he is going:

> Be of good courage, I begin to feel
> Some rouzing motions in me which dispose
> To something extraordinary my thoughts. . . .
> If there be aught of presage in the mind,
> This day will be remarkable in my life
> By some great act, or of my days the last. (1381–89)

What separates this speech from Samson's previous ones to Manoa, Dalila, and Harapha is an uncertainty different in kind to that of the tragedy's middle. While uncertainty is generated in the three major dialogues through a cacophony of competing truth-claims, it is generated here by the limits of human perception of the ends to which God inspires the hero of faith. Unlike in his refutations of Manoa, Dalila, and Harapha, Samson is here reduced to precisely the limited vision of outcomes that marks him as following divine will wheresoever it leads, rather than engaging in the human process of making plans and projecting outcomes.

This is why *Samson Agonistes* cannot have what Johnson would call a 'middle.' In order for Samson's final act to be justified, it cannot be causally related to the fleshly, rational concerns of his three major dialogues, and must instead take its impulse from the immediate divine illumination residing entirely outside of the events with which we are presented.[37] Samson must calm the human impulses that led him astray and follow the divine 'impulse' that is the guide of the Saint. Thus Milton presents his response to the issues raised by Trapp and Bullinger regarding Samson's heroism: it is by following the agency of the Spirit, rather than his own, that Samson ultimately escapes from his hubris and becomes a hero of faith. If, as Johnson complains, *Samson Agonistes* does not fully adhere to classical standards, it is because Milton is drawing our attention to a relationship between divinity and humanity fundamentally opposed to that of his classical sources. For Greek tragedians, Jean-Pierre Vernant observes, 'human action is not, of itself, strong enough to do without the power of the gods, not autonomous enough to be fully conceived without them.'[38]

Samson Agonistes, on the other hand, dramatizes a temporary removal of divinity from human action to show that in marrying Dalila and betraying the secret of his strength Samson is, to recall Trapp's hawking analogy, flying far from God. The hubris of the classical hero always carries with it a certain degree of divine impulsion, even if this exists only as the determination of the Fates. In Milton's Christian ontology, hubris is a byproduct of man's tendency to be, to use Augustine's phrase, 'inclinatus ad se ipsum minus esset' ('inclined to his own inferior being'), and the Saint is the one granted the divine illumination necessary to transcend this corrupt nature.[39] To recall Victoria Kahn's perceptive reading, *Samson Agonistes* is also unlike baroque drama, of which Benjamin gives an account in his book on *Trauerspiel*, in that the return of divine agency in the catastrophe lends action a significance beyond the world of the drama. That return of divine direction reclaims the classical significance of tragic action against Restoration drama's acting, which is only a stage property, thus reclaiming some elements of classical drama and placing them 'in the service of the "good old cause."'[40] Like the 'typology of difference' generated between Christ and Hercules, the dramatic development of *Samson Agonistes* adjusts the classical and Renaissance categories it evokes in order to account for a hero of faith different in kind to Hercules, Oedipus, Macbeth, or Christ in *Christos Paschon*.[41] None of these heroes ever flies far from his divinely appointed role.

This dramatic development is entirely consistent with Milton's plans for an Abraham or Phineas tragedy, to which plans Burns draws our attention in his excellent reading of *Samson Agonistes*.[42] These differ markedly from Milton's proposed Christ tragedy, where, after a brief scene showing Judas' betrayal, the tragedy simply provides 'noble expressions' by 'message & chorus' of Christ's 'agony' (*YP* 8: 560). In the projected Abraham tragedy, on the other hand, the Chorus speaks of 'Abrahams strange voyage,' 'discoursing as the world would of such an action divers ways,' and is left in confusion until finally the hero returns 'home with joy' (*YP* 8: 557–58).

Even more pertinent is the plan for a Phineas tragedy, where 'the Epitasis' shows 'contention' over the legality of Phineas' actions until finally the 'tumult' is quelled by 'the word of the lord . . . acquitting & approving phineas' (*YP* 8: 560). As in *Samson Agonistes*, the epitasis of the Abraham tragedy is not causally related to the catastrophe; it serves instead to highlight the hiddenness of the divine plan. The Phineas tragedy resembles *Samson Agonistes* in that it shows the insufficiency of legal proscript in interpreting the actions of the hero of faith, who, ultimately, is publicly justified by divine intervention. Each proto-tragedy accentuates the 'new acquist / Of true experience' (1755–56) granted to God's true servants by staging imperfect and misguided human understanding of the Saint's errand, the very point emphasized in the confusion over God's ways evident in the speeches of Manoa and the Chorus immediately following Samson's departure (1427–1540).

Also worth noting is that the Chorus's confused rendition of Samson's triumph is significantly more graphic than the Messenger's report, the speech that is often claimed as preventing us from viewing comfortably the divine origin of Samson's final action. Nowhere in the Messenger's description of the massacre do we see the kind of grisliness evident, for example, in Amphitryon's account in *Hercules furens* of Hercules' murders— as it appears in Jasper Heywood's translation, Hercules 'rolled' his first son until 'his head resoundeth out, / The sprynkled howses with the brayne / of him throwne owt are wet' (1978–81)—or in the Euripidean Messenger's description of the Bacchae's murder of Pentheus:

> One tore off an arm,
> Another a foot still warm in its shoe. His ribs
> were clawed clean of flesh and every hand
> was smeared with blood as they played ball with scraps
> of Pentheus' body.[43]

The Miltonic Messenger's very brief statement on the human cost of Samson's actions, by comparison, seems expressly designed not to grant the Philistines the status of human beings. Unlike the Chorus's more graphic description of miraculous 'slaughter,' which description incorrectly discerns God's ways, the Messenger's account glosses over human torment in a way that does allow comfortable attribution of the action to divine agency:

> The whole roof after them, with burst of thunder
> Upon the heads of all who sat beneath,

> Lords, Ladies, Captains, Councellors, or Priests,
> Thir choice nobility and flower, not only
> Of this but each *Philistian* City round . . . (1651–55)

We are never allowed to forget in these lines the victims' status as Philistine political elite and the attendant association of this class with oppression of Israel. The kind of human suffering that elicits our horror over Hercules' actions and complicates our response to Pentheus' hubris simply does not emerge in Milton's portrait of this massacre.

In downplaying the human cost of Samson's triumph, in showing the independence of Samson's final action from the rationalism and legality of the tragedy's middle, and in recalling in the climactic scene the immediate divine direction evident in Samson's first marriage, Milton presents a hero of faith achieving the saintly militarism described by Lawrence and Vane. That Samson's actions carry a horrific human cost does not preclude consideration of them as consistent with Providence, but rather serves as a reminder of the natural conclusions arising from, to employ Fredric Jameson's comments on *Paradise Lost*, the 'ideological closure' of 'ethical binaries of good and evil, to which the Providential vision is irredeemably shackled.'[44] In presenting a hero of faith whose ultimate achievement is Providential slaughter, Milton shows an ideology marginalizing the humanity of non-adherents—just as he had done in his satisfaction over the beheading of Charles, in his triumphalism over Cromwell's Irish slaughters, and in his advocacy in the final days of the republic of military suppression of the 'inconsiderate multitude['s]' desire for monarchy (*YP* 8: 446). Biblical narrative lends support to these conclusions in casting as inevitable God's vengeance upon the unfaithful.

II. Christian violence as impossible narrative

Both text and context provide ample evidence supporting those readings of *Samson Agonistes* that John Carey has declared impermissible. Critics who see the tragedy as uncomfortable with its hero's triumph tend simply to misread the text or ignore historical evidence. If Carey's piece in the *Times Literary Supplement* has value, it is in making explicit the cultural assumptions silently underpinning those critics' obfuscations. As we have seen, Carey makes much of terrorism's transformative effects so that he might elevate the reading of Milton to the level of crisis: either we argue for a 'subtle-minded poet' who necessarily would recoil from the actions he presents in his dramatic poem, or we be foolish enough to ignore his poetic achievement and see him as the kind of 'murderous bigot' who would praise the events of 9/11. Ezra Pound opted for the second alternative in his professed 'disgust' of Milton's 'beastly hebraism.' What is most disconcerting about this parallel between Carey and Pound is how completely their systems of literary value overlap. Both men offer interpretations of Milton predicated upon a politics of identity separating humanist endeavor from a race of 'beastly' sub-humans. Though they are on opposites sides of the fence with regard to Milton, the fence is much the same for each: just as 'Hebraism' is the Other to which Pound relegates Milton, 'Arabism' is the Other from which Carey rescues him.

We cannot, Carey argues, associate Milton with those 'pictures screened on British television in the immediate aftermath of September 11, which showed people in Arab dress dancing for joy in the streets' (16). The language with which Carey divorces this spectacle from the realm of culture is telling: these are not real-life Arabs with a literature and religion of their own, but rather television images of actors in fancy dress staging a macabre dumb-show. In Carey's view these 'murderous bigots' are entirely removed from the rarefied realm of 'human imagination.' This high-humanist argument betrays its own ideological closure in mounting a geopolitically coded opposition of good and evil in which Milton's radicalist sympathies are silenced.

That closure might alert us to a parallel closure in the thought of Milbank, despite its claims of inclusivity. When the procedures of criticism produce undesirable conclusions, critics have turned to vaguely formalist, 'post-modern' strategies emphasizing a poetic ambiguity that does not upset our moral sensibilities. Likewise, imposing contingency upon terrestrial events creates a space where moral intuition is freed from the given and the historical facts of Christian orthodoxy can be overlooked.

That is not an inherently flawed project, but is access to the divine gift equal? Tyler Roberts has observed that 'Milbank purchases his vision of Christian peace by constructing a narrative of human history that attributes violence as an inherent characteristic of non-Christian identities—whether secular or religious.'[45] Is that criticism just? Milbank does certainly assert that *only* Christianity offers a vision of harmony and escapes an ontology of violence: '[N]ot even Judaism,' he claims, creates the sense of idealized community 'unique' to Christianity. And Milbank does claim that in the Christian vision, and only in the Christian vision, violence is perceived to be a 'jarring note' in the universally available divine harmony that is the background music of Creation.[46] Only Christians, of course, ever say that Christianity is universal. But Milbank's is not as exclusive a position as it might initially seem, for he advances what he describes as a 'pre-modern' theology where identity is a divine gift rather than a byproduct of the individual will, so that difference is always a part of divine order.

That view tends to ignore the double-edged nature of divine gift in the Christian tradition. Grace carries a latent threat—it is a gift arriving with a card that reads, 'Please accept this token of my boundless affection (or else).' Augustine certainly confirms that threatening aspect of grace in his idea of predestination. There are 'two cities' for Augustine, 'two societies of human beings, one of which is predestined to reign with God for all eternity, the other doomed to undergo eternal punishment with the Devil.'[47] Milbank's disciple Simon Oliver turns to Pseudo-Dionysius the Areopagite as modeling the Neoplatonic sense of divine procession and return that understands church and society as 'composed of a hierarchy of harmonious differences of natures, talents, characters, wills, desires, and so on.'[48] This, too, is a partial reading, for the Pseudo-Dionysius' harmonious order is a rigid hierarchy where the knowledge of superior orders absolutely contains the knowledge of inferior ones, where bishops hold absolute authority over the arcanum of divine knowledge, and where participation in the sacraments is protected from the polluting influence of the impure. Dionysius erupts in outrage in his letter to Demophilus, who had interfered with a priest's pity for a penitent, not because the monk had violated the principle of charity but because he had violated hierarchical order: 'It is not permitted that a priest should be corrected by the deacons, who are your superiors, nor by the monks, who are at the same level as yourself, and this is so even if it would seem that he had in some way misused divine things and even if it could be shown that he had violated some other regulation.'[49]

Another way of saying this is that the Milbank school offers a beautiful vision of a fully inclusive divine order, so beautiful and so inclusive, in fact, that it cannot justly be termed Christian. It is a theistic post-modernism expressing itself in a loosely Christian idiom. By ignoring such concepts as sin and God's disfavor of non-believers, it has little to do with anything that has been accepted as an orthodoxy in any of Christianity's traditions and might more accurately be called 'radical heterodoxy.' That it terms itself an 'orthodoxy' justifies Tyler Roberts's criticism of its religious exclusivism. Its arguments for Christianity as the only belief system offering vision of a *societas perfecta* present Christian violence as an aberrancy where violence is fundamental to other belief systems. Though Milbank's own vision admirably divorces God's justice and creative energies from violence, by attributing his values to a pre-modern Christian tradition, he offers a spurious claim of the faith's original purity. While that claim is used to mount productive analysis of secular modernity, its own principle of equal difference is limited by a slanted account of the religion to which it subscribes.

Milton and his contemporaries took it for granted that the spiritual peace offered to the upright soul could express itself in justified slaughter if God so desired. It is no small achievement of subject-centered modernity to raise grave doubts about that view. If Milton holds especial importance in current political discussion, it is precisely because he frustrates the kind of narrativization of Christian and Western traditions that we have seen Milbank and Carey attempt. In examining his work, we are aware, to use Achcar's Benjaminian phrase, of how 'each civilization has its own barbarism.'[50] Even as humanistically 'pure' a speech-act as his pastoral elegy *Lycidas* is animated partly by anxiety over 'what the grim Woolf with privy paw / Daily devours apace' (128–29), thus voicing fear of the threat to homeland security posed by Catholic infiltration. His propagandist prose for the Protectorate mirrors the conflicted relationship between the discourses of liberty and conquest inhering in 'Operation Iraqi Freedom.' One of the most Miltonic statements of recent history is the Ayatollah Khomeini's (probably unwitting) paraphrase of *The Readie and Easie Way* on the eve of the Iranian Revolution, immediately before he would institute the brand of oligarchical, absolutist regime advocated in Milton's tract: 'Islam is fundamentally opposed to the whole notion of monarchy.'[51] Because Milton's literary achievements are undeniably great while sometimes exhibiting what we would now call religious extremism, honest and clear-sighted criticism of his work can lead us to challenge ontological separation of these modes of thought. Through such challenges we interrogate the coding of Christianity and Western culture as fundamentally non-violent, and turn a skeptical eye to any argument for the purity of a religious or cultural tradition.

5

Can the Suicide Bomber Speak?

> [W]hat are we to make of those who care nothing for life, not even their own? The truth is that we have no idea what to make of them, because we can sense that even before they've died, they've journeyed to another world where we cannot reach them.
>
> —Arundhati Roy, 'The Monster in the Mirror'

We have all by now become familiar with and rejected the trite aphorism 'one person's terrorist is another's freedom fighter,' which offers little insight on terrorism and engages in an unthinking relativism—though it is not as catchy, one could sooner countenance 'one person's terrorist who is also another's freedom fighter should be every person's murderer.'[1] The trite aphorism does, however, offer one important insight through its double possessive: the life of the terrorist is always already written and incorporated into an existing demonology or hagiology. This is particularly true of the suicide attacker, whose final action is not self-expression so much as a radical self-effacement on which the order of narrative is imposed. That this attacker leaves behind evidence of an active adoption of that narrative—the obligatory letter or video denouncing infidels and anticipating celestial reward—should not fool us into thinking that it constitutes entire fulfillment of his or her wishes. To think that it does is to take subjectivization to be subjectivity. As Spivak describes it, the training of the suicide bomber is 'coercion at the full'; groups such as 'Hamas or Islamic Jihad . . . coercively rearrange desires until coercion seems identical with the will of the coerced. . . . [If] in the imagination we do not make the attempt to figure the other as imaginative actant, political (and military) solutions will not remove the binary that led to the problem in the first place.'[2]

Indeed, experiences closer to home should not make this so difficult an imagining. We know that a good many undergraduates funding an education through the US Army may not answer the call to serve in Iraq or Afghanistan entirely willingly, no matter how many photos in uniform they leave behind. We often sense that the active soldier struggles with the conscientious objector within. Cultural distance can lead us to assume that the terrorist lacks this internal complexity, that the suicide bomber is a 'radical' and an 'extremist' so internally polarized as no longer to be imaginable as a fully human subject. This view could be accurate, but it also might not be. My point is not so much that it is wrong to see suicide bombers as individuals whose actions betray an inhuman subjectivity, but rather to see such a view in large part as a culturally mediated assumption underwritten by the power relationships typical of culturally mediated assumptions. We should be reluctant, as Talal Asad has shown, to claim knowledge of the suicide bomber's motives: '[M]otives themselves are rarely lucid, always invested with emotions, and their description can be contested. They may not be clear even to the actor. Most important, explanations in terms of motives depend on typologies of action that are conventionally recognized.'[3] In pointing to the attacker's 'systematic deprivation and humiliation' or to 'Islamic discourse,' commentators typically describe 'intention,' which 'occurs at a causal level,' rather than motive.[4] To put it in theory-speak, the self-immolation of the suicide bomber creates an aporia that narrative conventions of cause and effect can supplement but never fill.

This is a limit registered in current literary representation of the terrorist. Despite his newfound popularity, the terrorist as novelic character seems never to speak to us in our own language, and indeed speaks in a language conspicuously bereft of literary expressiveness and thus representing an inner life either pathological or other-worldly.[5] The example that comes first to mind is John Updike's *Terrorist*, which shows a master novelist providing an embarrassingly ham-fisted portrait of a suicide bomber. As Amitav Ghosh observes in his review of the novel, the speech of the lead character has a 'curious timbre: Although he is a native-born American and has never left the United States, he speaks as if he had learned English at a *madrassa* run by the Taliban. "I of course do not hate all Americans," he says. "But the American way is the way of infidels. It is headed for a terrible doom."'[6] Updike would make Ahmed's an American story, where the anxiety leading him to violence is the sense of miscegenation arising from the union of his black Egyptian father and Irish-American mother. In trying to make that anxiety part of the experience of a jihadist we are not led to imagine a subjectivity that leads us beyond a rigid separation of West and East. In fact we find quite the opposite: the novel stalls in trying to bridge this gap. Updike crafts an inner life for Ahmed that is reasonably plausible American high schooler on the one hand, and on the other an experience of Islam that seems derived from news reports and a knowledge of the *Qur'an* admirable in its own way but that has the human insight of an encyclopedia entry. It is an important effort, but one that dispiritingly fails. In that failure we see the limited imagining of a subjectivity.

Ghosh strongly suggests in his searing review that race plays a large role in the shortcomings of *Terrorist*. Updike, the quintessentially WASP American writer, fails in attempting for the first time to create a central character of color. The best and worst of the novel is revealed in the description of Ahmed's father, 'whose ancestors had been baked since the time of the Pharaohs in the muddy rice and flax fields of the overflowing Nile' (13). There are few who could craft this lovely turn of phrase, and one must admire the ear of a novelist-poet who can make its quiet use of assonance, sibilance, and alliteration seem effortless. These sound devices, however, also contribute to its exoticist tone: they associate the everyday fact of an exchange student's pigmentation with the aura of faraway lands and ancient civilizations. Updike does not go as far as Spenser and Milton do in suggesting that the muddy fields left behind by the overflowing Nile spring hermaphroditic monsters and drown armies, but we half expect him to.[7] He also seems to assume that brown people and those who love them are obsessed with the many shades melanin can produce, like Victorian ethnographers crafting tables of innumerable columns in which to place people, some who, like Ahmed's father, are 'perfectly matte, like a cloth that's been dipped, olive-beige with a pinch of lampblack in it' (90); others who, like Ahmed, are 'dun, a low-luster shade lighter than beige' (13); the appetizing variety who resemble 'cocoa and caramel and chocolate' (170); more still who are 'the color of walnut furniture-stain while it's still sitting up wet on the wood' (15). Ghosh's observation would seem justified by the fact that, to my knowledge, one does not find in Rabbit Angstrom's many pages of inner monologue comparable contemplation of the fleshly declensions of the color pink.

What do we make then of Mohsin Hamid's eponymous reluctant

fundamentalist, who seems equally to speak in a language not our own? Here there is no cultural gap between writer and character: like his narrator, Hamid is born and raised in Lahore and attends Princeton. This coincidence does yield some of the kind of insight of which Updike seems incapable. We see a character lured to the opportunities of the Western metropolis and struggling with conflicted emotions: affection for things American, shame over Pakistan's poverty, and resentment that the East was once the seat of the world's most advanced civilizations and has become, and become viewed as, hopelessly backward. One of the novel's keenest perceptions comes in the form of an allusion to the kipper episode in Salman Rushdie's *Satanic Verses*. In a fictionalized version of his own experiences at an English private school, Rushdie presents Changez Chamchawala struggling to remove the bones from a kipper while his 'fellow-pupils watched him suffer in silence; not one of them said, here, let me show you, you eat it this way. . . . Then the thought occurred to him that he had been taught an important lesson. England was a peculiar-tasting smoked fish full of spikes and bones, and nobody would ever tell him how to eat it.'[8] In *The Reluctant Fundamentalist*, Hamid's narrating character, who is not coincidentally named Changez, has quite a different experience with a Princeton classmate, Erica, in whom he has a romantic interest: 'I felt . . . that she was sharing with me an intimacy, and this feeling grew stronger when, after observing me struggle, she helped me separate the flesh from the bones of my fish without me having to ask.'[9] Despite this perceived intimacy, Changez is continually denied a fully realized romantic relationship with Erica. His fish experience seems also to hold an important lesson: America seems generously inviting in offering the belonging that it in fact jealously guards.

And yet the plausibility of Hamid's Changez quickly evaporates in the café scene where he recounts to his American interlocutor the moment on a business trip in the Philippines when he sees television images of the crumbling World Trade Center:

> Besides, my throat is parched; the breeze seems to have disappeared entirely and, although night has fallen, it is still rather warm. Would you care for another soft drink? No? You are curious, you say, and desire me to continue? Very well. I will just signal our waiter to bring a bottle for me; there, it is done. And here he comes, making such haste; one would think we were his only customers! Ah, delicious: this is precisely what I required.

> The following evening was supposed to be our last in Manila. I was in my room, packing my things. I turned on the television and saw what at first I took to be a film. But as I continued to watch, I realized that it was not fiction but news. I stared as one—and then another—of the twin towers of New York's World Trade Center collapsed. And then I *smiled*. Yes, despicable as it may sound, my initial reaction was to be remarkably pleased.
>
> Your disgust is evident; indeed, your large hand has, perhaps without your noticing, clenched into a fist. (72)

Who would not be disgusted by such contrived prose, in which a narrator of our day speaks like a castoff from a Graham Greene novel? We are prepared for Changez's immoral response to the collapse of the World Trade Center by the manner in which he drinks a soda—a very American act that he performs with ludicrously un-American formality. Before the account of the towers falling we are already in the realm of the *Unheimliche* in that the most quotidian of actions is altered in its details in such a way as to render it menacingly unfamiliar. In the novel's concluding anticipation of a shootout, this Changez again sounds as though he has his namesake's bowler hat lodged in his backside: 'Ah, we are about to arrive at the gates of your hotel. It is here that you and I shall at last part company. Perhaps our waiter wants to say goodbye as well, for he is rapidly closing in. . . . But why are reaching into your jacket, sir? I detect a glint of metal. Given that you and I are now bound by a certain intimacy, I trust it is from the holder of your business cards' (184). It is in such speeches—much more than in his declaration of sympathy with a 'Third World sensibility' or his accounts of growing up in Lahore (67)—that the character's radical alterity is established. Despite an experience that is recognizable in many ways, the fundamentalist speaks to us in a language conspicuously not our own, and as in Updike's novel we find his subjectivity rendered mysterious. Changez describes himself as capable of entering a mystic's state where his 'self would disappear' (12); perhaps his curious mode of expression is intended to suggest one who feels as though he has risen above human experience. That may be an accurate representation of fundamentalist self-perception; it also reflects a perception that the subjectivity of the fundamentalist is not fully articulable.

One senses in Thomas Pynchon's *Against the Day* a much more supple handling of terrorism. This novel's setting in the late nineteenth and early twentieth centuries leaves more open the parallels to our own time. In providing a portrait of radicalism, Pynchon points to anarchist disruption of the railroads intended to provide the infrastructure by which the periphery is brought under the influence of the center. We are reminded of America's own history as frontier, rather than center of world civilization (the landscape of the novel is untamed and unforgiving in a way we have come to associate with the mountains of Afghanistan); we see a history of radicalist resistance to American power in which Americans themselves have engaged; and we see the brutality of the bounty hunters and covert operatives whose ruthlessness differs little from that of the anarchists they pursue. In Pynchon's terms the radicals emerge as holding beliefs more admirable than those of the anti-terrorists who are the henchmen of corporate power. This narrative of power and resistance coincides with one of capitalist competition over scientific discovery, with rival factions seeking to harness the potentialities of the wireless network of the world's magnetic fields.[10]

As subtle-minded as are Pynchon's eleven-hundred pages—and one certainly cannot do justice to their nuances in a couple of paragraphs—they also evince what for his readers will be familiar concerns. Anarchist opposition to centralized institutions is very much in keeping with the paranoid handling of a national postal service in *The Crying of Lot 49*. Pynchon's skepticism regarding an Enlightenment triumph of reason and the progressivism of scientific truth-claims is equally displayed in *Gravity's Rainbow* and *Mason & Dixon*—the latter is quite close to *Against the Day* in interrogating the ability of applied sciences to impose order upon an American landscape and upon human nature. By enlisting the anarchist, who is reminiscent of the present-day terrorist, in these concerns, Pynchon implicitly renders terrorism an opposition to an Enlightenment triumph of reason and to the ever-expanding reach of the US Government. This narrativization of terrorist resistance arises more from concerns within the West than it does from an evaluation of the subjectivity of the Islamist; it enlists terrorism as a means of political resistance in a fundamentally secular view of history, thus implying that there is ultimately little that distinguishes its deployment by anarchists and jihadists. Pynchon's wisdom, which Updike could have followed, lies in his realization that his novel risks spectacular failure in attempting to do otherwise. We see in *Against the Day* the self-conscious strengths and limitations of an artist contemplating his perennial themes.

If Updike and Hamid show the *radical alterity* of the fundamentalist,

Pynchon evinces what we might term *the temptation of ipseity*. In the latter we project our own politics and cultural suppositions upon the terrorist's violent resistance, imagining it as an extension of our worldview. We see this in the reaction of those on the political left presenting 9/11 as an expression of their own objections to the inequities of global capitalism—as a sort of Battle in Seattle writ large. Noam Chomsky's and Jean Baudrillard's casting of the 9/11 terrorists as avatars of the world's resentment of America's role in global capitalism seems very much to inhabit this realm. They advance in part an understanding of terrorism but are also invested in confirming the fundamentally secular and materialist understanding of history threatened by the mobilizing power of radical religion. In the most perceptive argument of this kind, Gilbert Achcar addresses US support of radical Islamic movements throughout the Cold War—well beyond the familiar case of the *Mujahiddeen* during the Afghan-Soviet War—when organizations like the Muslim Brotherhood in Egypt were seen as the only viable opposition to the pan-Arabic socialism gaining steam under the charisma of Gamal Abdul Nasser.[11] Such financing shifted Sunni Muslim learning from its historical center in Cairo to Saudi Arabia, generating an infrastructure for the spread of the Wahabbite cancer that now afflicts Sunni Islam worldwide. In this view, religion speaks to popular hopes only in the absence of a socialist alternative. Achcar provides an incisive account of the conditions by which radical religion has spread, but one wonders if the fundamental materialism of that account can describe religion's allure. And its assumption of humanity's natural progress toward secular political movements assumes precisely the *telos* of modernity on which we have cast some doubt in chapter three.

Both an uncritical alterity and an uncritical ipseity do not perform the imaginative work that we have described as necessary to ethical reading in chapter two, where one hears the call of the Other as a demand to inhabit as sense that which is taken as nonsense. These modes opt instead for the comfort of familiar ideological ground. Rather than providing an articulation of his subjectivity, this narrative silences the terrorist even as it enlists him as a lead character.

I. Silence and the anxiety of interpreting 'Samson Agonistes'

If I emphasize such problems of articulation and somewhat grudgingly repair to some of the most worn of theoretical terms, 'aporia' and 'supplement,' it is because so much of the critical controversy surrounding *Samson Agonistes* revolves around a silence: the absence of Samson's prayer immediately before he pulls down the pillars of the temple upon the Philistine nobility. It is on this silence that the apologist critic striving to make this a text opposed to the idea of divinely inspired slaughter typically projects Samson's alterity and Milton's ipseity. The claim often repeated is that Milton's elimination of Samson's vengeful prayer from the Book of Judges—'I pray thee, only this once, O God, that I may be at once avenged of the Philistines for my two eyes' (16.28)—suggests that the strength allowing Samson to commit his final act is only physical and does not arise from God. On the evidence of this silence Carey claims that 'Milton's drama' is 'a drastic rewriting of the Samson story' that 'calls into question Samson's motivation, and whether he has any divine sanction for his suicide attack.'[12] That Milton's Samson bows his head 'as one who pray'd, / Or some great matter in his mind revolv'd' (1637–38) suggests that 'perhaps he prays, perhaps not';[13] where the Judges account clearly implies 'that God is involved,' Milton shrouds this moment in ambiguity. While Carey intends to question the 'dogmatism' of Stanley Fish's reading of *Samson Agonistes*, his view of the poem engages in its own dogmatic imposition of ambiguity, as does Joseph Wittreich's closed claim that 'to equivocate on Samson's prayer . . . is to equivocate on Samson's heroism.'[14]

That happens to be untrue. A negative view of Samson's prayer is not always and necessarily an argument against his heroism of faith or a denial of divine involvement in his final act. In the *Institutes* Calvin objects to Samson's 'vicious longing for vengeance' but maintains that God grants his 'perverted prayer.'[15] There is also no evidence within the text that removal of Samson's prayer serves the ends that Carey and Wittreich describe. In adopting their view of this silence, we must see it as motivated by a secular humanist discomfort with Samson's slaughter, and exploit this opportunity to advance our own cultural narrative, which would have Milton impregn this pause with the objection to murderous violence that a sensitive poet must have.

I would argue that this moment in *Samson Agonistes* shows Milton himself succumbing to the temptation of ipseity. In imposing a silence upon this suicide attacker, he advances his favored cultural narrative: God's special favor for heroes of faith and execution of justice upon His idolatrous enemies, be they the flower of Palestine or of Restoration England. Milton thus perfects the silencing of the historical Samson, who was likely an able military leader, a silencing begun by the biblical narrator in imposing on his biography an anticipation of Israel's kings and the divinely appointed errand described in Judges 13 and 16, and which is sustained in the Christian Bible in counting him among the heroes of faith in Hebrews 11.[16] Milton rewrites his biblical sources to bring Samson more fully into accord with his view of biblical history and its relevance to his cultural moment, impulses revealed throughout the catastrophe of this tragedy: he removes the human motivation of revenge for personal injury and emphasizes an objection to Philistine idolatry, an attunement to divine will, and an anticipation of the Apocalypse.[17] In this respect his Samson shares features with the view of Jesus that emerges over his entire poetic career, from the Nativity Ode to *Paradise Regained*, which tends to emphasize the arrival of Christ as the central moment in biblical history and to downplay the suffering on the cross. At the moment of his triumph, Milton's Samson is much less a human subject than he is a vessel of God's wrath, which wrath is an irruption of the divine into our world of the sort punctuating biblical history.

If we are to compare *Samson Agonistes* to the novels introduced in this chapter, we might find it most resembling *Against The Day*. Like Pynchon's, Milton's text is a contemplation of an artist's career-long concerns. Douglas Bush describes the tragedy as 'the most deeply humanized treatment of Milton's perennial theme, and it remains, not the most beautiful, but the most wholly alive, the most permanently moving, of all his works. Samson is a completely human being in a completely real world, a great man who has lived greatly and sinned greatly.' The lesson of the three long poems is one of self-rule in a corrupt world: Adam 'has no need of an earthly paradise, he has a paradise within him, happier far'; Jesus 'maintains his integrity against the allurements of the world'; and 'Samson, resisting selfish and sensual temptations, achieves an inner regeneration which makes his outward fate of no account.'[18] Milton applies this theme in a way that humanizes his blind hero's sense of failure and despair, but ultimately shows that heroism of faith lies beyond merely human subjectivity. This is visible in the irony of Samson's statement immediately before following the officer to the temple, shortly after he has felt his 'rouzing motions' (1382):

> Masters commands come with a power resistless
> To such as owe them absolute subjection;

> And for a life who will not change his purpose?
> (So mutable are all the ways of men)
> Yet this be sure, in nothing to comply
> Scandalous or forbidden in our Law. (1404–9)

The double entendre running through this passage is lost on the Philistine officer, but it will not be lost on the fit reader: it is the divine master that Samson has in mind, and the changing of human ways in view of eternal life. Samson's final 'change' vaults above human mutability in its absolute subjection to God's will.

Milton generates further distance between Samson and his Philistine audience in insisting that the hero's death is not a suicide. In Spivak's analysis of the suicide bomber, she suggestively describes it as simultaneous self-objectification and objectification of others: '[S]uicide bombing . . . is a purposive self-annihilation, a confrontation between oneself and oneself. . . . It is when one sees oneself as an object, capable of destruction, in a world of objects, so that the destruction of others is indistinguishable from the destruction of the self.' By seeking to imagine the subjectivity of the bomber here, Spivak is performing precisely the gesture that a culture endorsing religious violence wishes to frustrate in its rigid separation of martyr and infidel. Milton shows his participation in such a culture in his anxiety that Samson not be viewed as holding all life in disesteem. His is not the act of a nihilist—he kills himself '*by accident*' (*YP* 8: 138), 'self-kill'd / Not willingly, but tangl'd in the fold, / Of dire necessity' (1664–66)—he is presented as concerned with a life beyond life and participates in a transcendent ethics and justice.

Our own moment reveals that the silencing of personal motives is typical of the culture seeking to immortalize those self-sacrificing militants who, like Milton's Samson, are distanced from suicide. Among Tamil Tigers, the secular movement that is the world leader in suicide attack, the term *thatkodai* ('gift of the self') is used rather than *thatkolai* ('suicide').[19] The Palestinian *shaheed* ('martyr') is etymologically associated with the verb *shahada* 'to witness,' and *shahida*, which means 'tombstone' and refers to the sign of the index finger extended upward, or the 'one-way sign,' representing exclusive focus on things heavenly. True to this suite of meanings, memorials never show a martyr's physical injuries and emphasize divine service and reward. These memorials also conflate those innocently killed with those who die while killing; as in Hebrews 11, Abels and Enochs rest alongside Gideons and Samsons.[20] Milton's quiet Samson completes this conflation reaching across his three major poems, which claim over and again that divine favor is bestowed upon those who set aside worldly motives in God's service, that spiritual supersedes physical sight, and that the destruction of worldly iniquity is inevitable.

It is precisely this prospect—that *Samson Agonistes* takes for granted God's inspiration of mass slaughter—that Carey dramatically raises as the horrifying result of disagreeing with him. That horror lurks more silently behind a broad range of responses to the dramatic poem. Though, as Mark R. Kelley and Joseph Wittreich have recently described it, this text is 'the major site of contestation within Milton studies,' several of its agonists have united in their desire to distance it from religious violence, either by arguing for its opposition to the events it displays or by contrasting its radicalism to that of the present day.[21] We can observe this tendency in the ostensibly divergent readings of Stanley Fish, Joseph Wittreich, and David Loewenstein.

Albeit subtly, Carey's desire to dissociate Milton from religious violence is also evinced in the reading of *Samson* to which he objects, that of Stanley Fish in *How Milton Works*. In a reading from which he has now retreated, Fish describes the resolution of two plots at the end of Milton's dramatic poem, that of Samson's internal regeneration and that of his external revenge on the Philistines, with the violence of the latter calling into question its relationship to the former. Thus Milton's Samson takes his place alongside the heroes of faith of Hebrews 11, who, Fish claims, are praised for taking 'provisional actions . . . in the name of a certain faith,'[22] an entirely valid point if this provisionalness refers only to Samson's lack of foreknowledge regarding the effects of his 'rouzing motions' (*SA* 1382). To say that the worthies of Hebrews 11 are valued only for taking '*provisional* actions in the *name* of a certain faith' is to set the bar of spiritual heroism rather lower than Milton would allow, and especially to ignore the divine favor and reward fundamental to such heroism. This is what Milton emphasizes in his portrayals of other worthies of Hebrews 11: Michael reassures Adam in *Paradise Lost* that Abel's faith will be 'approv'd' by God and that he will 'Loose no reward' (11.458–59); that Enoch is removed from harm's way, 'Rapt in a balmie Cloud . . . to walk with God / High in Salvation' (11.706–8); that Noah is observed by God to be 'The one just Man alive' (11.818); and that in Moses we see what 'wondrous power God to his

Saint will lend' (12.200). Jesus tells us in *Paradise Regain'd* that the godly general Gideon shall enjoy the celestial reward of 'reign in *Israel* without end' (2.442; italics in original).[23] Milton's plan for a Phineas tragedy concludes with 'the word of the lord . . . acquitting & approving phineas' for running his javelin through a man of Israel and his Midianitish female companion (*YP* 8: 560; cf. Num 25.7–11).

Most pertinently, Abraham follows his 'Faith' not to ambiguous action but to the execution of God's plan for His elect: '[God] from him will raise / A mightie Nation, and upon him showre / His benediction' (12.123–25). Though he does not see the future of Israel clearly before him, Abraham is not praised simply, as Fish once claimed, for his 'resolution to keep moving, to see what happens, take a chance';[24] his heroism is predicated upon the special calling granted to him by God as a reward for his faith. Though they may see their actions as provisional, we are told repeatedly that what makes the men of Hebrews 11 exemplary is their ability to 'hear [God] call' (*PL* 3.185), a sensitivity to divine prompting that always and necessarily produces justified external action. To see Samson's final slaughter of the Philistines as a provisional action divorced from divine agency is to impose a sense of tragic outcome informed more by the present-day value of literary polysemy than by Milton's views on spiritual heroism and Christian tragedy. The reading of *Samson Agonistes* offered in *How Milton Works* tends, as Michael Lieb observes and Fish has now conceded, to run counter to the argument of the book by introducing doubt in the demonstration of the doctrine of the inner light that it describes as the Miltonic masterplot.[25]

Contributing to a series of essays on 'Why Milton Matters,' Fish similarly offers a poet unsettling to liberal sensibilities by limiting discussion of his works to literary performance. This comes despite Fish's criticism of the tendency among liberal academics to find in Milton a poet who has 'the right political values—their values,' a claim made in an argument skeptical of historicism and in favor of a formalist valuation of 'aesthetic achievement.'[26] Though he avoids a narrowly ideological formalism by recognizing that literary form is itself underwritten by history and politics—and that Milton's period especially is one where debates on literary genre are 'unintelligible apart from the issues of nationalism, political authority, and public morality'[27]—there is no room in his thesis for consideration of Milton's prose as illuminating the poetry. Once we admit in our examination of the poetry the significance of the anti-prelatical tracts or the defenses, we must also admit the significance of Joseph Hall, James Ussher, Claude Saumaise, Alexander More, and a host of others whose influence on Milton does not reside primarily in the field of poetics. In the terms of Fish's essay, this is impermissible. Form has its own history: '[Y]ou have to attend to the specificity of the discourse that has solicited your attention, and that means attending to its history, not to history in general (there is no such thing) but to the history of a form.'[28] Fish thus offers a Milton who 'matters' only insofar as we recognize the poet's aesthetic achievement and ignore the polemicist's sometimes unseemly political views. Though this is not a Milton marching in the cause of modern liberalism, it is nonetheless a Milton whose status within the liberal tradition remains largely uncomplicated by unsettling aspects of his political and religious thought.

If Fish at times implicitly displays liberal values in his reading of *Samson*, Joseph Wittreich does so explicitly in his claim that 'Milton *matters* because, in facing tragedy, he forces us to reach beyond an axis of good and evil in the world to a more ambiguous reality.' 'Poetry,' Wittreich tells us, 'repeals traditions and voids conventions'—a claim difficult to reconcile with the Renaissance repristination of traditions and conventions, literary and religious, in which *Samson Agonistes* is deeply engaged.[29] In *Shifting Contexts* he has described the relationship between Samson and Christ as a 'typology of difference' where 'Samson's slaying . . . sets him at odds with Christ's saving' and even from the 'moral bearing' and 'heroic character' of Hercules.[30]

With this view of Milton's pacifism in mind, Wittreich proceeds to critique current conservative politics, pointing to Margaret Thatcher's use of the Samson image in *Areopagitica* to rouse American militarism: 'Thatcher herself uses Milton differently than he would be used, far differently than he (and others) had used Euripides against those who would reduce a city to ruin and desolation and therefore as part of an appeal not to tear down—to create rather than destroy and thereby revive "expiring libertie."'[31] The closing reference to *The Readie and Easie Way* points to complications arising from an association of Milton's views with current liberalism: the comment on 'expiring libertie' to which Wittreich directs attention describes the inevitability of God's defense of an enlightened few in a tract advocating the suspension of the rights of the majority—a suspension, we learn in Milton's *Letter to a Friend*, to be implemented and sustained by military force, if necessary (*YP* 7: 330).[32] In this sense, Milton's revival of 'expiring libertie' does share some of the spirit of Margaret Thatcher's encouragement of American unilateralism. Wittreich's position, like Carey's, forecloses discussion of Milton's radicalism in an effort to present him as a poet sympathetic to the values of modern humanism.

Wittreich's comments are, however, animated by a timely and important concern that we not consider ourselves members of an enlightened age that has outgrown 'revenge fantasy.' If, he claims, we see Samson's heroism as Milton's imagined tearing down of the 'pillars of [Restoration] church and state,' then we posit that his 'excellence is his relevance to the seventeenth century and irrelevance to our own—with Milton, then, seeming to embrace the very values that, having outgrown them, we now oppose.'[33]

This presents a valid challenge to scholarly work offering increasingly specific location of *Samson* in its moment of publication.[34] This branch of scholarship has tended to argue for greater distance between Milton's contexts and our own in response to the discomfort of reading *Samson Agonistes* in an age of terror. David Loewenstein has recently reiterated the parallels between the tragedy and Quaker polemics for which he argues in *Representing Revolution*, but, perhaps to prevent alarmed objection, has added that while Milton's dramatic poem displays 'religious terror' it does not present us with 'terrorism,' a term that arises only after the French Revolution. 'We need,' Loewenstein claims, 'to make crucial distinctions, informed particularly by an understanding of religious terror in the tumultuous world [of] seventeenth-century England, before branding Milton's Samson with the pejorative name "terrorist," a word unknown to Milton and his contemporaries.'[35] These include Milton's removal of the vengeful prayer in Judges and his stipulation that Samson's death is not a suicide, as well as the fact that Samson does not plan his attack upon the Philistines or even actively seek Dagon's temple.

Such distinctions call into question the parallel between Samson and the 9/11 hijackers that Carey describes as 'obvious' but tend to skirt around a central similarity: that Samson, in Carey's words, 'destroys many innocent victims, whose lives, hopes and loves are all quite unknown to him personally.'[36] By emphasizing differences between Milton's Samson and the modern terrorist, Loewenstein's reading generates comfortable distance between seventeenth-century radicalism and that of the present day. This gesture allows us to explore Milton's radical religion without raising unsettling parallels to the violence of its current counterpart; in the process, it avoids subjecting the modern term 'terrorism' to the kind of 'discriminating analysis' and 'rational argument' that Loewenstein identifies as absent in 'political and cultural discourse.'[37] As I've argued in this chapter, those parallels suggest that the distinctions themselves—the removal of the prayer and the claim that the hero is no suicide—are the distinctions typical of religious violence, which distances its martyrs from motives of personal vengeance and emphasizes their divine calling. The distinctions may make the poem dissonant with the facts of a modern suicide attack, but they simultaneously show a consonance with the culture by which those attacks are immortalized.

II. Intellectual work in an age of terror

Each side of the great divide on *Samson Agonistes* can thus operate to cleanse Milton of association with present-day religious violence, either by vaccinating him with current liberal ideals or by consigning him to a distant and irrelevant past. We might see in this process Milton studies showing the tendency identified by poststructuralists of intellectual work to support the presuppositions of the political dominant. As Pierre Bourdieu claims, the critic's 'only hope of producing scientific knowledge—rather than weapons to advance a particular class of specific interests—is to make explicit to oneself one's position in the sub-field of the producers of discourse about art.'[38] In a similar vein, Michel Foucault observes in a conversation with Gilles Deleuze that the intellectual must 'struggle against the forms of power that transform him into its object and instrument in the sphere of "knowledge," "truth," "consciousness," and "discourse."'[39]

This certainly holds a valuable lesson for Milton studies as it turns its attention to the issue of terrorism: criticism should beware of the potential of perpetuating a discourse that has employed global terrorism to solidify its own power. The teleology of Bourdieu's and Foucault's statements, however, must come under suspicion: the hope of producing a 'scientific knowledge' that is not a weapon of specific interests, and the creation of a class of intellectuals engaged in genuine struggle against 'power' are aspirations employed to legitimize the theories of the practitioners who voice them. The very voices that these intellectuals would claim to make heard are marginalized and subordinated to an *a priori* narrative of class struggle—one is consistently aware that the workers on whose behalf the signs must burn have their desires and aspirations assumed and articulated for them by the poststructuralist theorist.

Attuned to such complications is Gayatri Spivak's theorization of the Native Informant in her *Critique of Postcolonial Reason*—commenting on the above-cited conversation between Foucault and Deleuze, she observes that 'the ventriloquism of the speaking subaltern is the left intellectual's stock-in-trade.'[40] In the terms of her argument, academic postcolonialism is a discipline especially fraught with the contradiction of making a show of resistance to the cultural dominant while operating within its terms.[41] 'Postcolonial informants' take professional advantage of an 'aura of identification with . . . distant objects of oppression,' and 'at worst, they . . . play the native informant uncontaminated by disavowed involvement with the machinery of the production of knowledge.'[42] In order to be more 'effective,' then, postcolonialism must acknowledge its complicity in the silencing of subaltern voices and the perpetuation of colonial relationships between the Western metropolis and the 'third world.'[43]

This may seem a far cry from Milton, but it is not. If early modern studies shares a quality with postcolonial studies, it is that it offers an aura of authority on a culture foreign to the uninitiated. Like the postcolonial informant Spivak identifies, current response to *Samson Agonistes* deploys an aura of identification with a distant culture in a way that silently affirms, and gains legitimacy by affirming, presuppositions of the current cultural dominant. Either by declaring Milton's sympathy with horror over religious violence or by asserting the irrelevance of his radicalism to the present day, such intellectual work declares its allegiance with Western values of non-violence and liberty and its uncomplicated cultural superiority to the religious violence of the Other.

This can be seen as only the latest episode in the long history of politically charged interpretation of Milton, and especially of his dramatic poem. It is no coincidence, as Sharon Achinstein has suggested, that the 'notorious missing middle is blotted out by the conservative Tory Samuel Johnson,' a gesture that radicalizes the text by shifting focus to its conclusion and supports Johnson's estimation of it as 'the tragedy which ignorance has admired and bigotry applauded.'[44] Achinstein's observation on Johnson's politicized aesthetic is borne out by Richard Cumberland's Whig rescue of the tragedy's middle in *The Observer* (1791).⁴⁵ What I am suggesting here is in some ways an extension of the brand of inquiry evinced in Joan S. Bennett's reading of Milton in light of current liberation theology. Drawing on Loewenstein's description of *Samson* as 'iconoclastic weapon,' Bennett concludes that 'Milton's biblical story-making is performative discourse and that iconoclasm is a very important part of the work being done. . . . The modern revolutionary identity more appropriately comparable to Milton than "terrorist" is perhaps, in a broad sense, "educator."'⁴⁶ This view of Milton as educator in resistance is undoubtedly true and is suggestive in its relationship to all of Milton's Restoration publications, not only the three major poems but also the *Artis Logicae*, the *Accedence Commenc't Grammar*, *The History of Britain*, and *Of True Religion*.

Surely one of the contexts that must now obtain is what Mark Juergensmeyer has described as the 'performance violence' of modern terrorism, where 'explosive scenarios are not *tactics* directed toward an immediate, earthly, or strategic goal, but *dramatic events* intended to impress for their symbolic significance.' When members of the culture that is the target of such attacks 'take them seriously' and 'begin to distrust the peacefulness of the world around [them,] the purposes of this theater are achieved.'⁴⁷ This seems precisely the reason for the particular horror of suicide bombing explored by Talal Asad, a tactic that, as he describes it, goes beyond other means of terrorist attack in its impact. 'Horror,' he argues, is distinguishable from 'terror, outrage, or the spontaneous desire for vengeance' in that it 'has no object'; it stems, rather, from the sense that '*our own* identities are precarious but also those of other humans—and not only the identity of individual humans but also that of human ways of life.'⁴⁸ In his exploration of the sources of this horror, most persuasive is his claim that a suicide bombing is shocking not only in that it is an 'unexpected suicide' occurring in public and involving 'the shattering of other human bodies and their belongings,' but it is also 'a sudden disruption of the patterns of everyday life, a violence in which death is unregulated by the nation-state.'⁴⁹

By this logic we might describe suicide bombing as civility's evil twin. Following Robert Pippin, Žižek connects civility to 'the rise of the autonomous free individual . . . the fragile web of civility is the "social substance" of free independent individuals, it is their mode of (inter)dependence. If this substance disintegrates, the very social space of individual freedom is foreclosed.'⁵⁰ Civility offers a code of conduct allowing members of a society to assure each other of their common acceptance of ideology, thus allowing the perception of a 'free' society where order is sustained without the ubiquitous policing of the totalitarian state. Suicide bombing shows us that it knows that code well enough to play along for a time and then to turn it against us. We are no longer comforted by civility. We can no longer sit in a café, or stand on a train platform, or take a flight without any suspicion of those around us who seem to share our knowledge of the intricate steps in the dance of everyday life. In the horror of that disruption, we see that the threat to 'our way of life' is not to its openness, but the failure of ideology fully to govern our day-to-day interactions. We long to have orderly conduct again become an assurance of law and order, and resent most of all the police-state measures introduced in the name of 'security.'

Milton's Samson is quite adept at this element of suicide attack. The Philistines, confident in having brought their enemy to heel, turn him into a liveried performer as a public sign of their conquest. The frequent double entendre and equivocation in his final speeches to which Balachandra Rajan draws our attention show that he knows how to play his part while sustaining revolutionary commitment—to adopt the code of civility while plotting against the political structures that it is meant to secure.⁵¹

If *Samson Agonistes* is in part a conduct manual for failed revolutionaries, then this seems an important part of its lesson. Samson's initial response to the Philistine officer is dismissive, and opts for isolation rather than service of a debased regime. Divine prompting leads him to a change of heart that allows him to give a show of service that will ultimately serve God's ends. The possibility of equivocation that is used throughout the period to justify intolerance of Roman Catholics is suggested here as a course of action for those sympathetic to the Good Old Cause. Simple retreat from public life will pose no challenge to a restored monarchy and episcopacy. Those who triumph will move at the center of power and wait for divinely granted opportunity.

We might add this element of the dramatic poem to the critique of baroque drama to which Victoria Kahn draws our attention. *Samson Agonistes*, she argues, is quite opposed to the world of a play like *Hamlet*, which, as Benjamin claims in his account of *Trauerspiel*, moves tragedy away from an Aristotelian imitation of action and toward acting, where the passions on the stage have an externality and self-conscious theatricality.[52] Thus the play within a play of *Hamlet* constitutes 'the playful miniaturization of reality and the introduction of a reflective infinity of thought into the finite space of a profane fate.'[53] With this in mind, it is revealing that unlike Joost van den Vondel, Milton distinguishes Samson's final action from acting. Where Vondel's Samson plays his own life in a masque re-dramatizing his own failings, Milton's Samson performs the feats of strength recalling those past triumphs that were an affliction to his Philistine audience. The Philistine audience's perception that God's strength can be appropriated by Dagon's revelers generates dramatic irony, though that audience will never be allowed the inner complexity of realizing their mistake. Where Hamlet stages his play within a play to prompt emotional response in his fellow characters, the climax of *Samson Agonistes* does not imply Philistine emotional conflictedness—a masque of the sort Vondel provides might suggest that at the moment of their death, some Philistines are for the first time encountering their enemy's human failings and the agonies of his blinding and imprisonment.

When we read this dramatic irony aright, we know that at this moment Samson is not fully *in proper persona*. And the terms of his acting are not confined to the world of the tragedy: they reach into the world of the viewer where action is equally governed by the promptings of grace and which is equally afflicted by earthly lords 'Drunk with Idolatry, drunk with Wine' (1670). By so reaching it truly translates the spirit of Attic tragedy into an English and Christian language, and is at odds, as Kahn shows, with an emerging 'aesthetic ideology' in that its transformation of 'passion into action is a critique of aesthetic contemplation.'[54]

Though it must be stressed that the performance violence of *Samson Agonistes* remains fictive, we cannot deny that its intervention in Restoration culture parallels the performance aspect of modern terrorism. In its every sinew *Samson Agonistes* strains against Restoration triumphalism, and reminds its readers that a defeated and ridiculed blind guide can carry within him the larger—and, in the chiliastic terms the text invites, the more menacing—triumph of divine illumination. It unsettles as illusory the peacefulness of restored monarchy, and affirms as irresistible the cosmic progress toward human liberty—a liberty equivalent in Milton's terms to the defeat of the ungodly and the justification of the elect.

This recognition of the text's performance violence is no new account of *Samson*, for it evokes the reading that Sir Walter Raleigh advanced over a century ago with his typical sensitivity and verve:

> Milton was thinking not very remotely of his own case when he wrote that jubilant semi-chorus, with the marvellous fugal succession of figures, wherein Samson, and by inference Milton himself, is compared to a smouldering fire revived, to a serpent attacking a hen-roost, to an eagle swooping on his helpless prey, and last, his enemies now silent for ever, to the phoenix, self-begotten and self-perpetuating. The Philistian nobility (or the Restoration notables) are described, with huge scorn, as ranged along the tiers of their theatre, like barnyard fowl blinking on their perch, watching, not without a flutter of apprehension, the vain attempts made on their safety by the reptile groveling in the dust below.[55]

In Raleigh's reading, literary complexity is not at all at odds with revenge ethic. The tragedy's imaginative achievements are ineluctably a part of its effectiveness as 'iconoclastic weapon': the text's literary complexity, religious piety, and virtuoso humanist adherence to ancient models are all necessary to its arraignment of the lesser achievements of Dryden and Davenant.

In seeking to avoid the conclusion unsettling within the discipline of Milton studies—that there was a place in Milton's view of Providence for divinely inspired slaughter—critics have tended toward positions a good deal more unsettling in their coincidence with current discourses of domination. The dissociation of Milton from current religious extremism has implicitly advanced narrativization of the moral enlightenment of Western liberal humanism. If Milton matters it is because he so clearly reminds us that even while we relish the greatest intellectual and artistic achievements of the Western tradition we would be remiss not also to recognize its barbarisms. If Milton prompts us to look beyond an axis of good and evil, it is because of, not despite, the unsettling parallels between *Samson Agonistes* and modern terrorism; in these parallels we see that even a subtle-minded poet energetic in his defense of liberty can promulgate an exceptionalist discourse privileging the rights of the elect. Grappling with Milton's complexities in these regards thus affords an opportunity for critical *agons* building resistance to too-easy determinations of alterity and ipseity, precisely the intellectual work that an age of war resists.

Epilogue

> Prometheus: I stopped mortals from foreseeing doom.
> Chorus: What cure did you discover for that sickness?
> Prometheus: I sowed in them blind hopes.
> Chorus: That was a great help that you gave to men.
> Prometheus: Besides, I myself gave them fire.
> Chorus: Do now creatures of a day own bright-faced fire?
> Prometheus: Yes and from it they shall learn many crafts.
>
> —Aeschylus, *Prometheus Bound*

In first approaching the issues raised in this book, I was determined to speak to the post-secular with no friendly voice.[1] I am now less certain. Secular dismissal of belief seems to me less an antipathy to superstition and valuation of reason than it does a triumph of *technē* stifling freedom from the given. There is more than a little merit to Creston Davis's claim that 'the portal to theology was opened precisely because capitalism is ultimately a self-enclosed structure, and so theology gives us a way to transcend capital,' a way that is 'premised on relationality and not on Ego.'[2] Even blind hopes, Prometheus suggests, can have the salutary effect of leading us to ignore our certain doom and to look beyond mere mortality. The granting of fire by which we learn the crafts of *technē*, by contrast, seems like a significantly less beneficial afterthought.

Citing Kant's *Contest of Faculties*, Žižek has incisively suggested that if there is such a thing as human progress, it is punctuated by triumphs of illusions—equality, liberty, justice—which have an ethical value that material gains do not. That is the significance, as he describes it, of Toussaint L'Ouverture's reception as an equal in the Popular Assembly of Revolutionary France. That is also the significance, he rightly discerns, of the election of Barack Obama, a centrist whose policies will contain only the faintest glimmer of progressivism. What those locked in a cynicism deeply skeptical of change fail to see, Žižek concludes, 'is their own naivety, the naivety of their cynical wisdom which ignores the power of illusions.'³

Milton marks for us the torment of a life without illusions through Satan in *Paradise Lost*. Satan's rebellion arises in no small measure from an over-estimation of the importance of existents and a rejection of those aspects of his relationship with God to be affirmed through belief: the unobservable act of his own creation; and the benevolence of the Son's vicegerent rule, which he takes to be an expression of divine authoritarianism. In denying these, he mocks an acceptance of truth beyond the hard facts of empiricism:

> That we were formd then saist thou? and the work
> Of secondarie hands, by task transferd
> From Father to his Son? strange point and new!
> Doctrin which we would know whence learnt: who saw
> When this creation was? remeberst thou
> Thy making, while the Maker gave thee being? (5.853–58)

The inability to embrace the idea of divine gift is simultaneously a turn away from the good. In his inner Hell, Satan can rationally discern the benefit of belief even as he can no longer experience it: '[N]ever can true reconcilement grow / Where wounds of deadly hate have peirc'd so deep' (4.98–99). Despite blustering to the contrary, his conquest over humanity is more imagined than believed, for in the Niphates speech of book 4 he rightly perceives that base motives must yield base results. Capable only of a self-consciously partial illusion, he is left with the material and the imagined. Blake is thus right to associate Satan with imagination, though wrong to include Milton in the devil's party. In Milton's terms hope resides in the believing soul's experiential connection to God; '[T]he fancy,' as Keats discerns, 'cannot cheat so well.'⁴

A re-evaluation of belief seems pressing in light of the Supreme Court's June 2010 decision in *Christian Legal Society v. Martinez*.⁵ On the surface, it is a triumph of liberal equality over retrograde orthodoxy. The case arises from the application of a chapter of the Christian Legal Society for recognition as a Registered Student Organization (RSO) of the UC Hastings College of the Law. The school denied the application, objecting to a 'Statement of Faith' that the organization requires of its members—which includes the predictable Christian fundamentalist clause on God's sanction only of married, heterosexual sex—on the grounds that it violates the university's Non-Discrimination Policy. As litigation proceeded, a former Dean declared that the school had traditionally interpreted that policy to mean that RSOs must accept 'all comers.' Any group receiving support through the program must be open to all students, lest students be required to support through their fees an organization that excludes them. Though the Christian Legal Society could not enjoy RSO status, it was not barred from campus and could still operate as a non-registered student group with access to certain facilities—as indeed it had done after its application was denied, and done with lamentable success.

Writing for the majority, Justice Ginsburg delivers a gleefully crushing decision in favor of the law school. She reserves especial ire for the attempt of the Christian Legal Society to claim that Hastings had actively interfered with its activities, not because the claim is incorrect but because it departs from facts stipulated at the summary judgment stage of proceedings: 'We reject CLS's unseemly attempt to escape from the stipulation and shift its target to Hastings' policy as written' (12). The Court eliminates from consideration the constitutionality of Hastings' Non-Discrimination Policy and focuses on the unwritten 'all-comers' practice as it relates to precedent concerning limited public fora, where 'any access barrier must be reasonable and viewpoint neutral' (13).[6] The policy is praised on both fronts, and for serving the significant pedagogical aim of encouraging 'tolerance, cooperation, and learning among students' (23).

We can guess who the four dissenters are in this 5–4 ruling. Writing on their behalf, Samuel Alito finds 'deeply disappointing' the majority's blow to regressive thought (2). He also scores some palpable hits. The 'all-comers' measure that the majority praises as assuring viewpoint neutrality is in fact directly opposed to faith-based organizations, which are founded upon the shared beliefs of members.[7] In this view the kind of inter-faith and cross-cultural dialogue that Hastings declares as an aim of its RSOs, and which Ginsburg praises, is in fact the assertion of a viewpoint opposed to strong belief rather than the implementation of viewpoint neutrality—Alito cites the *amicus* brief filed in support of the Christian Legal Society by Muslim, Sikh, and Jewish student organizations, which declares it 'fundamentally confused to apply a rule against religious discrimination to a religious organization' (22). What's more, despite its claim of allowing the group to operate as a non-registered organization, Hastings had engaged in silly tricks when the students attempted to book facilities for their events: on two occasions the same administrator who denied their application ignored e-mails making such requests, replying only after the date of the event had passed (11–12). The 'all-comers' practice that became central to the Court's finding of viewpoint neutrality was not cited in the school's initial decision, which referred only to the university's written Non-Discrimination Policy; indeed it did not emerge until litigation was under way, and even then the school adapted its terms to suit the emerging needs of the case. In excluding from consideration the constitutionality of the written policy, the Court had thus ignored the rationale initially offered as a denial of RSO status. To recall Ginsburg's language, it is not only the Christian Legal Society that had engaged in an unseemly attempt to adapt its position to emerging interests.

It is difficult to find inspiring either the opinion or the dissent. One offers a liberal proceduralism that catches bigots on technicalities and bureaucratic stalling tactics, and the other a supposed protection of belief that allows bigots to run amok. One claims to champion a public sphere open to all (but that marginalizes believers), and the other to champion belief (no matter how backward). Both base their conclusions in a relativistic acceptance of 'all comers,' differing only on where the principle should be applied, whether at the level of the individual or a 'step up' at the level of groups. Neither side of the bench directly confronts the elephant in the room, namely that a group requiring its members to endorse anti-gay discrimination is opposed to human equality, and therefore cannot be deemed a legitimate legal society.

It is the nature of court cases rarely to inspire, but in this instance uninspiring court proceedings point to a larger and equally uninspiring intellectual choice: that between liberal proceduralism and *modus vivendi* toleration. Neither of these seems willing to provide a robust sense of legitimate belief, on which Badiou has given us some direction in describing ethically viable truth as 'indifferent to differences.'[8] There is nothing inherently wrong with a statement of faith limiting admission to a group, so long as the faith demanded advances human harmony rather than frustrates it. Cynical proceduralism and conscientious bigotry are challenges to be overcome in a full embrace of such blind hopes as equality and justice.

Perhaps there is, then, much worth taking seriously in Derrida's 'messianicity without messianism' or in aspects of Milbank's 'radical orthodoxy.' The crimes of the secular state in the name of self-preservation must make us yearn for strong correctives to capitalist parliamentarian incarnations of democracy. But strong medicine, I have worried in these pages, can kill as often as it cures. Secularists are often right to take up a Rawlsean opposition to strong belief when it disregards compromise and consensus. The lack of sociality in the believer's adherence to truth will pay no heed to worldly institutions, or to fellow citizens, perceived to oppose truth, finding its most extreme political expression in the endorsement of religious violence. Those are dynamics to which reading Milton alerts us, with his consistently energetic arguments for the liberty of a fit few and his assurance that the enemies of truth will suffer defeat in God's time, as well as his deployment of language in a way that signals privileged access to truth: whether through the epic plain style by which truth is revealed in *Paradise Lost*; the rhetorical excess serving as cover for an ethos-based politics in *Areopagitica*; the rhetorical plainness removing authority over the enlightened from the realm of politics in *Civil Power*; or a hero of faith's impenetrable silence at a moment of divine inspiration, seen in *Samson Agonistes*.

At his finest, Milton subjects received wisdom to thoughtful scrutiny and argues for a sweeping away of institutions restricting human freedom. The inspiring energy of such moments should not blind us to the limits of his view of liberty; nor should the limits of his view of liberty blind us to the vigorous iconoclasm made possible by a commitment to truth. An unthinking secular liberalism can rest on the assumption that strong belief leads inexorably to slaughter in God's name, or that strong commitment to political truth leads inexorably to the crimes of totalitarianism.

Have wounds of deadly hate pierced humanity—and humanities scholars—so deep that we are no longer capable of blind hopes? Are illusions desirable, responsible, or even tenable, in an age so keenly aware of human and ecological catastrophe? The landfill of history has certainly been stuffed by the offal of strong belief, but cynical realism is not likely to yield the ethical and political commitment that might tame its burgeoning heaps. If post-secularity is a good thing, it will learn from the mistakes of its religious and secular predecessors by finding modes of belief enabling richer expressions of human harmony and programs of action broadening material sufficiency and spiritual fulfillment. But until belief is proven to unite rather than to atomize the human family, I trust we may be forgiven some skepticism.

Notes

INTRODUCTION

1. Bertolt Brecht, 'Portrayal of the Church,' in *Collected Plays*, ed. John Willet, Ralph Manheim, and Tom Kuhn, 8 vols., 1970–2003 (London, 2006), 5: 192–93.
2. Ibid., 5: 270.
3. John Willet and Ralph Manheim, Introduction to ibid., 5: xv, xxii.
4. Qtd. in ibid., 5: xxix.
5. See ibid., 5: 192.
6. Alain Badiou, *Being and Event* [*L'être et l'événement*, 1988], trans. Oliver Feltham (2005; pbk. London, 2007), 28: 'Ontology, insofar as it exists, must be the science of the multiple qua multiple.'
7. Charles Taylor, *A Secular Age* (Cambridge, Mass., 2007), 3 *et passim*. Alain Badiou, *Logics of Worlds: Being and Event 2* [*Logiques des mondes*, 2006], trans. Alberto Toscano (London, 2009), 9; italics in original.
8. Philip Gorski, 'Historicizing the Secularization Debate: Church, State, and Society in Late Medieval and Early Modern Europe, ca. 1300–1700,' *American Sociological Review* 65 (2000): 138–67.
9. See Gauri Viswanathan, 'Secularism in the Framework of Heterodoxy,' *PMLA* 123 (2008): 467.
10. Gorski, 'Historicizing the Secularization Debate,' 148–49.
11. Sir Henry Vane the Younger, *A Pilgrimage into the Land of Promise, by the Light of the Vision of Jacobs Ladder* ([London,] 1664; Wing V73), 66; Badiou, *Logics of Worlds*, 34.
12. Jacques Derrida, *The Gift of Death*, trans. David Wills (Chicago, 1996), 49.
13. John Milbank, 'Postmodern Critical Augustinianism: A Short *Summa* in Forty-Two Responses to Unasked Questions,' in *The Radical Orthodoxy Reader*, ed. Milbank and Simon Oliver (London, 2009), 49.
14. John Milbank, 'Knowledge: The Theological Critique of Philosophy in Hamann and Jacobi,' in *Radical Orthodoxy*, ed. Milbank, Catherine Pickstock, and Graham Ward (London, 1999), 32.

15. See John Milbank, 'The Double Glory, or Paradox versus Dialectics: On Not Quite Agreeing with Slavoj Žižek,' in *The Monstrosity of Christ: Paradox or Dialectic*, by Milbank and Žižek, ed. Creston Davis (Cambridge, Mass., 2009), 114–15.

16. John Milbank, 'An Essay against Secular Order,' *The Journal of Religious Ethics* 15 (1987): 206.

17. John Milbank, *Theology and Social Theory* (1990; Oxford, 2006).

18. Jürgen Habermas, 'Religion in the Public Sphere,' trans. Jeremy Gaines, *European Journal of Philosophy* 14 (2006): 15. Habermas also develops his position in *Between Naturalism and Religion*, trans. Ciaran Cronin (Cambridge, 2008); in his debate with Joseph Ratzinger, now Pope Benedict XVI, *The Dialectics of Secularization: On Reason and Religion*, ed. Florian Schuller, trans. Brian McNeil (San Francisco, 2006); and his published podium discussion with Norbert Brieskorn, Michael Reder, Friedo Ricken, and Josef Schmidt, *An Awareness of What Is Missing: Faith and Reason in a Post-Secular Age* (Cambridge, 2010).

19. See 'Zurich Allows Anti-Minaret Poster,' *BBC News*, 8 October 2009, accessed 8 December 2009, news.bbc.co.uk/2/hi/europe/8297826.stm; 'Swiss Muslims Open Mosque Doors,' *BBC News*, 7 November 2009, accessed 8 December 2009, news.bbc.co.uk/2/hi/europe/8348279.stm; and esp. Sally Neighbour, 'Fears of Eurabian Future Unfounded,' *The Australian*, 5 December 2009, accessed 8 December 2009, www.theaustralian.com.au/news/world/fears-of-eurabian-future-unfounded/story-e6frg6so-1225807133633.

20. Alain Badiou, *Handbook of Inaesthetics*, trans. Alberto Toscano (Stanford, Calif., 2005), 6.

21. On 'excess' as the language of hagiography, see Françoise Meltzer and Jas' Elsner, Introduction to *Holy by Special Application*, special issue, *Critical Inquiry* 35 (2009): 377.

22. Douglas A. Brooks similarly remarks that 'scholarly reliance on Milton's poetry to interpret and comment upon recent crises is not, of course, new' (Introduction to *Milton and the Jews* [Cambridge, 2008], 2 n. 5).

23. Nicholas von Maltzahn, 'The First Reception of *Paradise Lost* (1667),' *RES* n.s. 47 (1996): 480.

24. The comment is that of Roger L'Estrange, Milton's enemy and publisher; qtd. in von Maltzahn, 'The Whig Milton, 1667–1700,' in *Milton and Republicanism*, ed. David Armitage et al., Ideas in Context (1995; pbk. Cambridge, 1998), 235.

25. Anthony à Wood, from *Fasti Oxoniensis*, in *Early Lives of Milton*, ed. Helen Darbishire (1932; New York, 1965), 39; on Wood's biography and the 1688 *Paradise Lost*, see von Maltzahn, 'Wood, Allam, and the Oxford Milton,' *Milton Studies* 31 (1995): 155–77.

26. John Toland, *Life of John Milton*, in *Early Lives of Milton*, 139. An example of Presbyterian opposition to toleration is the 'inhuman Treatment' of his acquain-

tance Daniel Williams, a Presbyterian making efforts to reach out to Dissenters and who had been tarnished as a result with accusations of Socinianism—the gesture of solidarity is also one of self-defense, as Toland had been subjected to similar accusations.

27. Ibid., 86.

28. See Gordon Campbell, 'Milton, Sir Christopher,' in *ODNB* (Oxford, 2004), online edn. revised January 2008; and Steve Pincus, *1688: The First Modern Revolution* (New Haven, 2009), 260. On Dissenters' skepticism of James's intentions in repealing the Penal Laws and Test Acts, see Pincus, 202–5.

29. Joseph Wittreich, *Why Milton Matters: A New Preface to His Writings* (New York, 2006), 141; see also his *The Romantics on Milton: Formal Essays and Critical Asides* (Cleveland, 1970). Erik Gray has recently extended our awareness of this reception into the nineteenth century in *Milton and the Victorians* (Ithaca, NY, 2009).

30. G. Wilson Knight, 'The Frozen Labyrinth: An Essay on Milton,' in *The Burning Oracle: Studies in the Poetry of Action* (Oxford, 1939).

31. Douglas Bush, *'Paradise Lost' in Our Time: Some Comments* (New York, 1948), 6.

32. Ibid., 40. For more recent, precise accounts of *recta ratio*, see John Leonard, 'Douglas Bush in His Time and Ours,' in *Milton, Historicism, and Questions of Tradition: Essays by Canadians Past and Present*, ed. Feisal G. Mohamed and Mary Nyquist (Toronto, forthcoming); and Phillip J. Donnelly, *Milton's Scriptural Reasoning: Narrative and Protestant Toleration* (Cambridge, 2009), ch. 2.

33. Bush, *'Paradise Lost' in Our Time*, 4.

34. Douglas Bush, *The Renaissance and English Humanism* (1939; Toronto, 1965), 104.

35. See Douglas Bush, 'A.S.P. Woodhouse: Scholar, Critic, Humanist,' in *Essays in English Literature from the Renaissance to the Victorian Age: Presented to A.S.P. Woodhouse*, ed. Millar MacLure and F. W. Watt (Toronto, 1964), 321.

36. See Sharon Achinstein, 'Cold War Milton,' *Milton in America*, ed. Paul Stevens and Patricia Simmons, special issue, *University of Toronto Quarterly* 77 (2008): 801–36. Recent works attempting to stimulate the general reader's interest in Milton tend to describe him as an uncomplicated champion of liberty. In this vein Nigel Smith has claimed Milton can protect us from tyranny: 'Through the preservation of these works and their extended appreciation over time, the forces of tyranny and empire, of censorship, manipulation, and exploitation, are to be challenged, overcome even, with the teachings of free will' (Nigel Smith, *Is Milton Better than Shakespeare?* [Cambridge, Mass., 2008], 166; see my review of this book in *Milton Quarterly* 44 (2010): 58–61). See also David Hawkes's argument on the need for Milton's iconoclasm in our image-obsessed age in *John Milton: A Hero of Our Time* (Berkeley, 2009), and my review of this book in *Clio* 39 (2010): 245–50.

37. Wittreich, *Why Milton Matters*, 170.

38. See *YP,* 1: 679.

39. Linda Charnes, *Hamlet's Heirs: Shakespeare and the Politics of a New Millennium*, Accents on Shakespeare, ed. Terence Hawkes (New York, 2006), 6, 14.

40. Ewan Fernie, 'Shakespeare and the Prospect of Presentism,' *Shakespeare Survey* 58 (2005): 176, 179. See also Fernie's 'The Last Act: Presentism, Spirituality, and the Politics of *Hamlet*,' in *Spiritual Shakespeares*, ed. Fernie (Abingdon, 2005), 186–211.

41. See the brief Introduction to Hugh Grady and Terence Hawkes's *Presentist Shakespeares* (London, 2007). Robin Headlam Wells notes that awareness of the present is as discernible in 'old' as in 'New' historicism; see 'Historicism and "Presentism" in Early Modern Studies,' *Cambridge Quarterly* 29 (2000): 38–60. See also Sharon Achinstein's perceptive Introduction 'Cloudless Thunder: Milton in History,' *Milton Studies* 48 (2008): 7–11.

42. Wittreich, *Why Milton Matters*, 191.

43. Ibid., 188, 192.

44. Lucy Hutchinson, *Order and Disorder*, ed. David Norbrook (Oxford, 2001), 9.11–14.

45. Andrew Marvell, *The First Anniversary of the Government under His Highness the Lord Protector, Poems*, rev. ed., ed. Nigel Smith (Harlow, UK, 2007), 289–96.

46. James Paterson, *A Complete Commentary, with Etymological, Critical, and Classical Notes on Milton's 'Paradise Lost'* (London, 1744), 483 [n. on 12.101]. Milton's association of Ham with Africa—Tunisia, in this case—is also indicated in *PL* 4.275–77, on which Paterson comments: '*Cham*, or *Ham*; *Heb.* i. e. *Heat* or *Blackness*. . . . In the first *Division* of the *Earth, Syria, Arabia, Egypt*, and all *Africa* fell to his Share.' See Stephen Jablonski, 'Ham's Vicious Race: Slavery and John Milton,' *Studies in English Literature, 1500–1900* 37 (1997): 173–90; and William McKee Evans, 'From the Land of Canaan to the Land of Guinea: The Strange Odyssey of the "Sons of Ham,"' *The American Historical Review* 85 (1980): 15–43; and Martin Dzelzainis, 'Milton and Slavery,' The Ninth International Milton Symposium (London, 2008).

47. Milton's liberty of 'the people,' as Paul A. Rahe observes, is in fact a defense of the 'aristocratic principle of differential moral and political rationality that had underpinned both theory and practice in ancient Greece and Rome'; see *Against Throne and Altar: Machiavelli and Political Theory under the English Republic* (Cambridge, 2008), 109. See also Quentin Skinner, *Liberty before Liberalism* (Cambridge, 1998); 'John Milton and the Politics of Slavery,' in *Milton and the Terms of Liberty*, ed. Graham Parry and Joad Raymond (Cambridge, 2002), 1–22; and Sharon Achinstein, 'Imperial Dialectic: Milton and Conquered Peoples,' in *Milton and the Imperial Vision*, ed. Balachandra Rajan and Elizabeth Sauer (Pittsburgh, Penn., 1999), esp. 73–74. Though turning its attention away from the slave

trade, Milton's *De doctrina Christiana* is no less unsettling in drawing conclusions from the Curse of Ham. Noah's example proves that 'the most just men have thought it right that a crime committed against them should be atoned for by the punishment not only of the criminal but also of his children'; precedent for that idea is found in Vergil and in Thucydides, and is associated with the right of war (*YP,* 6: 387–88).

48. Paul Stevens, 'Intolerance and the Virtues of Sacred Vehemence,' in *Milton and Toleration*, ed. Sharon Achinstein and Elizabeth Sauer (Oxford, 2007), 247.

49. Hugh Grady comes closest to the kind of approach I describe here; see his *Shakespeare's Universal Wolf: Studies in Early Modern Reification* (Oxford, 1996), 7. We can explore present concern while also respecting the limits of anachronism described in Glenn Burgess's 'The "Historical Turn" and the Political Culture of Early Modern England: Towards a Postmodern History?,' in *Neo-Historicism: Studies in Renaissance Literature, History and Politics*, ed. Robin Headlam Wells, Burgess, and Rowland Wymer, Studies in Renaissance Literature 5 (Cambridge, 2000), 36: 'If you do not reconstruct [the past] non-anachronistically, you construct only a version of your self, your prejudices, a version of the present. . . . To encounter the other, you must first grasp the nature of its otherness. And, for historians and for the past, the *only* way of doing that is to attempt descriptions that avoid anachronism.' Paul Stevens provides excellent models of reading later events through earlier ones in 'Spenser and the End of British Empire,' *Spenser Studies* 22 (2007): 5–26, and 'Bunyan, the Great War, and the Political Ways of Grace,' *Review of English Studies* n.s. 59 (2007): 701–21.

50. Walter Benjamin, 'Theses on the Philosophy of History,' in *Illuminations: Essays and Reflections*, ed. Hannah Arendt, trans. Harry Zohn, pref. Leon Wieseltier (New York, 2007), 257–58, 262–63.

CHAPTER ONE

1. Jonathan Rosen, 'Return to Paradise,' *The New Yorker,* 2 June 2008, accessed 23 June 2008, www.newyorker.com/arts/critics/atlarge/2008/06/02/080602crat_atlarge_rosen?printable=true.

2. Nigel Smith, *Is Milton Better than Shakespeare?* (Cambridge, Mass., 2008), 182.

3. Joseph Wittreich, *Why Milton Matters: A New Preface to His Writings* (New York, 2006), 172. See also questionings of the religiosity of Milton's vision among other acolytes of the 'New Milton Criticism': Michael Bryson, *The Tyranny of Heaven: Milton's Rejection of God as King* (Newark, 2004), 12; and Peter C. Herman, *Destabilizing Milton: 'Paradise Lost' and the Poetics of Incertitude* (New York, 2005).

4. See Gauri Viswanathan, 'Secularism in the Framework of Heterodoxy,' *PMLA* 123 (2008): 467.

5. The phrase '*revanche de Dieu*' is borrowed from Gilles Kepel's title, available as *The Revenge of God: The Resurgence of Islam, Christianity, and Judaism in the Modern World*, trans. Alan Braley (University Park, Penn., 1994). On the Anglican controversy, see Robert Piggott, 'Rival Meeting Deepens Anglican Rift,' *BBC News*, 22 June 2008, accessed 23 June 2008, news.bbc.co.uk/go/pr/fr/-/2/hi/middle_east/7468065.stm.

6. See 'Bishops Criticise Anglican Leader,' *BBC News*, 23 June 2008, accessed 23 June 2008, news.bbc.co.uk/go/pr/fr/-/2/hi/middle_east/7468474.stm; Riazatt Butt, 'Williams Accused of Leading Church into Crisis,' *The Guardian*, 23 June 2008, accessed 23 June 2008, www.guardian.co.uk/world/2008/jun/23/anglicanism.religion; Dina Kraft and Laurie Goodstein, 'Anglicans Face Wider Split over Policy toward Gays,' *The New York Times*, 30 June 2008, accessed 29 June 2008, www.nytimes.com/2008/06/30/world/30anglican.html; Paul Elie's engaging profile of Rowan Williams, 'The Velvet Reformation,' *The Atlantic* (March 2009): 72–80; and Garrett Keizer, 'Turning Away from Jesus: Gay Rights and the War for the Episcopal Church,' *Harper's Magazine* (June 2008), 39–50. The last of these is notable for quoting Gene Robinson at some length.

7. Epigraph to this section from Geoffrey Hill, *Style and Faith* (New York, 2003), xiv.

8. Joseph Addison, *Spectator*, 8 vols., Number 285, 26 January 1712 (London, 1712–15), 4: 196; Addison bases this remark in part on the use of 'Idioms of other Tongues,' which he finds especially in the 'Beginning' of the poem—that is, the first two books (195). Thomas Stearns Eliot, 'Milton II,' in *Selected Prose of T.S. Eliot*, ed. Frank Kermode (Boston, 1975), 268. See Christopher Ricks, *Milton's Grand Style* (Oxford, 1963), 27; and Arnold Stein, *Answerable Style* (1953; Seattle, 1967), 133.

9. James Burnet, Lord Monboddo, *Of the Origin and Progress of Language*, 6 vols. (Edinburgh, 1773–92), 2: 355–59. I am indebted to John Leonard for alerting me to this source, who is discussed in Leonard's forthcoming omnibus survey of critical response to *Paradise Lost*, prepared for Columbia's *Milton Variorum Commentary*, ed. P. J. Klemp.

10. Monboddo, *Of the Origin and Progress of Language*, 3: 143.

11. Ibid., 3: 51–52.

12. Unless otherwise indicated, references to Milton's shorter poems are to *Complete Shorter Poems*, ed. Stella P. Revard (Malden, Mass., 2009); references to *Paradise Lost* are to the Barbara K. Lewalski edition (Malden, Mass., 2007).

13. William Blake, *The Marriage of Heaven and Hell, Complete Writings*, ed. Geoffrey Keynes (Oxford, 1974), Plates 5–6; *Stardust Memories*, writer and dir. Woody Allen, perf. Woody Allen, Charlotte Rampling, Jessica Harper, and Marie-Christine Barrault (United Artists, 1980).

14. See Ezra Pound, *ABC of Reading* (New York, 1960), 51.

15. As Peter Berek claims, '[We] need to consider the Heavenly style not as a

failed attempt to equal the eloquence of the debate in Pandemonium, but as another kind of use of language'; see his '"Plain" and "Ornate" Styles and the Structure of *Paradise Lost*,' *PMLA* 85 (1970): 238; see also Irene Samuel, 'The Dialogue in Heaven: A Reconsideration of *Paradise Lost*, III. 1–417,' *PMLA* 72 (1957): 601–11.

16. Geoffrey Hill offers a reading of this passage on Abdiel in his lecture 'Milton as Muse,' delivered during *John Milton: The 400th Anniversary Celebrations*, The Lady Margaret Lectures 2008, Christ's College, Cambridge; podcast available at www.christs.cam.ac.uk/milton400/lectures.htm.

17. John Leonard, ed., *Paradise Lost* by John Milton (London, 2003), n. at 5.906.

18. Richard Bentley, ed., *Milton's 'Paradise Lost': A New Edition* (London, 1732), n. at 5.907.

19. Matthew Arnold, *Literature and Dogma: An Essay Towards a Better Apprehension of the Bible* (New York, 1883), 9. Berek similarly observes of God the Father's repetition that its effect is 'never to explore the wide range of possible meanings for ambiguous human language, but instead to insist on the sole relevance of a single, doctrinally correct meaning for each word'; see his '"Plain" and "Ornate" Styles,' 240.

20. Ricks, *Milton's Grand Style*, 36. On rhetorical elements in the language of God the Father, see Jackson I. Cope, *The Metaphoric Structure of 'Paradise Lost'* (Baltimore, 1962), esp. 174; and J. B. Broadbent, 'Milton's Rhetoric,' *Modern Philology* 56 (1959): esp. 230–31, 235–36.

21. Also like *Paradise Regained*, where Jesus' statements of plain truth conclude the second and third books, Abdiel's speech, and the commentary on it, are at the end of book 5. Such placement gains greater emphasis still by contrast with the chaotic instability that soon follows in the War in Heaven. The element of the ridiculous pervasive especially in the second day of battle casts the war in Heaven, as Arnold Stein (*Answerable Style*, 24) and others have observed, more in the realm of mock-epic than epic. The observation is taken up by Paul Stevens in 'Intolerance and the Virtues of Sacred Vehemence,' in *Milton and Toleration*, ed. Sharon Achinstein and Elizabeth Sauer (Oxford, 2007), 250.

22. See *OED* 'respite' *v.* 1 and 3, and 'reprieve' *v.* 1 and 4.

23. See ibid., 'pity' *v.* 2.

24. See the entry, ibid., for 'Manna,' 3 and 8. Cf. the careful biblicism of Jesus' use of the word in *Paradise Regained*: 'Man lives not by Bread only, but each Word/Proceeding from the mouth of God; who fed/Our Fathers here with Manna' (1.349–51).

25. Lucan, *The Civil War*, trans. J. D. Duff, Loeb Classical Library (New York, 1928), 1.299–313. See William W. Batstone, 'A Narrative Gestalt and the Force of Caesar's Style,' *Mnemosyne*, ser. 4, 44 (1991): 126.

26. Cicero, *Brutus*, trans. G. L. Hendrickson, *Brutus and Orator*, Loeb Classical Library (Cambridge, Mass., 1942), 253, 258.

27. Ibid., 262.
28. Cicero, *Orator*, trans. H. M. Hubbell, *Brutus and Orator*, 76, 77, 79.
29. Ibid., 79, 81.
30. Ibid., 84–85.
31. Kenneth J. E. Graham, *The Performance of Conviction* (Ithaca, NY, 1994), 5–7.
32. John Calvin, *Institutes of the Christian Religion*, trans. Henry Beveridge (Grand Rapids, Mich., 1997), 1: 71–73 [I.vii. 4–5].
33. See Perry Miller, 'The Plain Style,' in *The New-England Mind: The Seventeenth Century* (New York, 1939); Jackson I. Cope, 'Seventeenth-Century Quaker Style,' *PMLA* 71 (1956): 725–54; John R. Knott, Jr., *The Sword of the Spirit: Puritan Responses to the Bible* (Chicago, 1980).
34. George Converse Fiske, *Lucilius and Horace: A Study in the Classical Theory of Imitation* (1920; Westport, Conn., 1971), 78–79.
35. Andrew Shifflett, *Stoicism, Politics, and Literature in the Age of Milton: War and Peace Reconciled* (Cambridge, 1998), 132 and 137.
36. On *urbanitas*, see Fiske, *Lucilius and Horace*, 84–85, 124–25; on Jonson, see William Trimpi, *Ben Jonson's Poems: A Study of the Plain Style* (Stanford, Calif., 1962).
37. John Keats, 'Lines on Seeing a Lock of Milton's Hair,' in *The Poems of John Keats*, ed. Jack Stillinger (Cambridge, Mass., 1978), 13.
38. Victoria Kahn, 'Aesthetics as Critique: Tragedy and *Trauerspiel* in *Samson Agonistes*,' in *Reading Renaissance Ethics*, ed. Marshall Grossman (New York, 2007), 104; see also Nicholas von Maltzahn, 'The War in Heaven and the Miltonic Sublime,' in *A Nation Transformed: England after the Restoration*, ed. Alan Houston and Steve Pincus (Cambridge, 2001), esp. 165.
39. Kahn, 'Aesthetics as Critique,' 109; cf. Walter Benjamin, *The Origin of German Tragic Drama*, intr. George Steiner, trans. John Osborne (1998; pbk. London, 2003), 80–86.
40. Kahn, 'Aesthetics as Critique,' 110.
41. Ibid., 116.
42. Epigraph from Alain Badiou, 'Democracy, Politics, and Philosophy,' Seminar presented at the European Graduate School, 1 May 2006, European Graduate School Video, 12 May 2007, accessed 29 October 2008, www.youtube.com/watch?v=5-gjz2yORJk.
43. Michael Hardt and Antonio Negri, *Multitude: War and Democracy in the Age of Empire* (New York, 2004), xi.
44. Walt Whitman, *Song of Myself, Leaves of Grass*, 150th Anniversary Edition, intr. Harold Bloom (London, 2005), chant 24; Theodor W. Adorno, *The Jargon of Authenticity*, trans. Knut Tarnowski and Frederic Will (Evanston, Ill., 1973), 6.
45. Hardt and Negri, *Empire* (Cambridge, Mass., 2000), 21 and 413.
46. Hardt and Negri, *Multitude*, 211; italics in original.

47. Paul Rabinow and Nikolas Rose, 'Biopower Today,' *Biosocieties* 1 (2006): 199.

48. Such emphasis on affirmation is most clearly expressed in Deleuze's *Nietzsche and Philosophy*, foreword Michael Hardt, trans. Hugh Tomlinson (New York, 2006), 23–24: 'For there is no being beyond becoming, nothing beyond multiplicity. . . . Multiplicity is the inseparable manifestation, essential transformation and constant symptom of unity. Multiplicity is the affirmation of unity; becoming is the affirmation of being. . . . Multiple affirmation is the way in which the one affirms itself.' See also Deleuze's *Pure Immanence*, intr. John Rajchman, trans. Anne Boyman (New York, 2001), esp. 74.

49. Hardt and Negri, *Multitude*, xvi.

50. Ibid., 65.

51. Hardt and Negri, *Commonwealth* (Cambridge, Mass., 2009), 40.

52. Avishai Margalit, 'Sectarianism,' *Dissent Magazine* (Winter 2008): 40, 42.

53. Tom Nairn, 'Make for the Boondocks,' rev. of *Multitude*, by Michael Hardt and Antonio Negri, *London Review of Books*, 5 May 2005, 6, accessed 16 June 2008, www.lrb.co.uk/v27/n09/print/nair01_.html. Page references are to a printout of this online source. For this reference I am indebted to Matt Hart and his entry in *Kritik,* the blog of the Illinois Unit for Criticism and Interpretive Theory, accessed 7 February 2008, unitcrit.blogspot.com/2008/02/being-medium-ten-paragraphs-on-national.html.

54. Slavoj Žižek, 'The Descent of Transcendence into Immanence, or, Deleuze as a Hegelian,' in *Transcendence: Philosophy, Literature, and Theology Approach the Beyond*, ed. Regina Schwartz (New York, 2004), 235–36.

55. Nairn, 'Make for the Boondocks,' 4.

56. Ibid., 6.

57. Ibid., 10.

58. Nairn, *Faces of Nationalism: Janus Revisited* (London, 1997), 25.

59. Ibid., 27; and 'Make for the Boondocks,' 12, 13.

60. Kenneth Graham makes similar claims in his discussion of conviction: '[T]he epistemological stalemate in which plainness participates may lead to a contest of wills. In this contest, language loses its rhetorical dimension as a realm in which truth is discovered (or perhaps manufactured) and decisions are made, leading to action; instead, the performance of conviction, insofar as it is truly antirhetorical, confuses language both with truth and with power. Truth and power consequently collapse into each other, and ethical value disappears both from the individual and from the public world' (221).

61. See my 'Globe of Villages: Digital Media and the Rise of Homegrown Terrorism,' *Dissent Magazine* (Winter 2007): 61–64; the argument for the Internet fostering a divorce of ideology and geography is developed by Kenneth Payne in 'Winning the Battle of Ideas: Propaganda, Ideology, and Terror,' *Studies in Conflict and Terrorism* 32 (2009): 114–15.

62. McLuhan's 1943 Cambridge dissertation has recently been made available in print as *The Classical Trivium*, ed. W. Terrence Gordon (Corte Madera, Calif., 2006).

63. Arianna Huffington, interview with Charlie Rose, *The Charlie Rose Show*, PBS, 4 December 2008, accessed 23 March 2009, www.charlierose.com/view/interview/9705.

64. This derisive laughter in the *Animadversions* is a non-response to Hall's quite defensible claim that 'no one Clergie in the whole Christian world yeelds so many eminent schollers, learned preachers, grave, holy, and accomplish'd Divines as this Church of *England* doth at this day' (*YP*, 1: 726).

65. Alain Badiou, *Saint Paul: The Foundation of Universalism*, trans. Ray Brassier, Cultural Memory in the Present (Stanford, Calif., 2003), 7; see also the perceptive engagement of issues surrounding identity politics in Hardt and Negri's *Commonwealth*, esp. 325–44.

66. Alain Badiou, *Saint Paul: La fondation de l'universalisme* (Paris, 1997), 13 (italics original): 'If, as we believe, only truths (thought) allow man to be distinguished from the human animal that underlies him, it is no exaggeration to say that such minoritarian pronouncements are genuinely *barbaric*' (Brassier trans. 12).

67. Badiou, *Saint Paul*, 10.

68. 'PRIZM NE Segmentation System,' *My Best Segments*, Neilsen Claritas Inc., accessed 26 March 2009, www.claritas.com/MyBestSegments/Default.jsp?ID=30&idi=2000.

69. Alain Badiou, *Being and Event*, trans. Oliver Feltham (New York, 2005), 329–30; the corresponding pages in the French original, *L'être et l'événement* (Paris, 1988), are 363–64.

70. Roland Boer, *Political Myth: On the Use and Abuse of Biblical Themes* (Durham, NC, 2009), 14.

71. Badiou, *Saint Paul*, 4–5.

72. Ibid., 18–19.

73. Ibid., 28.

74. Ibid., 33.

75. Ibid., 101–4.

76. Regina M. Schwartz, *The Curse of Cain: The Violent Legacy of Monotheism* (Chicago, 1997), 33 (italics in original). See also Schwartz's similar statement, and skeptical handling of Badiou, in *Sacramental Poetics at the Dawn of Secularism: When God Left the World*, Cultural Memory in the Present (Stanford, Calif., 2008), 140 and 177n3.

77. The phrase 'immanent break' appears in Badiou's *Ethics*, trans. Peter Hallward (London, 2001), where he explains that a truth is '"Immanent" because a truth proceeds *in* the situation, and nowhere else—there is no heaven of truths. "Break" because what enables the truth-process—the event—meant nothing ac-

cording to the prevailing language and established knowledge of the situation' (42–43; italics in original); for the examples of 'truths' cited here, see Badiou, *Being and Event*, 17.

78. Berek, '"Plain" and "Ornate" Styles,' 241.

79. Douglas Bush, *The Renaissance and English Humanism*, The Alexander Lectures (1939; Toronto, 1965), 102.

CHAPTER TWO

1. Peter Hallward, Translator's Introduction to Alain Badiou, *Ethics*, trans. Peter Hallward, Wos es War (London, 2001), vii. Hallward's remark is justified by the flood of works in philosophy concerning themselves with ethics, for example, James Gordon Finlayson, 'Adorno on the Ethical and the Ineffable,' *European Journal of Philosophy* 10 (2002): 1–25; Raymond Geuss, 'Outside Ethics,' *European Journal of Philosophy* 11 (2003): 29–53; Victor J. Krebs, '"Around the Axis of Our Real Need": On the Ethical Point of Wittgenstein's Philosophy,' *European Journal of Philosophy* 9 (2001): 344–74; Emmanuel Lévinas, *Humanism of the Other*, trans. Nidra Poller (Urbana, Ill., 2006); John Skoropuski, *Ethical Explorations* (Oxford, 2000); Martin Stokhof, *World and Life as One: Ethics and Ontology in Wittgenstein's Early Thought* (Stanford, Calif., 2002).

2. Paul de Man, *Allegories of Reading: Figural Language in Rousseau, Nietzsche, Rilke, and Proust* (New Haven, 1979), 206.

3. J. Hillis Miller, *The Ethics of Reading: Kant, De Man, Eliot, Trollope, James, and Benjamin*, The Welleck Library Lectures at the University of California, Irvine (New York, 1987), 51; cf. role of 'knowledge' on 48, which seems to suggest possibility of ethical act arising from 'knowledge.'

4. See Aristotle, *Nicomachean Ethics*, Loeb Classical Library, 617 [X.vii.7–8]; further references in parentheses.

5. Sigmund Freud, *The Interpretation of Dreams*, *The Basic Writings of Sigmund Freud*, trans. A. A. Brill (New York: 1938), 206 [ch. 2].

6. Jacques Derrida, 'Plato's Pharmacy,' in *Dissemination*, trans. Barbara Johnson (Chicago, 1981), 110–11.

7. In what follows, I am most indebted to the readings of *Areopagitica* in Stanley Fish, 'Driving from the Letter: Truth and Indeterminacy in *Areopagitica*,' in *Re-Membering Milton*, ed. Mary Nyquist and Margaret W. Ferguson (New York, 1987), 234–54; Nigel Smith, '*Areopagitica*: Voicing Contexts, 1643–45,' in *Politics, Poetics, and Hermeneutics in Milton's Prose*, ed. David Loewenstein and James Grantham Turner (Cambridge, 1990), 103–22; and esp. Christopher Kendrick, *Milton: A Study in Ideology and Form* (New York, 1986), 19–51.

8. For a few examples, see Derrida, 'Plato's Pharmacy'; Gayatri C. Spivak's Introduction to *Of Grammatology*, by Jacques Derrida (1976; Baltimore, 1998); and Sandra M. Gilbert and Susan Gubar's *Madwoman in the Attic* (New Haven, 1979), 5ff.

9. Herbert Palmer, *The Glasse of Gods Providence toward His Faithfull Ones*

(London, 1644; Wing P235), 57. See William Riley Parker, *Milton: A Biography*, 2nd ed., ed. Gordon Campbell (Oxford, 2003), 1: 263–64.

10. See Milton's references to polygamy in the Commonplace Book, *YP,* 1: 397, 400, 411–13. Alan Rudrum, 'Polygamy in *Paradise Lost,*' *Essays in Criticism* 20 (1970): 18–23; and Leo Miller, *John Milton among the Polygamophiles* (New York, 1974).

11. James Joyce, *Ulysses: The 1922 Text,* ed. Jeri Johnson, The World's Classics (Oxford, 1993), 199.

12. Jacques Lacan, *The Ethics of Psychoanalysis, The Seminar* VII, trans. Dennis Porter (New York, 1992), 76; I adjust here Lacan's definition of the encounter between the subject and *das Ding,* which he describes in terms of the pleasure principle (52).

13. The observation is Martin Dzelzainis's in the Introduction to *Political Writings,* by John Milton, Cambridge Texts in the History of Political Thought (Cambridge, 1991), xx.

14. Lana Cable, *Carnal Rhetoric: Milton's Iconoclasm and the Poetics of Desire* (Durham, NC, 1995), 127; see also Stephen M. Fallon, *Milton's Peculiar Grace: Self-Representation and Authority* (Ithaca, NY, 2007), esp. 142–45.

15. Edmund Spenser, *The Faerie Queene,* ed. A. C. Hamilton et al., Longman Annotated English Poets (Harlow, UK, 2001), 2.12.68–69.

16. Ludwig Wittgenstein, *Philosophical Investigations: The German Text with a Revised English Translation,* trans. G. E. M. Anscombe (Malden, Mass., 2001), esp. par. 269.

17. See *YP,* 2: 545: 'These are the fruits which a dull ease and cessation of our knowledge will bring forth.'

18. Thomas Fulton, '*Areopagitica* and the Roots of Liberal Epistemology,' *English Literary Renaissance* 34 (2004): 44.

19. Ibid., 48.

20. Ibid., 53.

21. Robinson, Fulton observes, argues that 'a person's understanding and apprehension are better disposed when given the freedom to choose,' Walwyn that 'a belief that enters a person's judgment by some means other than free reason (coercion or conformity) is epistemologically inferior,' thus both anticipate the claim in *Areopagitica* that intolerance 'is a violation of conditions that are essential to the possession of knowledge' (ibid., 58–59).

22. Ibid., 76.

23. Smith, '*Areopagitica,*' 107, 109–11.

24. Fulton, '*Areopagitica* and the Roots of Liberal Epistemology,' 58–59.

25. Phillip J. Donnelly, *Milton's Scriptural Reasoning* (Cambridge, 2009), vii, 32.

26. Fulton, '*Areopagitica* and the Roots of Liberal Epistemology,' 66.

27. Alain Badiou, *Being and Event,* trans. Oliver Feltham (London, 2005), 329–30; and Badiou, *Ethics,* 41.

28. Badiou, *Ethics,* 52; my square brackets.

29. See ibid., 28.

30. 'Wherever there is the performative, whatever the form of communication,' Derrida claims, 'there is a context of legitimate, legitimizing, or legitimated convention that permits it to neutralize what happens, that is the brute eventness of the arrivant ... if in a certain manner performativity encounters the event produced by language, it is also that which neutralizes the eventness of the event'; see Derrida, 'Performative Powerlessness—A Response to Simon Critchley,' trans. James Ingram, in *Derrida-Habermas Reader,* ed. Lasse Thomassen (Chicago, 2006), 112.

31. Ibid., 113.

32. Simon Critchley, 'Frankfurt Impromptu—Remarks on Derrida and Habermas,' in *Derrida-Habermas Reader,* 99.

33. Derrida, 'The Last of the Rogue States: The "Democracy to Come," Opening in Two Turns,' trans. Pascale-Anne Brault and Michael Naas, *The South Atlantic Quarterly* 103 (2004): 329, 330, and 331; this article is a translation of ch. 8 of *Voyous* (Paris, 2003), available as *Rogues: Two Essays on Reason* (Stanford, Calif., 2005).

34. Emmanual Lévinas, *Totality and Infinity,* trans. Alphonso Lingis (Pittsburgh, Penn., 1969). For a clear-sighted account of Lévinas and Benjamin on ethics, see Annabel Herzog, 'Levinas, Benjamin, and the Oppressed,' *The Journal of Jewish Thought and Philosophy* 12 (2003): 123–38.

35. Sharon Achinstein and Marshall Grossman, 'An Exchange Passing through the *Areopagitica,*' in *Reading Renaissance Ethics,* ed. Marshall Grossman (New York, 2007), 263.

36. Slavoj Žižek, *Iraq: The Borrowed Kettle* (New York, 2004), 1–4.

37. As an epigraph to his essay on *Areopagitica,* Nigel Smith provides a passage from Jean Baudrillard's *Mirror of Production*: 'In these instances [of revolution], there is speech before history, before politics, before truth, speech before the separation and the future totality.'

38. Terry Eagleton, 'Lenin in the Postmodern Age,' in *Lenin Reloaded: Toward a Politics of Truth,* ed. Sebastian Budgen, Stathis Kouvelakis, and Slavoj Žižek, SIC 7 (Durham, NC, 2007), 47.

39. Kendrick, *Milton,* 37.

40. On this *volte face* between the two editions of *The Tenure,* see Martin Dzelzainis, Introduction to *Political Writings,* xviii–xix.

41. 'Warrant issued to John Milton, 1650,' Rare Book & Manuscript Library, University of Illinois. An image of this warrant is available in Valerie Hotchkiss and Fred C. Robinson, *English in Print: From Caxton to Shakespeare to Milton* (Urbana, Ill., 2008), 104.

42. C[rawford] B[rough] Macpherson, *The Political Theory of Possessive Individualism: Hobbes to Locke* (1962; Oxford, 1979), 3; see also 263–64, and Joseph H. Carens, ed., *Democracy and Possessive Individualism: The Intellectual Legacy of C.B.*

Macpherson (Albany, NY, 1993). 'Possessive Individualism' is also described in the entry for 'Liberal' in Raymond Williams, *Keywords* (1976; London, 1993).

43. Sir Walter Raleigh, *Milton* (London, 1900), 41.

44. See, for example, Blair Hoxby, *Mammon's Music: Literature and Economics in the Age of Milton* (New Haven, 2002), 25–56.

45. For such statements on the liberty of the wise, see esp. *YP,* 2: 487, 489, 521, and 531.

46. Derrida, *Politics of Friendship*, trans. G. Coffins (London, 1997), 42; see Critchley, 'Frankfurt Impromptu,' 100.

47. Derrida, 'The Last of the Rogue States,' 323–41.

48. Critchley, 'Frankfurt Impromptu,' 109.

49. Derrida and Lieven de Cauter, 'For a Justice to Come: An Interview with Jacques Derrida,' in *The Derrida-Habermas Reader*, 268.

50. Badiou, *Ethics*, liii.

51. Ibid., 11.

52. Badiou, *Logics of Worlds: Being and Event II* [*Logiques des mondes*, 2006], trans. Alberto Toscano (London, 2009), 4.

53. Badiou, *Ethics*, 4.

54. Žižek, *In Defense of Lost Causes* (London, 2008), 114; for a perceptive critique of the authoritarian Marxism endorsed by Žižek, see Alan Johnson's review of *In Defense of Lost Causes* in *Dissent Magazine* (Fall 2009): 122–27.

55. Michael Hardt and Antonio Negri, *Commonwealth* (Cambridge, Mass., 2009), 36.

56. Michel Foucault, 'What Are the Iranians Dreaming About?,' *Le Nouvel Observateur,* 16–22 October 1978, in *Foucault and the Iranian Revolution: Gender and the Seductions of Islamism,* ed. Janet Afary and Kevin B. Anderson (Chicago, 2005), 206. In their indispensable book Afary and Anderson provide as an appendix all of Foucault's journalism on Iran and some key responses to it.

57. Salman Rushdie, *The Satanic Verses* (1988; New York, 1997), 376.

58. Afary and Anderson, *Foucault and the Iranian Revolution*, 143.

59. See ibid., 82, 123, and esp. Maxime Rodinson's critique of Foucault on 99–102 and 223–38.

60. Foucault, 'The Mythical Leader of the Iranian Revolt,' *Corriere della Serra,* 26 November 1978, in ibid., 222.

61. On Foucault's conflicts with feminist thinkers, see Margaret A. McLaren, *Feminism, Foucault and Embodied Subjectivity* (Albany, 2002), 1–18; and Irene Diamond and Lee Quinby, eds., *Feminism and Foucault: Reflections on Resistance* (Boston, 1988).

62. Foucault, 'What Are the Iranians Dreaming About?,' 206.

63. Afary and Anderson, *Foucault and the Iranian Revolution*, 73–74; see also Nikki R. Keddie, *Modern Iran: Roots and Results of Revolution*, rev. ed. (New Haven, 2006), 145, 167, 229–30, 257.

64. 'Atoussa H.,' 'An Iranian Woman Writes,' *Le Nouvel Observateur,* 6 November 1978, in Afary and Anderson, *Foucault and the Iranian Revolution,* 209.

65. Foucault, response to 'Atoussa H.,' *Le Nouvel Observateur,* 13 November 1978, in ibid., 210.

66. Foucault, 'Open Letter to Prime Minister Mehdi Bazargan,' *Le Nouvel Observateur,* 14 April 1979, in ibid., 261; see also 11–13 and the speech by Simone de Beauvoir available at 246–47.

67. Critchley, *Infinitely Demanding: Ethics of Commitment, Politics of Resistance* (London, 2007), 49.

68. 'Dialogue between Michel Foucault and Baqir Parham,' *Nameh-yi Kanun-i Nevisandegan* 1 (Spring 1979): 9–17, in Afary and Anderson, *Foucault and the Iranian Revolution,* 187.

69. Derrida, 'The Last of the Rogue States,' 332.

70. Badiou, *Ethics,* 10.

71. Gayatri Chakravorty Spivak, *A Critique of Postcolonial Reason: Toward a History of the Vanishing Present* (Cambridge, Mass., 1999), 399.

72. Spivak, *Other Asias* (Malden, Mass., 2008), 42.

73. Ibid., 23.

74. See ibid., 30: '[S]ocialism belongs to those axiomatics ... Yet, that the impulse to redistribute is based on training, and that an education without the humanities to train the imagination cannot foster the redistributive impulse, has been forgotten.' See also Spivak's comments on suturing 'the habits of democracy on to the earlier subject formation' (40).

75. See Krebs, '"Around the Axis of Our Real Need,"' 344–74.

76. Qtd. in ibid., 346.

77. Ludwig Wittgenstein, *Tractatus Logico-Philosophicus,* trans. C. K. Ogden, intr. Bertrand Russell (1961; London, 1974), 74.

78. Ibid., 11 [3.032].

CHAPTER THREE

1. Michael Walzer, *Politics and Passion: Toward a More Egalitarian Liberalism* (New Haven, 2004), 110–11, 126. See Walzer's 'Communitarian Critique of Liberalism,' *Political Theory* 18 (1990): 6–23, reprinted as the appendix of *Politics and Passion.* Richard Bellamy, *Liberalism and Pluralism: Towards a Politics of Compromise* (New York, 1999); Robert B. Talisse, *Democracy after Liberalism: Pragmatism and Deliberative Politics* (New York, 2005); Paul Edward Gottfried, *After Liberalism: Mass Democracy in the Managerial State,* New Forum Books 3 (Princeton, 1999).

2. Paul W. Kahn, *Putting Liberalism in Its Place* (Princeton, 2005), 1.

3. Ibid., 9. See also Kahn, *Out of Eden: Adam and Eve and the Problem of Evil* (Princeton, 2007), 180: 'The popular sovereign truly emerges when all members of the polity can experience the pain of politics. This is not a matter of extending

the franchise but of a revolution in the political imagination.' For analysis of the tension between law and sovereignty as it presents itself in the reciprocal relationship between terror and torture, see Kahn's *Sacred Violence: Torture, Terror, and Sovereignty* (Ann Arbor, 2008), esp. ch. 5.

4. See Slavoj Žižek, *For They Know Not What They Do: Enjoyment as a Political Factor* (London, 1991), 268; Kahn, *Putting Liberalism in Its Place*, 16, 18. Michel Foucault makes similar claims in his analysis of American neo-liberalism in *The Birth of Biopolitics: Lectures at the Collège de France 1978–79*, ed. Michel Senellart, trans. Graham Burchell (Houndmills, UK, 2008), 217–18.

5. Leon Wieseltier, 'Washington Diarist: That Night,' *The New Republic*, 19 November 2008: 48.

6. Sean Penn, 'Conversations with Chávez and Castro,' *The Nation*, 15 December 2008: 20; Michael Walzer, 'The Day After: Beginning Again,' *Dissent Up-Front*, 5 November 2008, accessed 8 January 2009, www.dissentmagazine.org/online.php?id=157.

7. See 'The Choice 2008,' *Frontline*, WGBH/PBS, transcript, posted 22 October 2008, accessed 20 November 2009, www.pbs.org/wgbh/pages/frontline/choice2008/etc/script.html.

8. Walzer, 'The Day After.'

9. Kahn, *Putting Liberalism in Its Place*, 68.

10. Ibid., 74, 77; for a historical overview of the Christian and liberal traditions of religious toleration, and discussion of their present-day legal implications, see Rex Ahdar and Ian Leigh, *Religious Freedom in the Liberal State* (Oxford, 2005), chs. 1–2.

11. See Thomas Kranidas, *Milton and the Rhetoric of Zeal* (Pittsburgh, Penn., 2005), 58.

12. Stella P. Revard, 'Milton and Millenarianism: From the *Nativity Ode* to *Paradise Regained*,' in *Milton and the Ends of Time*, ed. Juliet Cummins (Cambridge, 2003), 47–48; Susanne Woods describes the prose of the 1640s and of 1659–60 in terms similar to the ones I use here; see her '"That Freedom of Discussion Which I Loved": Italy and Milton's Cultural Self Definition,' in *Milton in Italy: Contexts, Images, Contradictions*, ed. Mario A. Di Cesare (Binghamton, NY, 1991), esp. 11, and 'Elective Poetics and Milton's Prose: *A Treatise of Civil Power* and *Considerations Touching the Likeliest Means to Remove Hirelings Out of the Church*,' in *Politics, Poetics, and Hermeneutics in Milton's Prose*, ed. David Loewenstein and James Grantham Turner (Cambridge, 1990), esp. 198–99.

13. Examples of such reports, all printed by Thomas Simmons, are Francis Gawler, *A Record of Some Persecutions Inflicted upon Some of the Servants of the Lord in South-Wales* (London, 1659; Wing G396); Edward Burrough, *A Declaration of the Present Sufferings of Above 140 . . . Called Quakers* (London, [23 April] 1659; Wing B5993); *To the Parliament of England. . . A Narrative of the Cruel, and Unjust Sufferings of the People of God in the Nation of Ireland* (London, 1659; Wing T1581).

Printed by Giles Calvert is *To the Parliament of England now Sitting in Westminster. Being a Brief Accompt Taken out of the Multitude of the Cruel Grievous and Bloody Sufferings and Persecutions of the People of God (called Quakers)* (London, 1659; Wing T1579A).

14. *Journal of the House of Commons*, vol. 7: 1651–1660 (London, 1802), 640, available at <www.british-history.ac.uk/catalogue.asp?gid=43>.

15. George Fox, *This is For You Who Are Called the Comon-Wealths-Men Both in the Army and Parliament* (London [printed for Simmons], 1659; Wing F2011), 4, 7.

16. George Fox, *Honest, Upright, Faithful, and Plain Dealing With Thee O Army of the Common-Wealth of England (So called)* (London [printed for Simmons], 1659; Wing F2005A), 7, 8.

17. Ibid., 9.

18. George Fox the Younger, *An Answer to Doctor Burgess his Book* (London [printed for Simmons], 1659; Wing F1743), 16, see also 41; Fox comments in this tract on the persecution resulting from tithing (17–18), and on the roots of the practice in the Hebrew Bible and the Roman church (19). For Milton's statement on university training in *Hirelings*, see *YP*, 7: 315–16.

19. See Edward Burrough, *To the Rulers and to Such as are in Authority* (London [printed for Simmons], 1659; Wing B6040A), 9; and *To the Parliament of the Common-Wealth of England, Who are in Place of Authority to do Justice* (London, 1659; Wing B6039). The latter tract, dated by Burrough 'the 6. of 8.mon. [that is, October] 1659,' does not indicate a printer.

20. See Burrough, *To the Parliament of the Common-Wealth of England, the Present Authority of these Nations assembled at Westminster* (London [printed for Simmons], 1659; Wing B6038A); *A Faithful Testimony Concerning the True Worship of God* (London [printed for Simmons], 1659; Wing B6002), 5; *A Discovery of Some Part of the War Between the Kingdom of the Lamb and the Kingdom of Antichrist* (London [printed for Robert Wilson], 1659; Wing B5999A), 11 and 12; and *A Declaration from the People Called Quakers* (London [printed for Simmons], 1659; Wing B5990), 5. See also *To All Freinds [sic] and People in the Whole Christendome* ([London, printed for Wilson, 1658]; Wing T1321), 17; William Bayly, *The Blood of Righteous Abel* (London [printed '3 month 4 day' for M.W.], 1659; Wing B1519), 4; John Crook, *Tythes no Property to, Nor Lawful Maintenance for a Powerful Gospel-Preaching Ministry* (London [printed for Simmons], 1659; Wing C7214bA), 3 and 10. [George Fox the Younger], *A Paper Sent Forth into the World from them that Are Scornfully Called Quakers* ([London, printed for Simmons, 1659]; Wing F1876), 8; Gawler, *A Record of Some Persecutions*, 28; Thomas Greene, *An Alarm to the False Shepheards* (London [printed for Wilson], 1660 [described by author as 'received from the Lord, the 24th. of the 12th. month 1659']; Wing G1839), 4 and 6.

21. See Job 7.1–2 and 14.6. Milton uses 'hire' in *A Reason of Church Government* (*YP*, 1: 769) and 'hireling' in *An Apology Against a Pamphlet* (*YP*, 1: 888). Also

relevant is Roger Williams, *The Hireling Ministry None of Christs* (London, 1652; Wing W2765). The first relevant use of the term 'hireling' cited in the *OED* is found in the 1582 Rhemist New Testament's rendition of John 10.13: 'The hireling fleeth because he is a hireling.' Wycliffe had used 'hirid hyne,' Tyndale 'heyred servaunt.' The AV/KJV adopts the Rhemist usage: 'The hireling fleeth, because he is a hireling, and careth not for the sheep.'

22. Burrough, *A Faithful Testimony*, 7 and 5.

23. Burrough, *To the Parliament . . . the Present Authority*.

24. Edward Burrough, *A Message to the Present Rulers of England. Whether Committee of Safety; (so called) Councell of Officers, or Others Whatsoever* (London [printed for Calvert], 1659; Wing B6015), 2; see also the direct appeal to eliminate tithes on 13 (misnumbered 11).

25. See John Anderson, *To Those that Sit in Counsel for Ordering the Affairs of the Nation* (London [printed for Simmons], 1659; Wing A3083), esp. 1; Bayley, *Blood of Righteous Abel*, esp. 1 and 4–5; Ester Biddle, *A Warning from the Lord God of Life and Power* (London [printed for Wilson], 1660 [p. 18 gives date of composition as '16th of the 12th moneth, 1659]; Wing B2866), *passim*; John Chandler, *A Narrative Plainly Shewing* (London [printed for the author], 1659; Wing C1927B), esp. 1, 10–11, and 15; and Dorothy White, *This to be Delivered to the Counsellors that are Sitting in Counsel* (London [printed for Simmons], 1659; Wing W1753), *passim*.

26. Sir Henry Vane, *The Retired Mans Meditations, or the Mysterie and Power of Godliness* (London, 1655; Wing V75), 184, 211.

27. Henry Stubbe, *A Light Shining out of Darkness* (London, 1659; Wing S6056); David Hawkes, 'The Concept of the "Hireling" in Milton's Theology,' *Milton Studies* 43 (2004): 76–77.

28. For the proceedings of Richard's Parliament, see *Journal of the House of Commons*, 7: 588–644.

29. See also *YP*, 1: 615–16, 704–5, and 941.

30. Crook, *Tythes no Property*, 5 and 11.

31. Ibid., 8.

32. Ibid., 1. Crook draws directly on Coke on p. 4.

33. Ibid., 4.

34. See, for example, *Eikonoklastes* 28: 'Next in order to the laws of *Moses*, are those of *Christ*, who declares professedly his judicature to be spiritual, abstract from Civil managements, and therefore leaves all nations to their own particular Lawes, and way of Government. . . . From hence, not to be tedious, I shall pass into our own land of Britain; and shew that Subjects heer have exercis'd the utmost of spirituall Judicature and more then spirituall against thir Kings, his Predecessors' (*YP*, 3: 587).

35. Though I cite here the second edition of *The Readie and Easie Way*, I deal with proposals also running through its immediate predecessors: the first edition

of *The Readie and Easie Way, A Letter to a Friend*, and *Proposalls of Certaine Expedients*.

36. See *Journal of the House of Commons*, 7: 796–97: 'The Question being propounded, That the Regiments of Colonel Morley and Colonel Okey, and so many of Colonel Mosse his Regiment, as attended at Paul's, be, and are hereby, required to guard the Parliament, and Places hereabout, this Night; And the Question being put, That this Question be now put; It passed with the Negative.'

37. See *Journal of the House of Commons* 7: 715: '[T]he Council conceive it necessary, that a Proclamation be issued, prohibiting all Horse-races, Cock-matches, Bullbaitings, Hurlings, and other Meetings of like Nature, as being a Means to colour the Designs of such as endeavour or intend the Disturbance of the publick Peace.'

38. For the debate on Milton's 'rejection' of Cromwell, see Martin Dzelzainis, 'Milton and the Protectorate in 1658,' in *Milton and Republicanism*, ed. David Armitage, Armand Himy, and Quentin Skinner, Ideas in Context (1995; Cambridge, 1998), 181–205; and Paul Stevens, 'Milton's "Renunciation" of Cromwell: The Problem of Raleigh's Cabinet-Council,' *Modern Philology* 98 (2001): 363–92. On Moses Wall, see also Nicholas von Maltzahn, 'Making Use of the Jews: Milton and Philo-Semitism,' in *Milton and the Jews*, ed. Douglas A. Brooks (Cambridge, 2008), 64–67.

39. James Harrington, *A Discourse Upon this Saying. . .* , *Political Works*, ed. J. G. A. Pocock, Cambridge Studies in the History and Theory of Politics (Cambridge, 1977), 742.

40. On the Ciceronian and Senecan elements in *Of Education*, see Martin Dzelzainis, 'Milton's Classical Republicanism,' in *Milton and Republicanism*, 12–13.

41. See ibid., 17; and Quentin Skinner, 'John Milton and the Politics of Slavery,' in *Milton and the Terms of Liberty*, ed. Graham Parry and Joad Raymond, Studies in Renaissance Literature 7 (Cambridge, 2002), 1–22.

42. For this sentiment in the *Second Defence*, see *YP*, 4: 636; in *The Readie and Easie Way*, *YP*, 7: 415–17 and 455.

43. See *Commons Journal*, 7: 805 [9 January 1660], 812 [14 January], 828 [1 February], 835 [6 February], 841 [13 February]. See also *YP*, 7: 132, though Woolrych overstates the reluctance of Vane, Ludlow, and Selwey. Ludlow's memoirs indicate fairly ready acquiescence to Lambert: '[We] met in one of the council-chambers at Whitehall, where Col. Lambert in the first place demanded of me, if I could give him my hand. I answered, that tho according to my information his part in the late action appeared to me very inwarrantable; yet if it might make me more capable of serving the publick, and recommend my endeavours for the peace of the nation, and the reconciliation of the differences among us, I could not only give him my hand but my heart also' (*Ludlow's Memoirs*, 2 vols., ed. C. H. Firth, [Oxford, 1894], 2: 143).

44. '*In domo justi viventis ex fide, etiam qui imperant, serviunt iis, quibus videntur imperare*' (*YP*, 4: 1133). See the catalogue of variants in the London editions of the *Defence* provided as Appendix F in volume 4 of *YP*.

45. Kahn, *Putting Liberalism in Its Place*, 68 n. 4.

46. John Rawls, *Political Liberalism*, John Dewey Essays in Philosophy 4 (New York, 1993), 148.

47. Ibid., 147.

48. Rawls, *A Theory of Justice*, rev. ed. (Cambridge, Mass., 2003), 340.

49. Rawls, *Political Liberalism*, 39.

50. Jürgen Habermas, 'Religion in the Public Sphere,' trans. Jeremy Gaines, *European Journal of Philosophy* 14 (2006): 1; see also Habermas, Norbert Brieskorn, Michael Reder, Friedo Ricken, and Josef Schmidt, *An Awareness of What Is Missing: Faith and Reason in a Post-Secular Age* (Cambridge, 2010).

51. Habermas, 'Religion in the Public Sphere,' 6.

52. Ibid., 4; italics in original.

53. Ibid., 15.

54. Ibid.

55. Cristina Lafont, 'Religion in the Public Sphere: Remarks on Habermas's Conception of Public Deliberation in Postsecular Societies,' *Constellations* 14 (2007): 242, 245.

56. Harrington, *A Discourse Upon this Saying*, *Political Works*, 745.

57. Lafont, 'Religion in the Public Sphere,' 254.

58. On Habermas's abandonment of the transformative public sphere, see Maeve Cooke, 'A Secular State for a Postsecular Society: Postmetaphysical Political Theory and the Place of Religion,' *Constellations* 14 (2007): 228–29.

59. See also Simone Chambers, 'How Religion Speaks to the Agnostic: Habermas on the Persistent Value of Religion,' *Constellations* 14 (2007): 'The claim seems to be that while many of us might have the gut feeling that there is something terribly wrong with human cloning, we do not have the language to fully articulate and defend that feeling with the tools of postmetaphysical philosophy' (218).

60. Karl Marx, 'On the Jewish Question,' in *Early Writings*, trans. and ed. David McLellan (New York, 1971), 93–94.

61. Ibid., 103; for recent engagement of this essay, see Žižek, *Defense of Lost Causes*, 5.

62. See Franklyn S. Haiman, *Religious Expression and the American Constitution* (East Lansing, Mich., 2003), 124.

63. The cases here mentioned are *Prince v Massachusetts*, 321 US 158 (1944); *Wisconsin v Yoder*, 406 US 205 (1972); *Employment Division, Department of Human Resources of Oregon v Smith*, 494 US 872 (1990); and *Church of Lakumi Babulu Aye v City of Hialeh*, 508 US 520 (1993). See Haiman, *Religious Expression and the American Constitution*, 99–106 and 109–10; and John T. Noonan, Jr., and Edward McGlynn Gaffney, Jr., *Religious Freedom* (New York, 2001), 537.

64. Akhil Reid Amar, *Bill of Rights* (New Haven, 1998); my italics.

65. Haiman, *Religious Expression and the American Constitution*, 11; italics in original.

66. See *Bruker v. Marcovitz* [Canada], [2007] 3 S.C.R. 607, 2007 SCC 54; Benjamin Berger, 'The Cultural Limits of Legal Tolerance,' *Canadian Journal of Law and Jurisprudence* 21 (2008): 245–77; Lisa Fishbayn, 'Gender, Multiculturalism and Dialogue: The Case of Jewish Divorce,' *Canadian Journal of Law and Jurisprudence* 21 (2008): 71–96; and Ayelet Shachar, 'Privatizing Diversity: A Cautionary Tale from Religious Arbitration in Family Law,' *Theoretical Inquiries in Law* 9 (2008): esp. 594–602.

CHAPTER FOUR

1. John Milbank, 'An Essay against Secular Order,' *Journal of Religious Ethics* 15 (1987): 213; italics in original.

2. Ibid., 208, 209, 210.

3. John Milbank, 'Postmodern Critical Augustinianism: A Short *Summa* in Forty-Two Responses to Unasked Questions,' in *The Radical Orthodoxy Reader*, ed. Milbank and Simon Oliver (London, 2009), 51–52.

4. Milbank, 'An Essay against Secular Order,' 211.

5. See ibid., 199; Marvell's *Horatian Ode upon Cromwell's Return from Ireland*, quoted from *Poems*, rev. pbk. ed., ed. Nigel Smith (Harlow, UK, 2007).

6. Henry Lawrence, *Militia spiritualis. Or A Treatise of Angels* (London, 1652; Wing L662), 140.

7. Ibid., 188.

8. Norman Mailer, *Why Are We at War?* (New York, 2003), 13.

9. Gilbert Achcar, *The Clash of Barbarisms: September 11 and the Making of the New World Disorder* [*Choc des barbaries*], trans. Peter Drucker (New York, 2002), 61–62. Others have aimed the Samson trope in rather different directions. Tariq Ali has stated that 'many Arab intellectuals see Israel as the biblical ass whose jaw has been borrowed by an American Samson to destroy the real and imagined enemies of the Empire' (*The Clash of Fundamentalisms: Crusades, Jihads and Modernity* [2002; New York, 2003], xxii). In support of the invasion of Iraq, W. H. von Dreele has offered a brief piece of conservative doggerel entitled 'Chirac Plays Samson'; though 'He doesn't have the hair,' the French President does his best to pull down the pillars of the United Nations Headquarters—if 'there's no place to veto in,/Jacques will, in French, boo-hoo' (*National Review*, 7 April 2003: 12).

10. John Carey, 'A Work in Praise of Terrorism?,' *Times Literary Supplement* 6 September 2002: 15–16; further references to this article are in parentheses. See also the letters to the editor resulting from this article in the issues of 13 September, 20 September—which includes a response from Carey—and 4 October, as well as D. D. Guttenplan, 'Is Reading Milton Unsafe at Any Speed?,' *The New York Times*, 28 December 2002, accessed 31 December 2002, www.nytimes.com/2002/12/28/

arts/28TANK.html; Christopher Shea, 'Was Samson a Terrorist?,' *Boston Globe*, 3 November 2002: D5. For further references in this vein, see Joseph Wittreich, *Why Milton Matters: A New Preface to His Writings* (New York, 2006), 225 nn. 1–2.

11. On this comment, see also Alan Rudrum, 'Milton Scholarship and the *Agon* over *Samson Agonistes*,' *Huntington Library Quarterly* 65 (2002): 466.

12. Jerry L. Martin and Anne D. Neal, *Defending Civilization: How Our Universities Are Failing America and What Can Be Done About It*, American Council of Trustees and Alumni, February 2002. This document has been removed from the ACTA website, but is available through the Wikipedia article 'American Council of Trustees and Alumni,' *Wikipedia.org*, accessed 22 January 2011, en.wikipedia.org/wiki/American_Council_of_Trustees_and_Alumni.

13. Thomas Stearns Eliot, *Milton* (London, 1947), 3; Ezra Pound, *Make It New* (London, 1934), 109.

14. See John Carey, *Milton*, Arco Literary Critiques (1969; New York, 1970), 138.

15. Stanley Fish, *How Milton Works* (Cambridge, Mass., 2001), 426.

16. Tucked almost imperceptibly among Carey's accusations of 'dogmatism' is the following: 'As Fish concedes, Milton's Samson cannot know whether his vengeance conforms to the divine purpose or not.' Michael Lieb similarly observes that Carey misreads Fish's argument on *Samson Agonistes*; see his 'Returning the Gorgon Medusa's Gaze: Terror and Annihilation in Milton,' in *Milton in the Age of Fish: Essays on Authorship, Text, and Terrorism*, ed. Lieb and Albert C. Labriola (Pittsburgh, Penn., 2006), 232–34. See also Lieb's reading of Samson in '"Our Living Dread": The God of *Samson Agonistes*,' in *The Miltonic Samson*, special issue, *Milton Studies* 33, ed. Albert C. Labriola and Michael Lieb (Pittsburgh, Penn., 1996), 3–25; and Stephen Fallon's review of *Milton in the Age of Fish*, in *Modern Philology* 107 (2010): E40–E44.

17. Fish, *How Milton Works*, 424.

18. Ibid., 425, 428. Derek Wood similarly argues that Milton's portrayal of Samson calls into question the sufficiency of works under the Old Law, and shows the limits of faith without 'the example of Christ living the lesson of charity in time' (122). In his review, David Urban interrogates Wood's claims on Miltonic nonviolence, citing Michael's approval in *Paradise Lost* of 'Joshua's bloody victories over the Canaanites' (*Milton Quarterly* 37 [2003]: 45; see *Paradise Lost* 12.261–69).

19. Samuel Johnson, 'Rambler 139,' in *Milton's 'Samson Agonistes': The Poem and Materials for Analysis*, ed. Ralph E. Hone (San Francisco, 1966), 102–3; Fish, *How Milton Works*, 413.

20. See John M. Steadman, '"Faithful Champion": The Theological Basis of Milton's Hero of Faith,' *Anglia: Zeitschrift für Englische Philologie* 77 (1959): 13–28; and Mary Ann Radzinowicz, *Toward 'Samson Agonistes': The Growth of Milton's Mind* (Princeton, 1978), esp. 274–79.

21. John T. Shawcross, *The Uncertain World of 'Samson Agonistes,'* Studies in Renaissance Literature 6 (Cambridge, 2001), 60; see also Shawcross's reading of the three episodes of the tragedy's middle, 116–33; and his '"What Is Faith, Love, Vertue unassaid": Some Literary Answers to Our Ever-Present Evils,' *Milton Quarterly* 42 (2008): 69–77.

22. See Alan Rudrum, 'Discerning the Spirit in *Samson Agonistes*: The Dalila Episode,' in *'All in All': Unity, Diversity, and the Miltonic Perspective*, ed. Charles W. Durham and Kristin A. Pruitt (Selinsgrove, Penn., 1999), esp. 248–50; and Rudrum, 'Milton Scholarship and the *Agon* over *Samson Agonistes*,' 483–84.

23. Seneca, *Hercules furens*, in *Jasper Heywood and His Translation of Seneca's 'Troas,' 'Thyestes' and 'Hercules Furens*,' ed. H. de Vocht (1913; Vaduz, 1963), 1768–79; Euripides, *Heracleidae*, trans. David Grene, in *Euripides I*, The Complete Greek Tragedies (Chicago, 1955), lines 349–51.

24. See F. Michael Krouse, *Milton's Samson and the Christian Tradition* (Princeton, 1949), 40–44. In his 1640 treatise *The General View of the Holy Scriptures*, Thomas Hayne presents a long point-by-point comparison of Samson and Christ, relating Samson's murder of the Philistines to Christ's judgment of the Jews and Romans (Krouse Plate IV).

25. John Diodati, *Pious and Learned Annotations Upon the Holy Bible*, 4th ed. (London, 1664; Wing D1508), sig.Bb3ᵛ [comment on Judges 16.30]; John Donne, *Biathanatos*, ed. Ernest W. Sullivan II (Toronto, 1984), 135 [3.5.4]; George Herbert, 'Sunday,' in *Complete English Poems*, ed. John Tobin (London, 1991), 47–49. For further examples of sixteenth- and seventeenth-century exegetical treatment of Samson, see Krouse, *Milton's Samson and the Christian Tradition*, 63–79; for an interrogation of Krouse's view of the tradition, see Joseph Wittreich, *Interpreting 'Samson Agonistes'* (Princeton, NJ, 1986), ch. 4. See also the encyclopedic commentaries of Cornelius à Lapide, *In Josue, Judices, et Ruth commentarii*, vol. 2 of *Commentaria* (Paris, 1642), 137–49; and Matthew Poole, *Annotations upon the Holy Bible* (London, 1683).

26. Joseph Wittreich, *Shifting Contexts: Reinterpreting 'Samson Agonistes'* (Pittsburgh, 2002), 49, 55.

27. John Trapp, *A Commentary or Exposition upon All the Epistles and the Revelation* (London, 1647; Wing T2040), 682–83; cf. Wittreich, *Shifting Contexts*, 84–85.

28. Heinrich Bullinger, *Sermonum decades quinque* (London, 1587; STC 4076), 166r [III.vi].

29. Norman T. Burns, '"Then Stood Up Phinehas": Milton's Antinomianism, and Samson's,' in *The Miltonic Samson*, 32.

30. Sir Henry Vane, *The Retired Mans Meditations, or the Mysterie and Power of Godlines* (London, 1655; Wing V75), 19.

31. Ibid., 382.

32. Apparently, some feel that Jimmy Carter's sense of peacemaking is also a

thing of the past. William Bennett's Americans for Victory Over Terrorism has placed Carter among those who 'fundamentally misunderstand the nature of the war we are facing' based on the former president's comment that the phrase 'axis of evil' is 'overly-simplistic and counter-productive.' See Jim Lobe, 'The War on Dissent Widens,' *Foreign Policy Focus,* 15 March 2002: 1, accessed 22 January 2011, www.fpif.org/articles/the_war_on_dissent_widens; Marilyn B. Young, 'Ground Zero: Enduring War,' in *September 11 in History: A Watershed Moment?,* ed. Mary L. Dudziak (Durham, NC, 2003), 13; Walter Shapiro 'Anti-anti-war Crowd Dreams up a Disloyal Opposition,' *USA Today,* 13 March 2002, accessed 27 December 2003, www.usatoday.com/news/opinion/shapiro/610.htm; and Seth Leibsohn, 'Response to Walter Shapiro Op-ed,' Americans for Victory Over Terrorism, 19 March 2002, accessed 28 December 2003, www.avot.org/stories/storyReader$58.

33. See Sharon Achinstein, '*Samson Agonistes* and the Drama of Dissent,' in *The Miltonic Samson,* 133–58; Janel Mueller, 'The Figure and the Ground: Samson as a Hero of London Nonconformity, 1662–1667,' in *Milton and the Terms of Liberty,* ed. Graham Parry and Joad Raymond, Studies in Renaissance Literature 7 (Cambridge, 2002), 137–62; David Loewenstein, *Representing Revolution in Milton and His Contemporaries: Religion, Politics, and Polemics in Radical Puritanism* (Cambridge, 2001), 269–91; Barbara Kiefer Lewalski, *The Life of John Milton: A Critical Biography* (Oxford, 2000), 525–36.

34. Laura Lunger Knoppers, Introduction to *'Paradise Regain'd' and 'Samson Agonistes,'* vol. 2 of *The Complete Works of John Milton,* ed. Thomas N. Corns and Gordon Campbell (Oxford, 2008), lxx–lxxiv. Knoppers refers to a copy held by the University of Illinois (821 M64 M3 1671).

35. See Blair Worden, *Literature and Politics in Cromwellian England: John Milton, Andrew Marvell, Marchamont Nedham* (2007; pbk. Oxford, 2009), ch. 15; Sonnet 17 is first published in George Sikes, *The Life and Death of Sir Henry Vane Kt.* ([London,] 1662; Wing S3780), 93–94.

36. John P. Rumrich similarly observes that 'past performance is no guarantee of future results. Perhaps God did impel Samson to marry the woman of Timna; that does not mean that Samson was right to marry Dalila'; see his 'Samson and the Excluded Middle,' in *Altering Eyes: New Perspectives on 'Samson Agonistes,'* ed. Mark R. Kelley and Joseph A. Wittreich (Newark, 2002), 314; see also Susanne Woods, 'Choice and Election in *Samson Agonistes*,' in *Milton and the Grounds of Contention,* ed. Mark R. Kelley, Michael Lieb, and John T. Shawcross (Pittsburgh, 2003), esp. 184–85; David Urban, '"Intimate Impulses," "Rousing Motions," and the Written Law: Internal and External Scripture in *Samson Agonistes*,' in *Uncircumscribed Mind: Reading Milton Deeply,* ed. Charles W. Durham and Kristin A. Pruitt (Selinsgrove, Penn., 2008), 292–306; and the essays on *Samson Agonistes* in *The Oxford Handbook of Milton,* ed. Nicholas McDowell and Nigel Smith (Oxford, 2009), by R. W. Serjeantson (613–31), Regina M. Schwartz (632–48), and

Elizabeth D. Harvey (649–66). For further discussion and a view opposed to that here presented, see Ashraf H. A. Rushdy, *The Empty Garden: The Subject of Late Milton* (Pittsburgh, 1992), 297–306.

37. Cf. Rumrich, 'Samson and the Excluded Middle,' 317, which notes that the Aristotelian term supporting Johnson's claim is *pefuken*, the 'natural' quality that should mark dramatic progress and that is defined according to the classical view that 'natural phenomena . . . act as they do through necessity.'

38. Jean-Pierre Vernant and Pierre Vidal-Naquet, *Tragedy and Myth in Ancient Greece*, trans. Janet Lloyd (Atlantic Highlands, NJ, 1981), 19.

39. Augustine of Hippo, *De civitate Dei*, Corpus Christianorum, Series Latina 48 (Turnhout, 1955), 434 [14.13].

40. Victoria Kahn, 'Aesthetics as Critique: Tragedy and *Trauerspiel* in *Samson Agonistes*,' in *Reading Renaissance Ethics*, ed. Marshall Grossman (New York, 2007), 116, 120.

41. Alan Fishbone has provided a fresh translation of *Christos Paschon*, a text significant in its Euripidean rendition of biblical subject matter, available in *Milton Quarterly* 36 (2002): 129–98. Mark R. Kelley tends to elide Milton's tragic hero with those of Euripides in his account of 'Milton's Euripidean Poetics of Lament,' in *Altering Eyes*, esp. 146, 156.

42. See Burns, 'Then Stood Up Phineas,' 32–33.

43. Euripides, *The Bacchae*, trans. William Arrowsmith, *Euripides V*, The Complete Greek Tragedies (Chicago, 1959), 1133–37.

44. Fredric Jameson, 'Religion and Ideology: A Political Reading of *Paradise Lost*,' in *Literature, Politics and Theory: Papers from the Essex Conference 1976–84*, ed. Francis Barker et al. (New York, 1986), 42.

45. Tyler Roberts, 'Toward Secular Diaspora: Relocating Religion and Politics,' in *Secularisms*, ed. Janet R. Jakobsen and Ann Pellegrini (Durham, NC, 2008), 301. See also the various essays skeptically handling Radical Orthodoxy in *Deconstructing Radical Orthodoxy: Postmodern Theology, Rhetoric, and Truth*, ed. Wayne J. Hankey and Douglas Hedley (Aldershot, 2005).

46. Milbank, 'Postmodern Critical Augustinianism,' 52.

47. Augustine of Hippo, *Concerning the City of God against the Pagans* [*De civitate Dei*], trans. Henry Bettenson (1972; London, 1984), 595 [15.1].

48. Simon Oliver, 'Introducing Radical Orthodoxy: From Participation to Late Modernity,' in *The Radical Orthodoxy Reader*, 7.

49. Pseudo-Dionysius, *The Complete Works*, trans. Colm Luibheid, ed. Paul Rorem, The Classics of Western Spirituality (New York, 1987), 272.

50. Achcar, *Clash of Barbarisms*, 64. Cf. Walter Benjamin, 'Theses on the Philosophy of History,' in *Illuminations: Essays and Reflections*, ed. Hannah Arendt, trans. Harry Zohn, pref. Leon Wieseltier (New York, 2007), 256: '[T]here is no document of civilization which is not at the same time a document of barbarism.'

51. Qtd. in Ali, *Clash of Fundamentalisms*, 129; cf. *YP,* 7: 359–60, 364. Though he does not connect Khomeini to Milton, Ali later describes Iranian resistance to the Shah as 'Islamic Jacobinism,' stating that 'nothing like this had been seen since the victory of Protestant fundamentalism in seventeenth-century England' (131).

CHAPTER FIVE

1. Epigraph from Arundhati Roy, 'The Monster in the Mirror,' *The Guardian*, 13 December 2008, accessed 26 November 2009, www.guardian.co.uk/world/2008/dec/12/mumbai-arundhati-roy/print.
2. Gayatri Chakravorty Spivak, 'Terror: A Speech after 9–11,' *boundary 2* 31 (2004): 96, 93–94.
3. Talal Asad, *On Suicide Bombing*, Welleck Library Lectures (New York, 2007), 64.
4. Ibid., 42.
5. On suicide terrorism as 'pathological,' see ibid., 41.
6. Amitav Ghosh, 'A Jihadist from Jersey,' rev. of *Terrorist* by John Updike, *Washington Post,* 4 June 2006, BW03, accessed 29 October 2008, www.washingtonpost.com/wp-dyn/content/article/2006/06/01/AR2006060101520_pf.html. Ghosh quotes Updike, *Terrorist* (New York, 2006), 39; all further references to this novel are in parentheses.
7. See *Faerie Queene* 1.1.21, and *Paradise Lost* 2.592–95.
8. Salman Rushdie, *The Satanic Verses* (1988; New York, 1997), 44.
9. Mohsin Hamid, *The Reluctant Fundamentalist* (New York, 2007), 29; further references to this novel are in parentheses.
10. Kathryn Hume argues for the novel's endorsement of anti-capitalist political resistance and post-secular Catholic theology, in 'The Religious and Political Vision of Pynchon's *Against the Day*,' *Philological Quarterly* 86 (2007): 178–83.
11. See Gilbert Achcar, *Clash of Barbarisms: September 11 and the Making of the New World Disorder* [*Le choc des barbaries*] (New York, 2002).
12. John Carey, 'A Work in Praise of Terrorism?,' *Times Literary Supplement* 6 September 2002: 15.
13. Ibid.
14. Joseph Wittreich, 'Forum,' *PMLA* 120 (2005): 1641.
15. John Calvin, *Institutes of the Christian Religion*, trans. Henry Beveridge (1845; Grand Rapids, 1989), 3.20.15; see my reply to Wittreich and Peter C. Herman in 'Forum,' *PMLA* 120 (2005): 1643–44.
16. See Jonathan Cohen, 'On Martyrs and Communal Interests: Rabbinic Readings of the Samson Narrative,' *Review of Rabbinic Judaism* 11 (2008): 49–72; and Nancy Rosenfeld, *The Human Satan in Seventeenth-Century English Literature* (Aldershot, UK, 2008), 188–89.
17. David Loewenstein comes to similar conclusions in his learned and per-

ceptive reading of *Samson Agonistes*; see his *Representing Revolution in Milton and His Contemporaries: Religion, Politics, and Polemics in Radical Puritanism* (2001; pbk. Cambridge, 2007), 273–76.

18. Douglas Bush, *The Renaissance and English Humanism* (1939; Toronto, 1965), 121, 123–24. For the view that my own reading of *Samson* is 'radical,' see Richard J. DuRocher, 'Samson's "Rousing Motions": What They Are, How They Work, and Why They Matter,' *Literature Compass* 3 (2006): 454.

19. Bruce Hoffman, *Inside Terrorism*, rev. ed. (New York, 2006), 141.

20. See Lori A. Allen's account of Palestinian martyr commemorations: 'In their design and immediate visual impression, there was often little to distinguish between posters of suicide bombers, armed fighters, youth shot during clashes, and ordinary civilians—men, women or children—killed in Israeli attacks. . . . The photographic portraits of the person in martyr posters reflect an image of the person in life, and never would a poster of this genre include an image of the martyr's death or show his or her wounds. Thus the poster captures what, in religious terms, is the kind of eternal life of the martyr who is not believed to be dead' ('The Polyvalent Politics of Martyr Commemorations in the Palestinian *Intifada*,' *History & Memory* 18 [2006]: 117); and Anne Marie Oliver and Paul F. Steinberg, *The Road to Martyrs' Square: A Journey into the World of the Suicide Bomber* (Oxford, 2005), xii.

21. Mark R. Kelley and Joseph Wittreich, ed., *Altering Eyes: New Perspectives on 'Samson Agonistes'* (Newark, 2002), 11.

22. Stanley Fish, *How Milton Works* (Cambridge, Mass., 2001), 417.

23. For astute analysis of the relevance of Milton's plans for tragedies to Samson's spiritual heroism, see Norman T. Burns, '"Then Stood Up Phinehas": Milton's Antinomianism, and Samson's,' in *The Miltonic Samson*, special issue, *Milton Studies* 33, ed. Albert C. Labriola and Michael Lieb (Pittsburgh, 1996), 27–46.

24. Fish, *How Milton Works*, 465.

25. Michael Lieb, 'Returning the Gorgon Medusa's Gaze: Terror and Annihilation in Milton,' in *Milton in the Age of Fish: Essays on Authorship, Text, and Terrorism*, ed. Michael Lieb and Albert C. Labriola (Pittsburgh, 2006), 230–31.

26. Stanley Fish, 'Why Milton Matters: or, Against Historicism,' *Milton Studies* 44, ed. Albert C. Labriola (Pittsburgh, 2005), 10.

27. Ibid., 8.

28. Ibid.

29. Joseph Wittreich, 'Joseph Wittreich on Why Milton Matters,' *Milton Studies* 44, 30–31, 34, revised as a portion of ch. 3 in Wittreich's *Why Milton Matters: A New Preface to His Writings* (New York, 2006); where possible, subsequent references will be to the book chapter.

30. Joseph Wittreich, *Shifting Contexts: Reinterpreting 'Samson Agonistes'* (Pittsburgh, Penn., 2002), 49, 55.

31. Wittreich, 'Joseph Wittreich on Why Milton Matters,' 24; see Margaret Thatcher, 'Advice to a Superpower,' *The New York Times*, Monday, 11 February 2002, A27.

32. Barbara Lewalski also tends to ignore these aspects of *The Readie and Easie Way* in her account of it only as a courageous defense of the republican cause; see 'Barbara K. Lewalski on Why Milton Matters,' *Milton Studies* 44, 16–17.

33. Wittreich, 'Joseph Wittreich on Why Milton Matters,' 23.

34. See above, ch. 4, nn. 32–33. Even when such historicist readings are temporally widened beyond the text's immediate Restoration context, they tend to look to *Samson* as artifact of abandoned ideas. In this vein a recent reviewer of Derek Wood's *'Exiled from Light'* has claimed that Milton's tragic hero is an unsettling portrait of the poet's 'powerfully anti-Semitic . . . understanding of the Hebrew Bible,' showing 'what Christians in the seventeenth century really thought about Judaism,' a reading that would turn Samson into a Miltonic Shylock; see Andrew Barnaby, rev. of *'Exiled from Light': Divine Law, Morality, and Violence in Milton's 'Samson Agonistes,'* by Derek N. C. Wood, *Renaissance Quarterly* 56 (2003): 1342. For incisive critique of Wood's use of biblical material, see Alan Rudrum, 'Milton Scholarship and the *Agon* over *Samson Agonistes*,' *Huntington Library Quarterly* 65 (2002): 485; and David Urban, rev. of *'Exiled from Light,' Milton Quarterly* 37 (2003): 43–46.

35. David Loewenstein, '*Samson Agonistes* and the Culture of Religious Terror,' Labriola and Lieb (2006), 208. See also Loewenstein's 'Milton's Double-Edged Volume: On Religious Politics and Violence in the 1671 Poems,' *Milton Quarterly* 44 (2010): 231–38.

36. Carey, 'A Work in Praise of Terrorism?,' 15.

37. Loewenstein, '*Samson Agonistes* and the Culture of Religious Terror,' 207.

38. Pierre Bourdieu, 'The Field of Cultural Production, or: The Economic World Reversed,' trans. Richard Nice, *Poetics* 12 (1983): 317.

39. Michel Foucault, 'Intellectuals and Power: A Conversation between Michel Foucault and Gilles Deleuze,' in *Language, Counter-Memory, Practice*, ed. Donald F. Bouchard (Ithaca, NY, 1977), 207–8.

40. Gayatri C. Spivak, *A Critique of Postcolonial Reason: Toward a History of the Vanishing Present* (Cambridge, Mass., 1999), 255.

41. Ibid., 358.

42. Ibid., 360; italics in original.

43. See ibid., xii and 309.

44. Sharon Achinstein, '*Samson Agonistes* and the Drama of Dissent,' in *The Miltonic Samson*, 135; Samuel Johnson, in *Milton's 'Samson Agonistes': The Poem and Materials for Analysis*, 103.

45. See Richard Cumberland, *The Observer: Being a Collection of Moral, Literary, and Familiar Essays* (Dublin, 1791), 3: 262 [no. 111]: 'Aristotle has said *that every whole hath not amplitude enough for the construction of a tragic fable; now*

by a whole, (adds he in the way of illustration) *I mean that, which hath beginning, middle and end.* This and no more is what he says upon beginning, middle and end; and this, which the author of the Rambler conceives to be a rule for tragedy, turns out to be merely an explanation of the word *whole*' (italics in original).

46. Joan S. Bennett, 'Asserting Eternal Providence: John Milton through the Window of Liberation Theology,' in *Milton and Heresy*, ed. Stephen B. Dobranski and John P. Rumrich (Cambridge, 1998), 237; see David Loewenstein, *Milton and the Drama of History* (Cambridge, 1990), 145. One of the strengths of Bennett's (pre-9/11) argument, however, is that rather than dismissing terrorism as a context significant to *Samson*, it invites broadened consideration of contexts that might allow '"first world" academics and students today' better to imagine 'someone with Milton's deep religiosity and profound humanism maintaining a revolutionary political commitment' (220).

47. Mark Juergensmeyer, *Terror in the Mind of God* (Berkeley and Los Angeles, 2000), 123 and 126; italics in original.

48. Asad, *On Suicide Bombing*, 68; italics in original. Asad follows here Stanley Cavell, *The Claim of Reason* (New York, 1999), 418–19.

49. Asad, *On Suicide Bombing*, 90.

50. Žižek, *Defense of Lost Causes*, 19; see Robert B. Pippin, *The Persistence of Subjectivity: On the Kantian Aftermath* (Cambridge, 2005), 229–38.

51. See Balachandra Rajan, 'Samson Hath Quit Himself/Like Samson,' *Milton Quarterly* 41 (2007): 3.

52. Victoria Kahn, 'Aesthetics as Critique: Tragedy and *Trauerspiel* in *Samson Agonistes*,' in *Reading Renaissance Ethics*, ed. Marshall Grossman (New York, 2007), 109–10.

53. Qtd. in ibid.

54. Ibid., 116.

55. Sir Walter Raleigh, *Milton* (1900; reprint, New York, 1967), 28–29.

EPILOGUE

1. Epigraph from Aeschylus, *Prometheus Bound*, trans. David Grene, Greek Tragedies, vol. 1, 2nd ed., ed. Grene and Richard Lattimore (Chicago, 1991), 250–57.

2. Creston Davis, Introduction to *The Monstrosity of Christ: Paradox or Dialectic?*, by Slavoj Žižek and John Milbank, Short Circuits (Cambridge, Mass., 2009), 3.

3. Slavoj Žižek, 'Use Your Illusions,' *London Review of Books,* 14 November 2008, available at www.lrb.co.uk.

4. John Keats, *Ode to a Nightingale*, in *Poems*, ed. Jack Stillinger (Cambridge, Mass., 1978), 73.

5. *Christian Legal Society Chapter of the University of California, Hastings Col-*

lege of the Law, aka Hastings Christian Fellowship, Petitioner v. Leo P. Martinez et al., 561 US 08-1371 (2010). The opinion and dissent are available at www.supremecourt.gov, and are hereafter cited parenthetically.

6. See also 15–16: '[T]his case fits comfortably within the limited-public-forum category, for CLS, in seeking what is effectively a state subsidy, faces only indirect pressure to modify its membership policies. . . . Hastings, through its RSO program, is dangling the carrot of subsidy, not wielding the stick of prohibition.'

7. See Stanley Fish, 'Being Neutral Is Oh So Hard to Do,' *Opinionator, NYTimes.com,* 19 July 2010, accessed 21 July 2010, opinionator.blogs.nytimes.com/2010/07/19/being-neutral-is-oh-so-hard-to-do/ .

8. Alain Badiou, *Ethics,* trans. Peter Hallward, Wos es War (London, 2001), 27.

Index

Achcar, Gilbert, 90–91, 106, 113
Achinstein, Sharon, 8, 44, 52, 99, 122
Adorno, Theodor, 33
Alito, Samuel, 129
alter-globalization movement. *See* globalization
Amar, Akhil Reid, 85
America, United States of, 19, 35, 67–68, 79, 84–85, 92, 110, 112, 113, 119–20
Aristotle, 1, 5, 16, 124; view of ethics, 44, 48–49
Arnold, Matthew, 17, 26
Asad, Talal, 10, 108, 123
Augustine, Saint, 6, 40, 101; *De civitate Dei* 79, 105; *Sermo de Samsone,* 96; *societas perfecta,* 88

Badiou, Alain: democratic concept of truth, 3–5, 7, 32, 37–41; ethics 43–44, 51, 53, 57–58, 61–63, 130; 'event' in, 3, 21, 38, 41, 51, 60–61, 65; militant fidelity, 41, 51, 57–58, 60–61; Saint Paul, view of, 8, 20–21, 38–40
Baudrillard, Jean, 113
Being, 3, 40–41
belief, 3–5, 9, 10, 19, 20, 35, 41–42, 43, 50–51, 81–82, 83, 95, 127–131
Benjamin, Walter, 5, 106; 'Theses on Historical Philosophy,' 18; baroque drama, views on, 31–32, 101, 124
Bennett, Joan S., 123
Bentley, Richard, 26
Berek, Peter, 41

Bible, 20, 52, 70, 80, 89, 94, 96, 98, 115; Abraham, 87, 98; biblical history, 30, 70, 71, 72, 74, 80, 89, 90, 115; biblical narrative, 50, 87–88, 89, 90, 103; Christ, 6, 46, 89, 96–97, 98, 101, 115, 119; Gideon, 89, 98, 117, 118; Ham, 15–16; Hebrews, Epistle to, 9, 96, 97, 115, 116–18; Job, Book of, 72; Judges, Book of, 97, 114, 115; Matthew, Gospel of, 89; Noah, 15–16, 30, 117; Samson, 9–10, 13, 14–15, 90, 97, 114–15, 117, 119
Blake, William, 11, 24, 128
Boer, Roland, 39
Bonaventure, Saint, 64
Bourdieu, Pierre, 121
Brecht, Bertolt, 1–3, 7
Bullinger, Heinrich, 97, 100
Burns, Norman T., 98, 101
Burrough, Edward, 71–73, 99
Bush, Douglas, 12, 42, 115
Bush, George W., 37, 84

Cable, Lana, 47
Calvin, John, 29, 114
Carey, John, 'A Work in Praise of Terrorism?,' 13, 91–93, 97, 103–4, 106, 114, 117, 120
Charnes, Linda, 14
Chomsky, Noam, 113
Cicero, 16, 28–30, 78
civility, 47, 123–24
Critchley, Simon, 8, 52, 57, 61
Cromwell, Oliver, 16, 76–77, 89, 103

Index

Cromwell, Richard, 73–74
Crook, John, 71–72, 75

Davis, Creston, 127
De Man, Paul, 8, 44, 58, 64
Deleuze, Gilles, 34, 121–22
democracy, 5, 32–33, 35, 37–38, 40–41, 52, 53, 57, 61, 63, 67, 83, 131
Derrida, Jacques, 3, 5–6, 56–57, 63, 130; *démocratie à venir* (democracy to come), 56–57, 61, 63; ethics, 51–53, 56–57; kettle logic in, 45; the Other according to, 8, 51–53, 61; text, 44–45, 51
Diodati, John, 96
Donne, John, 12, 21, 37, 42, 96–97
Donnelly, Phillip, 50

Eagleton, Terry, 53
Eliot, T. S., 12, 20–22, 26, 92
Ellison, Ralph, 14–16
equality, 3, 7, 33, 37–38, 53, 66, 81, 84, 85–86, 127, 128, 130
ethics, 2, 5–6, 8, 10, 37, 43–65, 82–83, 103, 113, 116, 127, 130–31
Euripides, 95, 98, 102, 119

fable, 8, 20, 39
faith, 3, 4, 9, 19–20, 21, 31, 35, 42, 66, 68, 78, 79, 80, 81, 83, 84, 86, 95, 96, 106, 118, 128–31. *See also* religion
feminism. *See* gender
Fernie, Ewan, 14
First Amendment (U.S.), 84–85
Fish, Stanley, 19, 91–93, 114, 117–119
Foucault, Michel, 8, 58–61, 121–122
Fox, George, 71–72, 99
Fox, George the Younger, 71
Foxe, John, 74–75
freedom. *See* liberty
Freud, Sigmund, 8, 44
Fulton, Thomas, 49–50

gender, 13, 20, 40, 46–48, 59–60, 62–3, 66, 85–86
Ghosh, Amitav, 108–9
Ginsburg, Ruth Bader, 129–30

globalization, 34–36, 113; alter-globalization movement, 36, 57
Good Old Cause, 73, 76–78, 98, 101, 124
Gorski, Philip, 4–5
Gottfried, Paul Edward, 9, 66
Graham, Kenneth, 29
grand style. *See* Milton, John, *Paradise Lost*
Grossman, Marshall, 8, 44, 52, 64

Habermas, Jürgen, 3, 7, 14; religion in the public sphere, 9, 69, 81–83, 85–86
Haiman, Franklyn S., 85
Hamid, Mohsin, 10, 109–10, 112
Hardt, Michael, 21, 33–35, 58
Harrington, James, 77–78, 82
Hawkes, David, 74
Heidegger, Martin, 8, 32, 58, 63
Herbert, George, 21, 97
Hercules, 95, 97, 98, 101, 102–3, 119
Herman, Peter, 31
Hill, Geoffrey, 21, 31
historicism, 14, 18, 49, 118
Hitler, Adolf, 12. *See also* Nazism; Second World War
Hobbes, Thomas, 55, 78
Horace, 22, 30
humanism, 12, 42, 92, 104, 114, 120, 126
human rights, 34, 37–38, 43, 58, 60, 62–63
Hutchinson, Lucy, 15–16

identity, 39, 67, 84, 123; as divine gift, 105; politics of, 37–38, 104. *See also* subjects
imagination, 4, 13, 19–20, 44, 62–65, 91, 104, 107, 113, 128
Iran, 58–60, 106
Iraq, 53
Islam, 7, 13, 58–59, 60, 84, 90, 106, 107, 108–9, 112, 113

Jameson, Fredric, 103
Johnson, Samuel, 13, 93, 100–101, 122
Juergensmeyer, Mark, 123

Kahn, Paul W., 9, 67–69, 79–80, 84
Kahn, Victoria, 31, 101, 124–25
Kant, Immanuel, 3, 5–6, 50, 52, 127

Keats, John, 11, 128
Kelley, Mark R., 117
Kendrick, Christopher, 53–54
Khomeini, Ayatollah Ruhollah, 58–60, 106
Knight, G. Wilson, 11–13
Knoppers, Laura Lunger, 99
knowledge, 3, 7–8, 19–20, 34, 38–40, 41, 43, 45, 47, 50, 51, 55, 59–60, 61, 64, 105, 121–22

Lacan, Jacques, 46, 49, 64
Lafont, Cristina, 82–83
Lawrence, Henry, 9, 89–90, 98, 103
Leavis, F. R., 12, 22
Leonard, John, 26
Lévinas, Emmanuel, 5, 8, 52
Lewalski, Barbara, 99
liberal democracy, 32, 37, 54, 63
liberalism, 9, 49–50, 54–55, 57, 58, 66–69, 79, 80, 81, 83, 84, 118–19, 121, 126, 128, 130, 131; communitarian critique of, 9, 66–67
liberty, 5, 16, 33, 49, 55–56, 74, 76, 78, 79, 126, 127, 131; of conscience, 72, 76, 77, 78–79, 80
Licensing Order (June 1643), 8, 43, 44, 56
Lieb, Michael, 118
Loewenstein, David, 99, 117, 120–21, 123
Lucan, 28, 30

Macpherson, C. B., 54–55
Mailer, Norman, 90–91
Margalit, Avishai, 35
Marvell, Andrew, 16, 88–89
Marx, Karl, 83–84
Marxism, 1, 54, 58–59
McLuhan, Marshall, 36
messianism, 5–6, 36, 52, 57, 130
Milbank, John: metaphysics in Christianity, 3, 6, 12, 104–6, 130; reading of pre-modern Christian orthodoxy, 10, 105; on *societas perfecta*, 6, 106; view of biblical narrative, 87–88, 90
Miller, J. Hillis, 44
Milton, John, 2–3, 12, 109, 131; heroism of faith in, 26, 96, 99, 101, 102, 103, 114–15, 119–21, 122–23, 126; as poet-prophet, 30, 36, 39, 42; politics of, 9, 10, 50, 53–54, 61, 68, 76–80, 98–99, 103, 104, 118; as pre-secular, 19–20, 86, 104, 106; reason in, 4–5, 12, 47, 50, 58. Works: Abraham tragedy, planned, 101; *Accedence Commenc't Grammar*, 123; *An Apology against a Pamphlet*, 47; anti-prelatical tracts, 51, 53, 70, 72, 74, 75, 119; *Artis logicae*, 29, 123; Christ tragedy, planned, 101; *De doctrina Christiana*, 4; *Defense* (1658), 79; divorce tracts, 45–47, 53, 55, 74; *Eikonoklastes*, 23, 76; *Hirelings*, 71–74, 76, 79; *The History of Britain*, 123; *The Judgement of Martin Bucer*, 74; *Letter to a Friend*, 120; *Lycidas*, 106; *A Mask Presented at Ludlow Castle*, 23; *Of Education*, 55, 78; *Of Reformation*, 23, 69–70, 74, 79; *Of True Religion*, 123; *Paradise Regained*, 23, 27, 29–30, 95–98, 100, 115, 118; Phineas tragedy, planned, 102, 118; *The Readie and the Easie Way*, 76–79, 106, 119; *The Reason of Church Government*, 23, 47, 70; *Second Defense*, 78, 94; *The Tenure of Kings and Magistrates*, 11, 47, 54, 78; *A Treatise of Civil Power*, 30, 32, 69–71, 73–74, 77–80, 131
— *Areopagitica*, 119; ethics in, 8, 43–56, 61, 63–64, 131; kettle logic of, 45, 48, 54; rhetorical excess of, 8, 43, 53–54, 131; truth in, 50–51, 63–64
— *Paradise Lost*, 10, 12, 15–16, 46, 63, 94, 103, 117, 128; Abdiel, 8, 25–26, 27, 30; Belial, 27–28; God the Father, 8, 23–24, 25, 26, 30, 39, 40, 41; grand style in, 8, 21–23, 24, 26, 27, 31; Moloch, 28; plain style in, 7–8, 20–21, 23–32, 39–41, 43, 68, 131; Satan, 12, 22–23, 25, 26, 63, 128
— *Samson Agonistes*, 9, 13–17, 31–32, 90–103, 113–15, 119–26; Chorus, 102; Dalila (character), 93–96, 99–101; Harapha (character), 93, 95–96, 100; Manoa (character), 93, 94, 100, 102; middle, 93, 96, 100, 122–23; 'rouzing motions,'

31–32, 100–103, 115–18, 124–25, 131; Samson's prayer in, 113–15; suicide in, 116–17, 120, 121
Monboddo, James Burnett Lord, 22–23
Morrison, Toni, 15–16
Mueller, Janel, 99

Nairn, Tom, 35–36
Nazism, 1, 58, 61. *See also* Second World War
neo-roman thought, 12, 17, 55, 79
Negri, Antonio, 21, 33–35, 58

Obama, Barack, 37, 67, 127
Oliver, Simon, 105
Other, the, 43, 65, 90, 104, 113, 122; according to Derrida, 5, 8, 51–52, 61; according to Lacan, 47; according to Spivak, 8, 44, 61–62, 107, 116; divine or transcendent, 5, 51–52; historical, 10, 14, 17–18; as victim, 58, 62

Palmer, Herbert, 45–46
Parliament, 54, 72, 73, 74; Long, 68, 69, 71, 75; Rump, 76–77, 79
Paterson, James, 16
Paul, Saint, 8, 20–21, 38–40
plain style, 20, 28–31, 43, 68. *See also* Milton, John, *Paradise Lost*
Plato, 32, 44
politics, erotic character of, 37, 67, 79
post-secularity, 3–7, 8, 10, 18, 20, 81, 83, 86, 127, 131
Pound, Ezra, 12, 24, 92, 104
Presbyterians, 11, 50–51, 52, 61, 70–72
pre-secularity, 5, 7, 10, 18, 19–20, 86
presentism, 12–18
property, 6, 34, 55–56, 75
prophecy, 30–31, 36, 73
Pseudo-Dionysius, 105
public sphere, 9, 49, 55, 69, 80–83, 84, 130
Pynchon, Thomas, 111–13, 115

Quakers, 71, 72–74
Qur'an, 59, 60, 90, 109. *See also* Islam

Rabinow, Paul, 34
'radical orthodoxy,' 6, 90, 104, 105–6, 130. *See also* Milbank, John
Radzinowicz, Mary Ann, 93
Rajan, Balachandra, 124
Raleigh, Sir Walter, 42, 55, 126
Rawls, John: limits upon comprehensive doctrines, 32, 37, 80, 82–83, 84, 131; recognition of modes of living, 9, 80
reason, 4–5, 6, 8, 19, 32, 37, 42, 45, 47, 50, 66, 67, 79, 81, 82, 112, 127; *recta ratio*, 4, 12
Reformation, Protestant, 20, 29–30, 36, 49, 69, 74–75, 80, 98
religion, 2, 3, 5, 7, 9, 12, 15, 20, 30, 37, 38, 50, 59, 60, 61, 66, 68, 69, 70, 71, 73, 77, 78, 79, 80–86, 94, 95, 98, 104, 106, 113, 121, 129
religious violence, 9, 86, 90, 91–92, 104, 106, 116–22, 131. *See also* suicide bomber; terrorism
Restoration, the, 9, 76, 80, 98–99, 114, 120, 123, 125
Revard, Stella, 69
Ricks, Christopher, 24, 27
Roberts, Tyler, 104, 106
Rose, Nikolas, 34
Rosen, Jonathan, 19
Rudrum, Alan, 95

Schwartz, Regina, 41
Second World War, 1–2, 11–12, 58
sectarianism, 17, 20, 35–37, 99
secularism, 2, 4, 6, 7, 19–20, 31, 50, 81, 83, 85, 89, 127, 131
secular state, the, 7, 81, 82–84, 86, 130
September 11 (9/11), 13, 53, 90, 91, 104, 110–11, 113, 120
Shakespeare, William, 13, 14, 17, 31, 35, 37, 101, 124–25
Shawcross, John, 93
Shifflett, Andrew, 30
Sikes, George, 98–99
Sirluck, Ernest, 50–51
skepticism, 2, 12, 32, 42, 128, 131

Skinner, Quentin, 49, 55
slavery, African, 15–16
Smith, Nigel, 19, 50–51
Spenser, Edmund, 20, 47, 109
Spivak, Gayatri, 8, 64; analysis of the suicide bomber, 107, 116; ethics of reading, 44, 62–63; the subaltern Other, 44, 61–62, 122
Steadman, John M., 93
Stevens, Paul, 16–17
subjects and subjectivity, 3, 4, 5, 6, 7, 22, 35, 39, 44, 47, 52, 62, 63–65, 81, 83, 106, 107, 108, 109, 111, 113, 115, 116
suicide bomber, 10, 90, 91, 97, 107, 108, 116, 121; civility and, 123–24; distanced from suicide, 116; literary representation of, 108–13
Supreme Court of Canada, *Bruker v. Marcovitz*, 85–86
Supreme Court of the United States, 85; *Christian Legal Society v. Martinez*, 128–30

Talisse, Robert B., 9, 66
Taylor, Charles, 4
terrorism, 35, 57, 91, 92, 103, 107, 108, 111–13, 120–21, 123, 125, 126. *See also* religious violence; suicide bomber
Thatcher, Margaret, 119–20
Toland, John, 11
toleration, 11, 16–17, 50, 67, 80, 81, 84, 130
transcendence, 3, 4, 5, 6, 32, 36, 37, 49, 51, 52, 57, 64–65, 116

Trapp, John, 97, 100–101
truth, 2, 3, 4, 5, 6, 7–8, 10, 17, 20–21, 23, 27, 28, 30, 32–33, 36, 37–38, 39, 40–42, 43, 45, 50, 51–52, 56, 58, 60–61, 64, 68, 69, 71, 74, 79, 112, 121, 128, 130–31. *See also* Badiou, Alain

Updike, John 10, 108–12

Vane, Sir Henry the Younger, 5, 9, 55, 73, 79, 98, 99, 103
vanguard, 53
Vernant, Jean-Pierre, 101
Viswanathan, Gauri, 4
Vondel, Joost van den, 125
von Maltzahn, Nicholas, 31

Waldensians (Vaudois), 74–75, 80
Wall, Moses, 77
Walzer, Michael, 66–67
Worden, Blair, 49, 99
Wittgenstein, Ludwig, 44, 48, 64
Wittreich, Joseph, 11, 19, 31, 114; presentism of, 13–15, 19, 119–20; *Samson Agonistes*, reading of, 97, 114, 117, 119–20
World Trade Center. *See* September 11
Wycliffe, John, 74–75

X, Malcolm, 15–16

Žižek, Slavoj, 35, 67, 127–28; civility, 123–24; Iraq War and 'kettle logic,' 8, 53; revolutionary intellectuals in, 58, 61

Cultural Memory in the Present

Pierre Hadot, *The Present Alone Is Our Happiness, Second Edition: Conversations with Jeannie Carlier and Arnold I. Davidson*

Yasco Horsman, *Theaters of Justice: Judging, Staging, and Working Through in Arendt, Brecht, and Delbo*

Jacques Derrida, *Parages*, edited by John P. Leavey

Henri Atlan, *Sparks of Randomness, Volume 1: Spermatic Knowledge*

Rebecca Comay, *Mourning Sickness: Hegel and the French Revolution*

Djelal Kadir, *Memos from the Besieged City: Lifelines for Cultural Sustainability*

Stanley Cavell, *Little Did I Know: Excerpts from Memory*

Jeffrey Mehlman, *Adventures in the French Trade: Fragments Toward a Life*

Jacob Rogozinski, *The Ego and the Flesh: An Introduction to Egoanalysis*

Marcel Hénaff, *The Price of Truth: Gift, Money, and Philosophy*

Paul Patton, *Deleuzian Concepts: Philosophy, Colonialization, Politics*

Michael Fagenblat, *A Covenant of Creatures: Levinas's Philosophy of Judaism*

Stefanos Geroulanos, *An Atheism that Is Not Humanist Emerges in French Thought*

Andrew Herscher, *Violence Taking Place: The Architecture of the Kosovo Conflict*

Hans-Jörg Rheinberger, *On Historicizing Epistemology: An Essay*

Jacob Taubes, *From Cult to Culture*, edited by Charlotte Fonrobert and Amir Engel

Peter Hitchcock, *The Long Space: Transnationalism and Postcolonial Form*

Lambert Wiesing, *Artificial Presence: Philosophical Studies in Image Theory*

Jacob Taubes, *Occidental Eschatology*

Freddie Rokem, *Philosophers and Thespians: Thinking Performance*

Roberto Esposito, *Communitas: The Origin and Destiny of Community*

Vilashini Cooppan, *Worlds Within: National Narratives and Global Connections in Postcolonial Writing*

Josef Früchtl, *The Impertinent Self: A Heroic History of Modernity*

Frank Ankersmit, Ewa Domanska, and Hans Kellner, eds., *Re-Figuring Hayden White*

Michael Rothberg, *Multidirectional Memory: Remembering the Holocaust in the Age of Decolonization*

Jean-François Lyotard, *Enthusiasm: The Kantian Critique of History*

Ernst van Alphen, Mieke Bal, and Carel Smith, eds., *The Rhetoric of Sincerity*

Stéphane Mosès, *The Angel of History: Rosenzweig, Benjamin, Scholem*

Pierre Hadot, *The Present Alone Is Our Happiness: Conversations with Jeannie Carlier and Arnold I. Davidson*

Alexandre Lefebvre, *The Image of the Law: Deleuze, Bergson, Spinoza*

Samira Haj, *Reconfiguring Islamic Tradition: Reform, Rationality, and Modernity*

Diane Perpich, *The Ethics of Emmanuel Levinas*

Marcel Detienne, *Comparing the Incomparable*

François Delaporte, *Anatomy of the Passions*

René Girard, *Mimesis and Theory: Essays on Literature and Criticism, 1959-2005*

Richard Baxstrom, *Houses in Motion: The Experience of Place and the Problem of Belief in Urban Malaysia*

Jennifer L. Culbert, *Dead Certainty: The Death Penalty and the Problem of Judgment*

Samantha Frost, *Lessons from a Materialist Thinker: Hobbesian Reflections on Ethics and Politics*

Regina Mara Schwartz, *Sacramental Poetics at the Dawn of Secularism: When God Left the World*

Gil Anidjar, *Semites: Race, Religion, Literature*

Ranjana Khanna, *Algeria Cuts: Women and Representation, 1830 to the Present*

Esther Peeren, *Intersubjectivities and Popular Culture: Bakhtin and Beyond*

Eyal Peretz, *Becoming Visionary: Brian De Palma's Cinematic Education of the Senses*

Diana Sorensen, *A Turbulent Decade Remembered: Scenes from the Latin American Sixties*

Hubert Damisch, *A Childhood Memory by Piero della Francesca*

José van Dijck, *Mediated Memories in the Digital Age*

Dana Hollander, *Exemplarity and Chosenness: Rosenzweig and Derrida on the Nation of Philosophy*

Asja Szafraniec, *Beckett, Derrida, and the Event of Literature*

Sara Guyer, *Romanticism After Auschwitz*

Alison Ross, *The Aesthetic Paths of Philosophy: Presentation in Kant, Heidegger, Lacoue-Labarthe, and Nancy*

Gerhard Richter, *Thought-Images: Frankfurt School Writers' Reflections from Damaged Life*

Bella Brodzki, *Can These Bones Live? Translation, Survival, and Cultural Memory*

Rodolphe Gasché, *The Honor of Thinking: Critique, Theory, Philosophy*

Brigitte Peucker, *The Material Image: Art and the Real in Film*

Natalie Melas, *All the Difference in the World: Postcoloniality and the Ends of Comparison*

Jonathan Culler, *The Literary in Theory*

Michael G. Levine, *The Belated Witness: Literature, Testimony, and the Question of Holocaust Survival*

Jennifer A. Jordan, *Structures of Memory: Understanding German Change in Berlin and Beyond*

Christoph Menke, *Reflections of Equality*

Marlène Zarader, *The Unthought Debt: Heidegger and the Hebraic Heritage*

Jan Assmann, *Religion and Cultural Memory: Ten Studies*

David Scott and Charles Hirschkind, *Powers of the Secular Modern: Talal Asad and His Interlocutors*

Gyanendra Pandey, *Routine Violence: Nations, Fragments, Histories*

James Siegel, *Naming the Witch*

J. M. Bernstein, *Against Voluptuous Bodies: Late Modernism and the Meaning of Painting*

Theodore W. Jennings, Jr., *Reading Derrida / Thinking Paul: On Justice*

Richard Rorty and Eduardo Mendieta, *Take Care of Freedom and Truth Will Take Care of Itself: Interviews with Richard Rorty*

Jacques Derrida, *Paper Machine*

Renaud Barbaras, *Desire and Distance: Introduction to a Phenomenology of Perception*

Jill Bennett, *Empathic Vision: Affect, Trauma, and Contemporary Art*

Ban Wang, *Illuminations from the Past: Trauma, Memory, and History in Modern China*

James Phillips, *Heidegger's Volk: Between National Socialism and Poetry*

Frank Ankersmit, *Sublime Historical Experience*

István Rév, *Retroactive Justice: Prehistory of Post-Communism*

Paola Marrati, *Genesis and Trace: Derrida Reading Husserl and Heidegger*

Krzysztof Ziarek, *The Force of Art*

Marie-José Mondzain, *Image, Icon, Economy: The Byzantine Origins of the Contemporary Imaginary*

Cecilia Sjöholm, *The Antigone Complex: Ethics and the Invention of Feminine Desire*

Jacques Derrida and Elisabeth Roudinesco, *For What Tomorrow . . . : A Dialogue*

Elisabeth Weber, *Questioning Judaism: Interviews by Elisabeth Weber*

Jacques Derrida and Catherine Malabou, *Counterpath: Traveling with Jacques Derrida*

Martin Seel, *Aesthetics of Appearing*

Nanette Salomon, *Shifting Priorities: Gender and Genre in Seventeenth-Century Dutch Painting*

Jacob Taubes, *The Political Theology of Paul*

Jean-Luc Marion, *The Crossing of the Visible*

Eric Michaud, *The Cult of Art in Nazi Germany*

Anne Freadman, *The Machinery of Talk: Charles Peirce and the Sign Hypothesis*

Stanley Cavell, *Emerson's Transcendental Etudes*

Stuart McLean, *The Event and Its Terrors: Ireland, Famine, Modernity*

Beate Rössler, ed., *Privacies: Philosophical Evaluations*

Bernard Faure, *Double Exposure: Cutting Across Buddhist and Western Discourses*

Alessia Ricciardi, *The Ends of Mourning: Psychoanalysis, Literature, Film*

Alain Badiou, *Saint Paul: The Foundation of Universalism*

Gil Anidjar, *The Jew, the Arab: A History of the Enemy*

Jonathan Culler and Kevin Lamb, eds., *Just Being Difficult? Academic Writing in the Public Arena*

Jean-Luc Nancy, *A Finite Thinking*, edited by Simon Sparks

Theodor W. Adorno, *Can One Live after Auschwitz? A Philosophical Reader*, edited by Rolf Tiedemann

Patricia Pisters, *The Matrix of Visual Culture: Working with Deleuze in Film Theory*

Andreas Huyssen, *Present Pasts: Urban Palimpsests and the Politics of Memory*

Talal Asad, *Formations of the Secular: Christianity, Islam, Modernity*

Dorothea von Mücke, *The Rise of the Fantastic Tale*

Marc Redfield, *The Politics of Aesthetics: Nationalism, Gender, Romanticism*

Emmanuel Levinas, *On Escape*

Dan Zahavi, *Husserl's Phenomenology*

Rodolphe Gasché, *The Idea of Form: Rethinking Kant's Aesthetics*

Michael Naas, *Taking on the Tradition: Jacques Derrida and the Legacies of Deconstruction*

Herlinde Pauer-Studer, ed., *Constructions of Practical Reason: Interviews on Moral and Political Philosophy*

Jean-Luc Marion, *Being Given That: Toward a Phenomenology of Givenness*

Theodor W. Adorno and Max Horkheimer, *Dialectic of Enlightenment*

Ian Balfour, *The Rhetoric of Romantic Prophecy*

Martin Stokhof, *World and Life as One: Ethics and Ontology in Wittgenstein's Early Thought*

Gianni Vattimo, *Nietzsche: An Introduction*

Jacques Derrida, *Negotiations: Interventions and Interviews, 1971-1998*, ed. Elizabeth Rottenberg

Brett Levinson, *The Ends of Literature: The Latin American "Boom" in the Neoliberal Marketplace*

Timothy J. Reiss, *Against Autonomy: Cultural Instruments, Mutualities, and the Fictive Imagination*

Hent de Vries and Samuel Weber, eds., *Religion and Media*

Niklas Luhmann, *Theories of Distinction: Re-Describing the Descriptions of Modernity*, ed. and introd. William Rasch

Johannes Fabian, *Anthropology with an Attitude: Critical Essays*

Michel Henry, *I Am the Truth: Toward a Philosophy of Christianity*

Gil Anidjar, *"Our Place in Al-Andalus": Kabbalah, Philosophy, Literature in Arab-Jewish Letters*

Hélène Cixous and Jacques Derrida, *Veils*

F. R. Ankersmit, *Historical Representation*

F. R. Ankersmit, *Political Representation*

Elissa Marder, *Dead Time: Temporal Disorders in the Wake of Modernity (Baudelaire and Flaubert)*

Reinhart Koselleck, *The Practice of Conceptual History: Timing History, Spacing Concepts*

Niklas Luhmann, *The Reality of the Mass Media*

Hubert Damisch, *A Theory of /Cloud/: Toward a History of Painting*

Jean-Luc Nancy, *The Speculative Remark: (One of Hegel's bon mots)*

Jean-François Lyotard, *Soundproof Room: Malraux's Anti-Aesthetics*

Jan Patočka, *Plato and Europe*

Hubert Damisch, *Skyline: The Narcissistic City*

Isabel Hoving, *In Praise of New Travelers: Reading Caribbean Migrant Women Writers*

Richard Rand, ed., *Futures: Of Jacques Derrida*

William Rasch, *Niklas Luhmann's Modernity: The Paradoxes of Differentiation*

Jacques Derrida and Anne Dufourmantelle, *Of Hospitality*

Jean-François Lyotard, *The Confession of Augustine*

Kaja Silverman, *World Spectators*

Samuel Weber, *Institution and Interpretation: Expanded Edition*

Jeffrey S. Librett, *The Rhetoric of Cultural Dialogue: Jews and Germans in the Epoch of Emancipation*

Ulrich Baer, *Remnants of Song: Trauma and the Experience of Modernity in Charles Baudelaire and Paul Celan*

Samuel C. Wheeler III, *Deconstruction as Analytic Philosophy*

David S. Ferris, *Silent Urns: Romanticism, Hellenism, Modernity*

Rodolphe Gasché, *Of Minimal Things: Studies on the Notion of Relation*

Sarah Winter, *Freud and the Institution of Psychoanalytic Knowledge*

Samuel Weber, *The Legend of Freud: Expanded Edition*

Aris Fioretos, ed., *The Solid Letter: Readings of Friedrich Hölderlin*

J. Hillis Miller / Manuel Asensi, *Black Holes / J. Hillis Miller; or, Boustrophedonic Reading*

Miryam Sas, *Fault Lines: Cultural Memory and Japanese Surrealism*

Peter Schwenger, *Fantasm and Fiction: On Textual Envisioning*

Didier Maleuvre, *Museum Memories: History, Technology, Art*

Jacques Derrida, *Monolingualism of the Other; or, The Prosthesis of Origin*

Andrew Baruch Wachtel, *Making a Nation, Breaking a Nation: Literature and Cultural Politics in Yugoslavia*

Niklas Luhmann, *Love as Passion: The Codification of Intimacy*

Mieke Bal, ed., *The Practice of Cultural Analysis: Exposing Interdisciplinary Interpretation*

Jacques Derrida and Gianni Vattimo, eds., *Religion*

The authorized representative in the EU for product safety and compliance is:
Mare Nostrum Group
B.V Doelen 72
4831 GR Breda
The Netherlands

www.ingramcontent.com/pod-product-compliance
Lightning Source LLC
Chambersburg PA
CBHW030111170426
43198CB00009B/572